THE BALLAD OF KARLA FAYE TUCKER

THE BALLAD OF KARLA FAYE TUCKER

MARK BEAVER

University Press of Mississippi † Jackson

The University Press of Mississippi is the scholarly publishing agency of
the Mississippi Institutions of Higher Learning: Alcorn State University,
Delta State University, Jackson State University, Mississippi State University,
Mississippi University for Women, Mississippi Valley State University,
University of Mississippi, and University of Southern Mississippi.

www.upress.state.ms.us

The University Press of Mississippi is a member
of the Association of University Presses.

Copyright © 2023 by University Press of Mississippi
All rights reserved
Manufactured in the United States of America

First printing 2023

∞

Library of Congress Control Number: 2022060192 (print)
Library of Congress Control Number: 2022060193 (ebook)
Hardback ISBN: 9781496846624
Paperback ISBN: 9781496850324
Epub single ISBN: 9781496846631
Epub institutional ISBN: 9781496846648
PDF single ISBN: 9781496846655
PDF institutional ISBN: 9781496846662

Library of Congress Cataloging-in-Publication Data available at
https://lccn.loc.gov/2022060192

British Library Cataloging-in-Publication Data available

*In memory of my mother,
Norma Fay Beaver*

If someone dies, will they live again? All the days of my hard service I will wait for my renewal to come. You will call and I will answer you; you will long for the creature your hands have made. Surely then you will count my steps but not keep track of my sin.

—Job 14:14–16

CONTENTS

Prologue: All Five. 3
Chapter 1: Sweet Woman of God. 12
Chapter 2: Your Very Own Gethsemane. 19
Chapter 3: Looking for Something to Do 28
Chapter 4: Evangel. 39
Chapter 5: Fish and Ketchup 53
Chapter 6: Puppet Show 60
Chapter 7: And That's the Way with Jesus. 72
Chapter 8: Well, Hell Yes 93
Chapter 9: The Thing Is Quickly Enough Done 103
Chapter 10: Here and Happy 118
Chapter 11: Until She Be Dead 126
Chapter 12: The Ballad of Karla Faye Tucker. 137
Chapter 13: The Real Debbie Thornton 143
Chapter 14: Southern Gothic. 152
Chapter 15: This Mess That Some People Call Life 159
Chapter 16: I Will Wait for You 166
Chapter 17: The State of Texas, Office of the Governor, Austin. . . 176
Chapter 18: The Son's Execution Date. 192
Acknowledgments 195
Notes 197

THE BALLAD OF KARLA FAYE TUCKER

PROLOGUE: ALL FIVE

They have come here to a small town called Jackson, an hour south of Atlanta, to watch a woman die. Just shy of a dozen visitors follow guards across the grounds of the Georgia Diagnostic and Classification Prison, headed toward a tiny cinderblock building in the deep recesses of the compound. It's September 30, 2015, an evening of mist and drizzle, just a few minutes past midnight. After a day of steady rainfall, the air is thick and humid—it's *heavy*, like the occasion. The witnesses for the state are the first to file through the door, followed by one of the woman's lawyers and four members of the media who are forbidden to bring their own pens and notebooks (they are provided instead with blunt pencils and pads of paper). The guards escort the visitors toward three wooden church pews, separated from the execution chamber by a glass partition. This observation area, twenty feet by twelve feet, is only slightly larger than the eight-by-twelve space where, momentarily, Kelly Renee Gissendaner will be administered a drug, pentobarbital, that will render her unconscious, shut down her brain, and stop her heart.

Gissendaner has been waiting for them. When the observers take their places, the forty-seven-year-old woman is already tied down on a gurney facing them, her body slightly inclined, her head tilted above her feet—though she has to strain slightly in order to view those who have gathered to watch her last few minutes of life. She surveys the crowd in silence as the people settle onto their seats, her arms strapped to boards extending from her rib cage, an intravenous tube already attached to each of them and a sheet draped over her legs and stomach. Her body is stationary, but her eyes are active, flitting incessantly, lighting on everyone in the room but no one for very long.

Kelly Gissendaner is here on this execution gurney because her husband died eighteen years ago, in 1997. She was convicted of malice murder. Yet she did not, by her own hand, kill him or anyone else.

In the most circulated photo of Douglas Gissendaner, he looks like your typical husband and dad, circa the 1990s: he wears a polo shirt with multicolored vertical stripes, a watch, and slightly oversized glasses. He props his chin atop his thumb and grins a friendly, even somewhat goofy, grin; he's got dark brown hair cut in the most staid and conventional of styles, with a few strays standing starkly against the white background, and a reddish mustache. If someone told you he was an accountant, or a cook at the Red Lobster, or an assistant manager at the CVS near the strip mall by the highway, you'd believe them, unhesitatingly. Doug Gissendaner looks like someone who bowls on Tuesday nights; someone who believes he could win big on *The Price Is Right* if he ever made it to (and out of) the studio audience; someone whose biggest indiscretion might be squeezing in an extra trip to the soup-n-salad bar at the Ruby Tuesday when the waitress isn't looking. You would believe he is what he is—a loving and often doting father to his three children. The picture sends off no signals that Doug Gissendaner's life is anything but ordinary; certainly nothing here suggests anyone would want to see him dead.

Yet his wife, Kelly Gissendaner, did very much want him to die. So much so that she and her lover Gregory Owen concocted a scheme to bring about that end—one that began with Gregory lying in wait in the dark of the Gissendaners' home with a hunting knife and a nightstick. When thirty-year-old Doug returned home late that night—he'd been tinkering on a church friend's car—Gregory emerged from the shadows, approached Doug from behind, and set the knife blade against his neck. He told Doug he wanted to go for a ride; he directed Doug back to his car, a Chevy Caprice, and with the knife perched in his lap, he ordered Doug to drive them to a desolate area out Luke Edwards Road. When they arrived at the stretch of unincorporated Gwinnett County where the woods grew dense with brush and thicket, Gregory told Doug to park the car, and on foot they staggered together down a rain-slicked embankment to the bottom of a ravine. There, he forced Doug to his knees; and as Kelly Gissendaner had instructed, he took Doug's watch and wedding band, to make it look like a robbery. Then, with Doug's back turned to him, Gregory swung the nightstick and struck Doug flush in the head. Doug slumped forward, out cold before he hit the ground, silent and motionless. Gregory then stabbed Doug at least eight times in the jugular with the hunting knife.

All while Kelly Gissendaner was at a local bar called the Shack, dancing and drinking with friends.

As planned, it wasn't long before she arrived at the site in her car. After assuring themselves Doug was dead, they doused his vehicle with kerosene and sent it up in flames, black blankets of smoke spiraling toward the night sky. Kelly then drove Gregory home—to what they hoped would be ten grand of insurance money and the beginning of a new life together. The next morning, she continued the ruse, contacting authorities to report her husband missing. She called her in-laws too, asking if they'd heard from Douglas.

Two weeks later, law enforcement found what remained of the car, a torched husk, and eventually the body, picked over by wildlife. In Doug Gissendaner's clothing was a blood-soaked pay stub and a black wallet stamped with race-car driver Dale Earnhardt's #3.

For a time, Kelly played the role of grieving wife. She broke down in tears as she recounted to police her last exchange with her husband before his death. She appeared on TV, pleading for any information about his whereabouts. She attended his funeral and played inconsolable. But soon law enforcement learned about her affair with Gregory Owen, who confessed to the murder and implicated her.

Both Kelly and Gregory were offered plea bargains. On advice of her lawyer, she rejected hers. "I should have pushed her to take the plea," her trial attorney, Edwin Wilson, would say, "but did not because I thought we would get straight-up life if she was convicted." It seemed a logical gamble, because she hadn't actually killed her husband *and* she was a woman. But Gregory accepted his plea bargain and testified of Kelly's involvement in the murder. As a result, on this night that Kelly Gissendaner will die, Gregory Owen is still very much alive, eligible in fact for parole as early as 2022. This is how the judicial system works sometimes.

The Gissendaners' three children want to see their mother live. They say their father would not want her to die—he would not want the state to take away their sole remaining parent. Despite their fond memories of him as the one stable parent in their upbringing, putting them to bed at night and waking them the next morning, they believe Kelly has become something in their young adulthood that she never was in their childhood: a genuine mother. Kayla Gissendaner, who was only seven when Kelly arranged her father's death, says of her mother, "She's all that we have left." The children add that she ministers to fellow inmates who are suicidal; that she has earned a theological degree while imprisoned, even writing a seminar paper on Bonhoeffer.

Pope Francis has called for her clemency too. And of course, more than a hundred opponents of capital punishment are assembled tonight outside the prison walls in the rain, their umbrellas a futile defense against the humidity curdling their signs that read NOT IN MY NAME and 2 WRONGS DON'T MAKE A RIGHT. Together, the umbrellas create a stunning array of cheerful pastels—lime and hot pink and purple and fuchsia—but the spitting rain and the presence of law enforcement, equipped in riot gear and armed with body shields and sleek batons, pose a stark contrast.

This is Kelly Gissendaner's third execution date. A snowstorm halted her first and a "cloudy" batch of pentobarbital her second. But now, in the death chamber, four correctional officers stand guard in each of the corners of the room, and three other people stand ready to conduct this order of business that will escort Kelly into eternity. A nurse, the prison warden, and a chaplain each have responsibilities to perform here.

Kelly is offered the opportunity to make a final statement. The room is silent as the onlookers on the other side of the glass wait for her to speak. There is a pause, then finally, her voice, amplified by a microphone, fills the tight space. "Bless y'all," she begins, then she promptly starts to cry. She makes eye contact with her lawyer, seated in the second row. "I love you, Susan." Silently, Susan Casey reciprocates the sentiment, mouthing the words before burying her face in her hands. "You let my kids know I went out singing Amazing Grace," Kelly continues. "And tell the Gissendaner family I am so sorry that amazing man lost his life because of me. If I could take it back, if this would change it, I would've done it a long time ago. . . . I just hope they find peace, and they find some happiness. God bless you."

The chaplain offers his prayer. The warden reads aloud the warrant authorizing the execution. Then the microphone is shut off. Kelly averts her eyes from the observers, stares at the ceiling, and appears to begin praying silent prayers. The chaplain touches her shoulder, the last human contact Kelly will ever know, and follows the warden out of the chamber, leaving the nurse practically alone with this condemned woman. Only the correctional officers, still stationed in the four corners of the room, remain in the space.

It's then that Kelly Gissendaner does a remarkable thing. She begins to sing. The microphone is off, but everyone separated from her by the glass partition can still hear the song clearly. *Amazing grace, how sweet the sound,* she sings, *that saved a wretch like me. I once was lost, but now I'm found. Was blind, but now I see.* It's of course the old traditional hymn, composed in 1772 by Englishman John Newton, a one-time slave trader with a reputation for verbal debauchery who converted to Christianity and repented of his many sins. By America's Second Great Awakening, the song became a standard call-to-the-altar climax to countless camp meetings, especially in the South. It's been closing sermons here, and serving as a testimony to transformed souls, ever since. It, in short, bears witness to the claim that God's forgiveness can redeem even the darkest of souls.

Her voice loud and curiously full of what can only be described as joy, Kelly sings her way through the first verse before the drugs start to take effect. She licks her lips. She yawns. She stops, then starts up the second verse, then stops again. The sedative is taking hold. There will be no more singing tonight. Gradually, then quite abruptly, her chest goes still.

Afterward, Rhonda Cook, one of the journalists with a prison-authorized pencil and notepad who witnessed the event, wrote, "I have never attended a woman's execution, but it was hard to tell she actually was one. She has a very masculine appearance and has put on so much weight in prison she was bigger than some of the men I've seen executed."

Kelly Gissendaner was only the second woman to be put to death legally in Georgia's history—the first since Lena Baker, an African American maid who had killed a white man, in 1945. Yet as Cook notes, she was not feminine or attractive by any of the means we usually measure such things in American culture, which might account for why her death failed to trigger the hue and cry you might expect. Cook and other journalists indeed provided coverage, but there was nothing to rival the media blitz afforded to one Karla Faye Tucker almost twenty years ago, in early 1998, when as Sam Howe Verhovek of the *New York Times* put it, an inmate became "a virtual guest in American living rooms" and "put a particularly human face on those condemned to death." Tucker was the rarest of death-row offenders—and her unique combination of traits forced America to examine its attitudes toward and practice of capital punishment. Whether Tucker's case *should* have provoked such self-reflection is another matter altogether. "The real question we should ask ourselves," said David Dow, a University of Houston law professor, at the time, "is why so many people saw Tucker's humanity but refuse to see it in others. Because the truth is that almost all execution victims are like Tucker. Most come to regret that they killed. Most have families who love them. Many find religion. Many are articulate. Some are even physically attractive."

But for a brief few weeks, as we perched on the precarious edge of Y2K, the End Times, or maybe only a new millennium, we did pause to have a meaningful national conversation about the merits of putting a person to death—a conversation we've not since mustered the wherewithal to have again in such a concentrated way. Karla Faye Tucker illuminated *us*, forcing Americans to reconsider everything we believed about topics as disparate as the death penalty, gender, the Christian right, the South, and, ultimately, the nature and possibility of redemption. If you were part of that conversation, you asked hard questions with no easy answers. Why was the South putting people to death at accelerated rates? How much political clout did the evangelical right really have? Was Texas's governor, a man named George W. Bush, ironically making a stand *for* gender equality by refusing to differentiate Tucker's case from others? Or was he just weighing the political expediencies as he positioned himself for a run at the Oval Office? And there were theological mysteries to explore here, too. Could the soul of a woman who had murdered two people in brutal fashion really be redeemed? Had God forgiven Karla? And if He had, why couldn't we? For a brief window of time, we grappled with these questions and a whole litany of others related to them, and by the time the state of Texas flushed her veins with poison, we knew Karla Faye Tucker was a murderer, yes, but also a human being. By any measure, she was a different person than the one who had killed two people almost fifteen years earlier.

According to Professor Dow, Tucker possessed the magical alchemy that made her story irresistible to the American public. "She was a woman, white, attractive, articulate, and a Christian," he said at the time. "A lot of people on death row have three of those characteristics; some have four. But very few have all five, and I simply don't see another case commanding this amount of attention."

Dow's words have proved prophetic. In the decades since her February 3, 1998, execution, no case has focused our attention on capital punishment and invited the various arguments for and against it in such a sustained and meaningful way. No single inmate has served as a lightning rod for our debate, embodying all the traits that would bring *us* to the surface. The fact is that in the twenty-first century, public support for the death penalty has been steadily dwindling; one can point to Karla Faye Tucker's case and view it as a genuine turning point in cultural attitudes. A 2016 Pew Research Survey found that nationwide support had fallen below fifty percent for the first time in almost half a century. Even Tucker's home state of Texas, long a steadfast defender of the practice of putting people to death, has reduced the number of executions in recent years. After a peak of forty executions in 2000, the last four years have seen the Lone Star State put thirteen, nine, seven, and three people to death, clearly a sustained downward trend.

Kelly Gissendaner's 2015 death prompted in me a desire to go back and revisit the run-up to Karla Faye Tucker's 1998 execution—to review the strange intersection of cultural forces that made her case such a captivating story. And it also provoked me to take another look at where I fit in that story, at a time when I was wrestling with my own spiritual identity and was plodding through the apprenticeship that all young writers must endure before they can put words on a page that might prove moving and meaningful to readers.

This book is no defense of Tucker, twenty years too late. It's not an attempt to litigate the death penalty or scold its proponents. On the night Kelly Gissendaner met her Maker in Jackson, Georgia, I wasn't under one of those pastel umbrellas, holding a cardboard sign and waiting for the news to come from the death house. I was seventy miles away, in my home in the Atlanta suburbs, asleep probably. Like many Georgians, I'd been following Gissendaner's story from a safe distance, both physical and emotional, vaguely acquainted with the contours of her case but a little tired of the familiar tropes.

But when it was all over and I heard about her breaking into song as the state of Georgia administered pentobarbital, I realized Gissendaner's story had almost all the same ingredients as Karla Faye Tucker's. If Gissendaner was already receding into cultural oblivion as meekly as she had surfaced in the first place, then maybe revisiting Tucker's case could be a way of reviving that conversation and asking those questions, again.

Down here in the Bible Belt, it's blasphemous to talk *resurrection* about anybody but the Risen Savior. But even Jesus, they say, was flanked on both sides by criminals. Let's raise the Pickax Murderess from the dead. Let her speak again. See if she says anything that, today, we might need to hear.

Chapter 1

SWEET WOMAN OF GOD

I was closing in fast on my thirtieth birthday and mired in a prolonged spell of what the Baptist folk I grew up among would call *backsliding*, when my father asked me to write a letter on his behalf to George W. Bush. It was early 1998, and Bush was then governor of Texas. A woman named Karla Faye Tucker had been sentenced to die in his state. Unless Bush granted clemency, Tucker would be the first female on Texas's death row to be executed since the Civil War—and the first anywhere in the US in more than a decade.

A new millennium was drawing nigh, or maybe the End Times, and all the gruesome details of Tucker's crime were making national news. In a drug-induced haze in June 1983, when Tucker was twenty-three years old, she and her boyfriend broke into a Houston apartment at around three in the morning and slaughtered two people—one a sworn enemy, the other an utter stranger. By the time the pair fled the scene, they had punctured Jerry Lynn Dean just shy of thirty times with a pickax, and embedded the weapon seven inches deep in Deborah Thornton's chest. As if these grim facts weren't sensational enough, many of the news reports specified that the pickax pierced Thornton's heart.

Though Dad was a veteran of Korea, a law-and-order Republican, and typically a staunch advocate of eye-for-an-eye retribution, he nevertheless wanted to see Karla Faye Tucker live. He was a Southern Baptist deacon, too, and Tucker had become a poster child of sorts within the evangelical community. Her face and story were cycling through the Christian media, including Pat Robertson's *The 700 Club*, where Dad first heard her personal testimony of how she found Jesus on death row. Tucker told him and the rest of Robertson's washed-in-the-blood viewers that she stole a Bible from the prison ministry program and commenced skimming through the pages in her cell. "I didn't know what I was reading," she claimed in a gentle Texas drawl that sounded completely at odds with the brutality of her crime. "Before I knew it, I was in the middle of my cell floor on my knees. I was just asking God to forgive me."

At the time Tucker was sentenced to die, your typical evangelical like my father opposed abortion and euthanasia but supported capital punishment. To them, the moral gymnastics required to arrive at such a conclusion weren't all that complicated. The difference, in their view, was clear: God gives life and only God can take it away—unless the murderer forfeits her own right to life by taking away another's. They invited you to consider Genesis 9:6: "Whoso sheddeth man's blood, by man shall his blood be shed: for in the image of God made he man."

All the wrestling America had been doing over executions for decades seemed only to clear the way for the arrival of this woman who stood just five foot, three inches tall, sported a splotchy birthmark that looked as though she'd spilled chocolate milk on her forearm, and called herself "a really huggy, touchy-feely person." In 1972, in a group of cases called *Furman v. Georgia*, the US Supreme Court voted five to four to strike down the death penalty, ruling it was "so wantonly and freakishly imposed" that it constituted "cruel and unusual punishment" and violated the Eighth Amendment. Newspaper headlines across the country proclaimed some version of "Capital Punishment is Dead," and death row lost over six hundred inmates overnight. But the National Association of Evangelicals rebelled, rendering this official statement regarding the topic: "If no crime is considered serious enough to warrant capital punishment, then the gravity of the most atrocious crime is diminished accordingly. It follows then that the attitude of criminals will be affected. From the biblical perspective, if capital punishment is eliminated, the value of human life is reduced and the respect for life is correspondingly eroded." As a result, when the death penalty was reinstated for the January 1977 execution of Gary Gilmore by a firing squad in Utah, evangelicals believed justice had been restored. The fact that Gilmore himself pleaded for death made it seem to them that the scales of the spiritual universe were returning to balance. Man's law and God's were again aligning.

But now, two decades after Utah obliged Gilmore's choice between death by noose or by bullet—"I'd prefer to be shot," he said—here came Karla Faye Tucker. She was no ordinary candidate for the needle. Evangelicals saw her as a prime example of what God can do for even the most depraved and unregenerate heart. Moral Majority leader Jerry Falwell took to the media to declare that, though he'd always been an advocate for the death penalty, Tucker had convinced him to think otherwise about her. "I just knew instantly," he said, "that girl had been touched by the Lord and ought to be spared."

Falwell's considerable clout aside, it was televangelist Pat Robertson who became Tucker's most vocal and ardent supporter. In the early nineties, long before other Christians got on board, he was already drawing attention to her case, and now in the run-up to her scheduled execution in early '98, he was using his TV show *The 700 Club* essentially as an infomercial for her cause. He posited Governor Bush as the man standing between Tucker and life. If Bush "lets this sweet woman of God die," Robertson proclaimed, "he's a man who shows no mercy."

Texas was often considered the buckle of the Bible Belt, and you might expect them to side with these vocal Christian leaders. But the populace was still holding firm in its commitment to capital punishment. A year earlier, in 1997, the number of executions nationwide easily had surpassed the figure for any year since reinstatement of the penalty, and the Lone Star state led the charge. Texas executed thirty-seven people that year, equal to all other states combined. Polls showed that three-quarters of Texans supported the death penalty. The vast majority of them identified as Protestant Christians.

Karla Faye Tucker, then, was creating a showdown within the American evangelical community between supporters of a longstanding moral and political position and their brethren who were lobbying for this rare exception. Add to the drama George W. Bush himself. A devout Methodist with a come-to-Jesus story of his own, the governor stood at the fulcrum of the divide. Like evangelicals in general, he too drew a stark contrast between abortion and capital punishment. He believed executions could serve as a deterrent and ultimately prevent violence, whereas abortion fails to protect innocent life. In his 1999 biography *A Charge to Keep*, that's the way Bush distinguished between abortion and the death penalty: "It's the difference between innocence and guilt," he wrote.

Meanwhile, as her execution date drew closer, Tucker was leading Bible studies for other inmates. She decorated the prison's day room with crocheted handiwork. She maintained a perfect disciplinary record behind bars. By all accounts, her life had been genuinely transformed by what she called the saving grace of Jesus Christ. In a televised interview from that same prison day room shortly before her scheduled execution, her cheery decor hung in the background. Her face aglow, Tucker said, "I'm not afraid of dying. I know where I'm going. I know Jesus has already gone to prepare a place for me. I know that if I have to go February 3 that he's gonna come and he's gonna escort me personally. I believe that."

It was this woman that Dad wanted to see live—not the one who, during her trial fourteen years ago back in 1984, confessed she had bragged about experiencing orgasmic pleasure with every swing of her pickax.

Which is where I came in.

I suspect my father had two reasons for asking me to write a letter to George W. Bush. The first likely had to do with the precarious state of my soul. I'd become a Christmas and Easter Christian at best—one who darkened the doors of the church only under absolute obligation. Worse, I'd become versed in books other than the Bible, many of which didn't necessarily jibe with the notion that scripture came straight from the tongue of God and served as His inerrant Word and the final say on all matters of debate.

But Dad's second reason for asking me to compose a letter to Bush was more practical. I'd been telling the world I was a writer. I was finishing up the prolonged adolescence of my twenties and, much to my father's chagrin, in August I would be quitting a scrap heap of part-time jobs and delaying full adulthood yet again by vacating my apartment in the Atlanta suburbs and moving to North Carolina. There, I'd be entering an MFA program with a stockpile of pipe dreams, chief among them writing the classic Great American Novel. To this point, Dad had been indulging my literary ambitions with a kind of bewildered amusement—it was an unfortunate phase that would run its course as soon as I, to use his word, "matured." The sooner the better, to be sure.

But Karla Faye Tucker's predicament afforded Dad an opportunity. Though he was by nature a reticent man and generally suspicious of words unless they were God's—divinely inspired and recorded in the Bible—he recognized I was a convenient resource, despite my backsliding ways. Owner of a high-school diploma so tentative it seemed practically on loan, Dad understood his own verbal shortcomings. With a fellow Christian's life hanging in the balance, he simply needed someone who might be trusted to make his subjects and verbs agree. If I was a writer, well, maybe I could string together a few lines that might make a difference in this fallen world. And maybe, too, this whole experience could bring me back home to the faith of my youth.

So, my charge was clear: Dad wanted me to use whatever "writerly" talents I possessed to persuade Governor Bush to spare this woman that the twenty-four-hour news cycle was labeling "The Pickax Murderess." He wanted me to save Karla Faye Tucker's life with my words.

Lest I convey the wrong impression that my father was an inveterate rabble-rouser always firing off missives to elected public officials, pressuring them to act in accordance with his beliefs, I should make clear that his plea to George W. Bush was entirely out of character. This was not his typical way. He was a devotee of the electoral process, a citizen convinced that his voice could be expressed through his vote. He trusted the ballot booth, and to my knowledge never took any additional strides to express his opinions.

Sometimes this approach put him out of sync with his Baptist brethren. I'm thinking, for example, of the time our congregation got swept up in a nationwide fervor among Christians to censor the TV show *Soap*, a primetime sitcom spoofing daytime soap operas. Each episode of *Soap* was a bawdy romp exploring American sexual mores circa 1977. Each line of dialogue was full of innuendo, titillation, and camp—another match thrown on the inferno for believers convinced pop culture already had become a Sodom and Gomorrah landscape. The *New York Times* said the show "concerns the sexual predilections of members of two families, featuring a philandering husband and an impotent one, a transvestite son and a promiscuous daughter who is having an affair with a tennis pro who is having an affair with her promiscuous mother." Clearly, this type of premise did not endear the show to evangelicals. But perhaps it was the character of Jodie Dallas, played by newcomer Billy Crystal, who ignited the most ire among the Born Againers. Jodie Dallas was an uncloseted gay man—primetime TV's first—who was carrying on a romance with an NFL quarterback.

Months before the show's premiere, *Newsweek* published a mostly exaggerated preview of its upcoming debut on ABC, characterizing it as a sex farce and (falsely) asserting it featured a scene in which a priest is seduced in a church. Across Christendom, pushback was immediate—despite the fact no one had yet seen the show. Preachers and priests alike encouraged their parishioners to write letters to the show's sponsors, exhorting them to withdraw their advertising from such unwholesome programming—else Christians nationwide would be boycotting their products. It's estimated that thirty-two thousand people wrote letters.

My father was not one of them. I was only nine at the time and generally disinterested in my parents' social views, but I remember how resolved he was to avoid this particular fray. When the rest of the church deacons organized our congregation's letter-writing campaign, Dad somehow managed to sidestep the topic so deftly that no one questioned his refusal to participate. Somewhere in him he must have decided conflict would only deepen an already existing divide. The notion of tension leading eventually to greater reconciliation must have seemed like a fairytale at odds with the way things usually work out. He continued circulating the offering plate during worship services, singing the hymns off-key, visiting the shut-ins who couldn't make it to church, tithing 10 percent of his salary, and otherwise kept his opinions to himself.

As it turns out, perhaps Dad's refusal to add his own letter to those sent by our church was a wise choice. When *Soap* premiered in September of 1977, viewer discretion was advised. But as often happens, the controversy actually stoked viewership and helped sell the series. The first episode swept its time slot and snared 39 percent of the viewing audience. The show ranked #13 for the 1977–1978 season, ran for four years, launched a spin-off in *Benson*, and made a star of Billy Crystal.

I can only imagine what set of factors convinced Dad, this one time, he should make an exception to his longstanding strategy of bypassing controversy. I can only assume there was something in the power of Karla Faye Tucker's testimony, the way she looked you in the eye and told you what she believed, that made him, in turn, believe her.

Chapter 2

YOUR VERY OWN GETHSEMANE

Here's some irony: my parents named me after a writer. My namesake authored the earliest gospel in the New Testament. Mark was almost certainly male and Jewish—but otherwise we know little about him. He wrote in Greek, for Gentiles. Like the scribes of the other gospels, he never met Jesus. And as for his narrative, it covers only Jesus's baptism through his death and, in later versions, the discovery of his empty tomb. Nothing about his birth, upbringing, or post-Resurrection appearances. In Mark's version, Jesus's death is less victorious than in the others. His final words, in fact, are a bit of a downer: "My God, my God, why have you forsaken me?"

Apparently Matthew and Luke later used Mark's narrative to inform their records of Jesus's life and make his death more triumphant, to signal the fulfillment of the savior's divine mission. Then with the Gospel of John's emphasis on Jesus's divinity and his importance as *the* source of eternal life, we have a text that was instrumental to the survival of Christianity in its early centuries. Over time the Church came to regard these later gospels as superior to Mark's, primarily because Mark is conspicuously silent about the birth and resurrection that figure so prominently in the Christian narrative.

Today, scholars generally agree that Mark was writing theology, not history. He is prophesying a vision, not profiling a man. But the man that Mark gives us? He's irritable and impatient. He's got a temper. He doesn't suffer fools and doesn't stand on ceremony. He's full of advice about how to live, most of it contradictory of the prevailing customs of the time, but he reminds us none of it much matters anyway because the end is at hand. And maybe because we're all on borrowed time, he's also big on forgiveness. He even lays down an ultimatum. "But if ye do not forgive," he warns, "neither will your Father which is in heaven forgive your trespasses."

My parents were concocting no plan for me to follow in Mark's vocational footsteps as a scribe—they only wanted to forge my connection to Christianity and the Bible from the very beginning. (They named my older brother David, after the Old Testament king.)

But bless them, my parents. They got more than they bargained for.

They raised me in a house containing exactly one novel—a doorstopper-sized tome which none of us ever read. What my father called our "library" consisted of a couple of shelves stocked with every imaginable English translation of the Bible, automotive repair manuals, and that novel. Dad was a Baptist deacon, all right, so alongside the Bibles he also collected dozens of concordances and commentaries—all manner of books about one or another of the sixty-six books canonized in the Good Book. The repair manuals he stocked because he was a postman, a blue-collar stiff who had neither the compunction nor the discretionary income to pay some jake to do what he could figure out how to fix himself. Then there was that novel, a hard cover of *Gone with the Wind* that Dad probably purchased at a yard sale only because he figured he'd have to forfeit his Southern citizenship if he didn't own a copy.

I offer this summary of my scant literary upbringing in order to then state a question that has mystified me for now half my lifetime: of all the things the boy growing up in that brick ranch in Atlanta's suburbia could have become—a rain, sleet, snow, and dark of night postman; a mechanic with grease under his fingernails and calluses on his hands; an evangelist traveling the Sawdust Trail from one Holy Ghost tent meeting to the next, saving souls from Tallahassee to Tupelo—of all the paths I could have chosen, however did it come to be that I was telling my father I wanted to become a *writer*?

Mom and Dad raised me to play the part of a good Baptist boy, and I stuck to the script throughout my childhood. Perhaps my earliest memory is tagging along with my father when he joined his fellow deacons in the pastor's office before Sunday morning worship services. There, under the watchful gaze of a honey-haired, blue-eyed Jesus wearing a crown of thorns, these twelve men circled up, huddled shoulder-to-shoulder, and squeezed just tight enough to make room for me, even though my cowlick barely grazed their belt buckles. Pastor Davis led us in prayer, summoning God to dwell among us, to help us spread the Good News to the Lost, of whom there were many. I felt an intense sense of belonging that, even now, makes me think of home. In those days, it would have been impossible for me to imagine a future in which I wouldn't be part of that circle.

It was during that decade of the seventies, the heyday of horror movies, when evangelical filmmakers started producing their own flicks aimed at scaring the literal hell out of people. The popularity of 1972's *A Thief in the Night*, about a girl who misses the rapture, kick-started a whole series of motion pictures aiming to prepare us for Armageddon. The first time I saw one of these shoestring budget productions, I was seven years old. A deacon hit the lights, the reel-to-reel film began spooling through the projector, and within minutes our church sanctuary was transformed from a staid room full of middle-class worshippers into the fiery furnace of Hades. That was the end goal here—to dramatize hell according to the apocalyptic book of *Revelations*. To make clear what was at stake for all of us gathered here on this October night in 1975.

One scene stands out in my memory: a man lying on his back, his face smeared with ash, his tongue parched as he cries out for a single drop of water. Once this visual is established, here comes the narrator, his voice gone guttural with doom, offering a hypothetical anecdote I'm still unable, all these years later, to shake from memory. "Picture a mosquito flying around the earth," the narrator says. "Picture him, that common pest, circling the globe over and over. See him flap his wings and chip away at the dust till he whittles the earth to its very core—to a ball tiny enough to hold in the palm of your hand. Consider how many years of human history such a task would take to complete." He hesitates just long enough for us to contemplate how incomprehensible a time this process would take to unfold. Then, at just about the moment a putrid sickness starts roiling around in our lower intestines: "*That*, dear sinner, is one second in eternity."

It was that night, when the deacons cued up the horror flick, that I swore my allegiance with the Born Againers. In Dad's Chevy Malibu on our way home, my parents told me how I could escape such a fate as I'd witnessed tonight. They explained about the sinner's prayer. All you have to do, they said, is confess you need God's grace, and invite Jesus into your heart. With this easy transaction, you'll be assured of salvation and washed whiter than snow. If you were to die tonight, Jesus would count you among his own. You wouldn't have to worry about that mosquito. By the time we pulled into our driveway on King Arthur Drive, I was saved.

Baptism came later, at age thirteen, by which time I suppose I seemed well on my way to achieving my mother's goal for me: to become a missionary to some godforsaken land on the far side of the globe. She wanted me to share with the natives the good news of our Lord and Savior. But it was in those adolescent years that the straight and narrow became a tight squeeze. The culprits were typical—hormones, Miss September, Daisy Duke, MTV—all the things Pastor Davis regularly summed up as the *flesh*. I attended a record burning in a church parking lot, just to witness how it all went down, and almost cried in front of Jesus and all the holy assembled around the bonfire when the youth minister tossed a copy of one of my favorite records, Prince's *Dirty Mind*, into the flames.

Still, if the church doors were open, my parents made sure I was holding down a pew. For good luck I kept a Bible verse tucked inside my sock during basketball games. I said my prayers before tests in school. I annually attended an evangelical summer camp called SuperWOW.

In tenth grade, any pretensions I might have had toward becoming a writer got off to an inauspicious start when I approached the sponsor of the school newspaper—we'll call him Mr. Hayden—about securing a spot on his staff.

Hayden was lounging at a table in the cafeteria. He was doing lunch duty with a couple of other teachers, swigging a carton of chocolate milk, wearing the perpetual scowl he reserved for everyone except the most attractive variety of female students.

Hayden was an institution in our school. He'd taught journalism for a couple decades, coached girls soccer, wrote a pithy column in our hometown rag about the local sports teams. A couple of my buddies were already on staff. They reported that you never had to do any work in journalism class. Hayden gave you a hall pass and allowed you to roam the school in search of a "story." They said the staff was full of senior girls. I didn't want to seem intrusive, so I was standing a polite distance away and waiting for Hayden to acknowledge my consumption of his oxygen and summon me into his inner sanctum.

But this invitation did not appear to be forthcoming. As he continued chugging his milk and offering no-doubt cynical comic asides to his colleagues, Hayden seemed oblivious to my presence. He wiped his Fu Manchu with the back of his hand.

Finally, suspecting he might simply be testing my initiative, I stepped forward and spoke up. "Mr. Hayden?" I said.

He raised his head, squinted me into view. I saw now that, chocolate milk notwithstanding, he also was furiously working a wad of gum. "You need something?" he asked.

I wanted to sound confident. I suppose what I was really after here was a chance to kill seventh period each day chatting with older girls or exploring the distant hinterlands of the campus with my hall pass—but I wanted to sound like I was just the guy to take his paper to the next level. This man was our school's version of a writing guru, and I wanted him to know I indeed had gumption and guts aplenty. If there was a story out there, I could chase it down. "I'd like to register for your journalism class," I told him.

Hayden's forehead wrinkled; he knitted his brows. He clutched his gut as though that chocolate milk were taking a wrong turn in his digestive system.

The man must have taken pity on me, though. Eventually, after making me jump through hoops—requiring me to secure two teacher recs and provide a writing sample of an essay I wrote for English class—Hayden would begrudgingly admit me to his staff. For the next two years, he assigned me gigs covering the tennis team and interviewing members of the debate club. I spent the whole of that time clamoring to write a provocative article about teen pregnancy, an idea he summarily shot down—until my senior year when he assigned it to someone else.

But first, in this school cafeteria with hair-netted ladies in the backdrop and lime Jell-O cubes on the floor tiles, Hayden burped into his fist and looked me up and down as though questioning why I would have the audacity to even suggest I might belong in his tribe. Then he proceeded to provide as appropriate an introduction to the writing life as any I could have received.

"I don't even know who the hell you are," he said.

A few years before I would ever hear Karla Faye Tucker's name, I graduated college with a thoroughly impractical degree in psychology and a mediocre transcript from an unremarkable community school that kept the lights on by admitting anyone with a pulse. It was 1991. The US was mired in a deep funk recession, and no employers were responding to all the white space on my resume. It should have come as no surprise to anyone, myself least of all, that I couldn't get a job. Bereft of options, I moved back into my parents' house and took up residence in my old bedroom.

The décor was the same as I had left it four years ago, as though all along my folks had been milking suspicions they weren't yet shut of me. The same Prince posters covered the walls; the same Nerf hoop hung over the door. I dismantled the bed frame and slept on a mattress on the floor, because I wanted to convey the notion that this arrangement was temporary, a brief layover, and I'd soon be moving out and on to the brighter destiny that surely awaited me. In the meantime, each morning I wrestled the mattress onto its side and leaned it against the wall in order to create space for whatever completely insurrectionary activity I would conduct there. I just had to figure out what it was.

But after much rumination, I came to a conclusion: it's hard to trigger a revolution from your old room in your parents' house. Sure, I spent the expected time doing what anyone could have predicted a twenty-three-year-old boy would do in that space, especially one who was surly and petulant because the universe was stubbornly denying him the chance to get the job that would trumpet his transition to manhood. Sure, I listened to my stereo and ate whole bags of Cheetos and ignored my mother's entreaties from the other side of the wall. But unexpectedly, sort of by happenstance, what I also ended up doing in that space was a lot of reading and writing.

I read library and used bookstore copies of the classics. Steinbeck, Faulkner, Hemingway, and Warren. Chopin, Welty, O'Connor. Toomer, Hurston, Baldwin. I finished Ellison's *Invisible Man* and promptly flipped the book over, turned to page one, and commenced rereading it. I filled my copy of *Cathedral* with almost as much marginalia as Carver had provided in the text. I read long past the due dates of those library books and until the yellowed pages of those cheap, used volumes broke loose from their spines. I remember plucking a hardback edition of Faulkner's *These Thirteen* off the shelf and rubbing my fingertips across the lines as though I were trying to absorb his language into my bloodstream. I didn't quite believe Faulkner sat at the right hand of God; but when I held his book in my hands I regarded where I stood as holy ground.

And I wrote to figure out where to go from here. In journals, I filled pages with the big questions—the ones people usually don't spend much time pondering because they're gainfully employed. For starters I asked, *Who am I?*—then proceeded on to the next tier of human philosophy: *What should I do with my life? What's my passion? What does success look like?* It's probably best that those journals have been lost to the annals of time, because I no doubt plumbed new depths in solipsism.

Nevertheless, I'm glad I wrote them. In those blue-lined pages I didn't necessarily come up with any concrete answers, but if nothing else, writing helped me to recognize the dire nature of my current predicament—and created in me desperation to escape it. And there's this: I conjured the vague outlines of a future.

Somewhere in that reckoning I came to the notion I wanted to do unto others what Faulkner and the rest had done unto me. I wanted to be a writer. I longed to tell stories that would serve as my *Kilroy was here* and exist immortally after I was gone. Surely I understood an apprenticeship would be required, a time in the wilderness. But I was twenty-three, healthy, unburdened by adult responsibility, so there was adventure in it, the kind of perverse contentment that comes with enduring your very own Gethsemane.

Resolved to change my trajectory, I returned to school with plans to earn a teaching certificate at the community college, figuring I might occupy my days talking books with high schoolers until I wrote one of my own that would take its rightful place in the canon of what they were required to read. Along the way, I enrolled in a creative writing class, somehow still convinced, despite all evidence to the contrary, I had a gift. I remember carrying into my first workshop a strange confidence resulting not from having written anything of merit, only the biding conviction that I one day would. I expected my teacher to recognize this kernel of artistic potential and to acknowledge it with something resembling rousing endorsement. The way I imagined it, he would proudly designate himself my mentor and begin composing his version of Rilke's letters to me, his young artist. He would even quote Rilke: "If your daily life seems poor, do not blame it; blame yourself: tell yourself you are not yet poet enough to call forth its riches." He'd badger, wheedle, pester, and cajole me into dredging up whatever sludge my life might contain.

To his everlasting credit, my teacher did nurture me and offer encouragement, but overall he gave off no overt signs of believing I possessed anything resembling promise. If I succeeded at anything, it was convincing him of this: I badly wanted to be good.

He invited Ernest Gaines, whom I regarded as a literary deity, to the school, and introduced me cordially. Gaines was warm, generous with his attention. He signed my copy of *A Lesson before Dying*. On the title page, he wrote my name and "Best to you always." Afterward my teacher informed me that Gaines had said of me, "I could tell that young man was a writer." My teacher probably exaggerated that remark beyond all recognition, but it worked: I lived off it for the next year of my life.

It's probably fair to say, when I first heard Karla Faye Tucker's name, I was living off it, still.

Chapter 3

LOOKING FOR SOMETHING TO DO

It was already three days old, this ongoing binge that featured marijuana, heroin, and speed; Dilaudid, Mandrex, and methadone; Percodan, Soma, and Valium. And alcohol—lots and lots of alcohol: rum and tequila and Jack Daniel's practically by the bucketful. And barbecued ribs too, on the gas grill in the backyard. Friday, Saturday, Sunday—June 10, 11, and 12, 1983—the party had dragged on through the afternoons and the long nights too. It had also been three days of chatter—endless shit-talk about how much they hated one Jerry Lynn Dean's guts, how he was a wuss of a man, puny and stringy and just flat-out weak, all of which meant he had no damn business owning a Harley Davidson. He didn't deserve it. He was custom-building the motorcycle in his living room, piece by piece, and *he did not deserve it*. They could be doing the world a favor and upholding a standard of justice by relieving such a guy of his bike. Three days of shit-talk and not a wink of sleep and now, on Sunday night, the party coalesced into a hazy scheme that would irreversibly alter the rest of Karla Faye Tucker's life: let's break into Jerry's apartment.

A motley assortment was gathered at Tucker's rented three-bedroom house at 2205 McKean Street in northwest Houston. There was twenty-three-year-old Tucker; her boyfriend, thirty-seven-year-old bartender Danny Garrett; Jimmy Leibrandt, a thirty-year-old maker of excellent bathtub speed who would turn out to be a third-wheel accomplice; Tucker's sister Kari and Kari's ex-husband Ronnie Burrell, who served as Jimmy Leibrandt's partner in the speed-making business. "It was all a bunch of big, bad, dope talk," Karla said. "You sit around in circles like that, and you talk about things that never really develop, never turn into anything but talk." There were two pit bulls on the premises. A twelve-gauge pump shotgun behind the couch. A cast of sketchy minor characters coming and going all weekend, looking to satisfy a jones for drugs and sex and shit-talk. Supremely bored, tired of simply jabbering, Danny Garrett found a stray sheet of paper and started sketching out the floor plan to Jerry's apartment. Karla's man was ex-Navy, a Vietnam vet, a self-proclaimed expert on all matters related to reconnaissance, just the kind of guy who could lead this charge, if everybody fell in line with his plan. Intrigued by the idea, Karla disappeared into another room and returned with the keys to Jerry's apartment and car. How'd she come by the keys? Her best girlfriend, Shawn Dean, just happened to be Jerry's estranged wife. A week ago, she'd been washing Shawn Dean's jeans and found the spare set in a pocket.

So, okay. Danny Garrett knew the layout to Jerry's place, and Karla had a key—they could actually do this. They could ride over there and shake things up a bit.

For several weeks now, Karla had been reveling in the possibility of, to borrow her vernacular, "offing" Jerry and making off with his Harley. She believed she had more than enough reasons to justify a little larceny. Beyond what she viewed as his general assholishness, Jerry had given Karla reasons aplenty to hate his guts. For starters, her girlfriend Shawn Dean was currently sporting a broken nose and busted lip courtesy of her ex-husband Jerry. What's more, the twenty-seven-year-old cable installer had once destroyed a photo album of Karla's, including a picture of her now-dead mother. He'd stabbed the picture full of holes. She'd already exacted a measure of revenge by laying into him like a hellcat and punching him in his eyeglasses, an attack that resulted in a trip to the emergency room to get glass removed from his eye—but they were not yet even. And finally, as if she didn't already have enough motivation, there was the matter of the motorcycle. Jerry loved that motorcycle. Karla hated it. She adored Harleys, all Harleys in general, but despised this one because it was his. She was nursing a grudge because Jerry had once parked his leaking bike in her living room. Oil all over the carpet. That scene was in fact her intro to Jerry. She had just returned from another two-week spot as a prostitute in Midland, and when she walked in the door of her apartment, there it was, somebody's motorcycle. "I'd been married to a biker," Karla said, "so I understood that. It was just that—coming home from out of town, doing what I was doing—I was ready to come home, crawl in my bed and rest for a week." And when she saw the bike and then went upstairs to find Shawn Dean and this scrawny man she didn't know in *her* bed, well, it didn't make for a good first impression. She served notice to Shawn Dean: you can come over anytime, but don't bring that loser with you. She said she'd off him; for his part, Jerry was more diplomatic in reciprocating his particular brand of antipathy—he said he didn't want to kill Karla, only take a flare gun to her pretty face so she'd be scarred and disfigured for the rest of her days.

Anyway, despite all the talk of violence, they did not go over to Jerry's apartment at 4000 Watonga aiming to kill him, Tucker said later. No murderous intent at all. "We were very wired," she said, "and we was looking for something to do." The plan tonight was just to "case the joint out"—they wanted to survey the premises so that maybe later that night, if things got really dull, they could circle back this way and steal Jerry's motorcycle. Strip it clean of its parts. Make off with a mother lode and maybe build her own bike. If she got a chance to intimidate him a little, well, all right then. He had it coming.

So here we are. On June 13, 1983, at sometime around three in the morning, the threesome of Karla, her boyfriend Danny Garrett, and their buddy Jimmy Leibrandt climbed into Garrett's 1977 blue Ranchero and rode the five miles over to Jerry's apartment. They probably rolled the windows down—the temp was in the low seventies, but the humidity exceeded 90 percent, and scattered clouds hung like scraps of dirty rags in the sky.

It was predawn, a Monday. The time when the night is at its most vulnerable hour, when you wake up to stumble down the hall to the bathroom and feel suddenly struck by how temporary the world is; when that thick void in the middle of the night comes like a pall over your consciousness and smothers you in every insecurity you can imagine. The hour you feel compelled to check on your children, just to make sure they're still sleeping, that no evil has befallen them during the night.

Karla and Danny Garrett were dressed for action. She was wearing a dark T-shirt, jeans, kicker boots. He was wearing a black Harley shirt, jeans, motorcycle boots. He was getting locked into his military mindset and taking special pride in being prepared and organizing undercover ventures like tonight's. He was carrying gloves and the shotgun he kept behind the couch, but Karla would later insist this did not mean they came to do violence. It was merely protocol. "We never went anywhere without a weapon," she claimed. "Danny always carried his little .38 pistol in his boot.... It would have been stupid to go there and walk around at three or four in the morning and not have some kind of protection. You certainly didn't go to case a place out and not be prepared for unexpected trouble lurking around a corner. Besides, in our circle of friends, you were always prepared for unexpected occurrences." When they arrived in the parking lot of the Windtree apartment complex, Karla and Danny Garrett urged Jimmy Leibrandt to join them in their stealth mission and go inside. But the third wheel made one of the few truly judicious decisions of his life. He chose his own role in the operation. He would scout out Jerry's El Camino. It had to be somewhere around here in the parking lot.

Karla and Danny Garrett went in the first-floor apartment, #2313, alone. Karla unlocked the door with the key she'd found in Shawn Dean's jeans; Danny Garrett slipped past her and led the way. It was a small apartment, 723 square feet. Linoleum in the kitchen, carpet toward the back. It didn't take long for them to cover the space, especially since Danny Garrett had been here and knew the floor plan. Once inside, Karla used a flashlight to locate the motorcycle. As expected, it wasn't intact. Jerry indeed had been restoring it, and parts and tools were strewn all over the place.

It was then that a voice, male, called out from one of the bedrooms in the back. "What's going on?"

Instead of hitting the door and escaping into the night, Danny Garrett led Karla down the hallway, toward the voice, toward the rear of the apartment. The room they entered was an outright mess, full of boxes, work tools, a couple of stepladders, everything silhouetted by a crack in the curtains and a sliver of light breaking through. On the floor was a mattress—no bedframe, just a mattress. On it lay Jerry Lynn Dean, naked, long hair and a mustache, five-seven and 142 pounds according to the autopsy report.

Here's where Karla plopped herself down atop Jerry, pinning him down, and laid out tonight's one and only rule. "Don't move, motherfucker," she told him, "or you're dead."

Maybe this was supposed to be the part where she intimidated him. Roughed him up a little. Put a little scare in him. Good clean fun—all according to plan. "My idea of getting even with him meant confronting him," she said. "Standing toe to toe, fist to fist." So this is what it had come to.

But then Jerry broke the one rule and panicked and reached out to grab for Karla's hands—doing the kind of thing you do when you wake at three in the morning to find somebody sitting on you, straddling your waist.

Danny Garrett leapt into action and shoved Karla onto the floor. And according to Karla, it was then that he veered from their stated plan.

Danny Garrett began wailing on Jerry with a hammer. Roundhouse swings upside his head.

It's impossible to know for certain what synapses were firing inside Karla's brain at that moment. Was she shocked by what he had just done? Did it really go against their intentions—or was this their scheme all along? Given the veritable pharmacy clouding her thinking, could she even process it? Was her next move what she had set out to do from the beginning? All we know is what she claimed: they had come here just to "case the joint out."

Danny Garrett hit Jerry with the hammer and hit him some more, over and over—until somehow in the ruckus, his victim finally ended up face down on his mattress. Maybe satisfied with the work he'd done, Danny Garrett then left the room. He started loading an armful of motorcycle parts into the bed of his Ranchero. Just like they'd come to do.

Alone now with Jerry Lynn Dean, Karla became, well, *distressed* by the sound coming from the dying man's body. A gurgling noise. Blood and fluid flowing into his lungs. Danny Garrett had hit Jerry atop the cranium so hard and so many times that his whole head became unhinged from his neck, which resulted in blood and mucus filling his breathing passages and, okay, Karla didn't know the science of it all—all she knew was she could not take it. It was like her nemesis was exacting revenge, taunting her with his refusal to die.

She turned on the overhead light. Maybe she turned on the radio too—when police showed up the next morning the radio was blasting rock 'n' roll, even though nobody's rightly sure who cranked it up. But no amount of light or music could drown out what was coming from this man lying half on, half off the mattress. "That sound," Karla later said during her trial. "All I wanted to do was stop him from making that noise."

Jerry Lynn Dean cobbled together a living from a number of jobs, one of which was with the cable company. He laid cable from telephone poles to houses. Dirty, hot, grunt work. Digging a trench anywhere surely is hard labor, requiring a sturdy instrument, but digging one in Houston's reclaimed swampland is another matter altogether. Jerry used a pickax to get the job done, four-feet long with a handle thick as a baseball bat and an iron head two-feet across, tip to tip. An ax blade on one side of the head and an adze on the other. He gripped the handle and brought the heavy tool up over his shoulder and brought it down, fast, into ground baked hard as concrete by the unforgiving Texas sun. He wrestled roots from the soil, busted dirt clods, unearthed rocks. Sometimes what he was swinging on was concrete. You can conjure the sound of such a tool reducing cement to rubble. What I'm saying is this: if a pickax were a person, it'd be a mean son of a bitch.

Jerry's pickax was leaning against the wall, right there among the boxes and garden tools and stepladders and more boxes. Karla saw it there, right about time she needed to make that gurgling noise stop.

"I reached over and grabbed it," Karla said. And here there's no hesitation in describing what comes next. It's as though there's only one thing she can do, once the tool is in her grip. "And I swung it and hit him in the back with it—four or five times."

It's hard to imagine her swinging a weapon that heavy and unwieldy several consecutive times. Even a woman as tenacious as Karla, a woman who dreamed of being the first female quarterback in the NFL, a woman with a history of fistfights, would need a break. Maybe in between each swing of the fifteen-pound ax she paused, resting, her chest heaving and her ear cocked, listening for that sound, wishing it gone.

But the gurgling continued.

It was around this time that Jimmy Leibrandt entered the apartment for the first time. He'd located Jerry's El Camino in the parking lot and was likely getting antsy about what was taking so long—or maybe he was just here to help Danny Garrett move motorcycle parts to the truck. When he stepped through the front door, he heard the gurgling noise that he would later say sounded "like an aquarium pump that was broken."

He entered the bedroom just in time to glimpse Karla standing with one foot on Jerry's body covered with a sheet, working the pickax loose from his back, wriggling it by the handle.

"She finally got the ax out," Jimmy Leibrandt said, "got it up over her head, turned and looked at me and smiled, and hit the dude again."

When Jimmy Leibrandt saw Karla smile and bring the ax down again, he decided he'd seen too much already. His next move was a good one, almost as good as choosing to stay outside while his two partners in crime broke into Jerry's place in search of a motorcycle. He did next what you and I and most anybody would've done, if we bore witness to such a heinous sight.

In the words of both Karla and Danny Garrett, their boy Jimmy Leibrandt "tucked tail and ran."

While Karla was laying into Jerry, Danny Garrett returned from loading Harley parts into his Ranchero. He heard the gurgling and saw Karla struggling to make it stop. He figured he had a method that would take care of the problem. So he proceeded to roll Jerry over face-up; then he took up the pickax himself, and brought it down squarely into Jerry's chest.

With that, Jerry Lynn Dean finally quit making that infernal noise.

Danny Garrett returned to the business of hauling motorcycle parts to his vehicle; Karla again stayed in the room, just she and Jerry's corpse.

Only, sometime about now she made a discovery: she and Jerry weren't alone. Someone was hiding against the wall under the bedsheets. Throughout the whole ordeal—the hammer and the gurgling and the pickax and the gurgling and the pickax splitting open Jerry's chest—a woman had been in the room, overhearing every gruesome detail and no doubt praying somehow could she get out of this apartment with her life. Deborah Thornton was a thirty-two-year-old office worker. She'd had a big fight with her husband, and perhaps with revenge on her mind she met Jerry at a pool party that very afternoon and maybe had a little too much to drink and then made a fateful decision: she made arrangements for her two kids to be taken care of and went home with him. She brought with her a change of clothes, a dress that police would find hanging in the bathroom the next morning, and planned to go straight to her job as a bookkeeper at a mortgage company. Under the bed sheets, right this moment, she was wearing only a T-shirt and some jewelry. She was a stranger to both Karla and Danny Garrett, but because she had borne witness to Jerry's murder, she too would have to die. The way Karla saw it, there was really no other recourse. Collateral damage.

Karla commenced picking Deborah Thornton, too. She squeezed the pickax and hoisted it and swung it again and brought it down on—but not through—the woman's shoulder. Deborah Thornton came up fighting, clawing for her life, trying to get hold of that pickax and avoid the same fate as the man she'd met this afternoon. But around this time Danny Garrett again returned to the room and wrestled the weapon away from the two women. It was quite a scrap—later Danny Garrett would speak of Deborah Thornton with admiration when he recalled how much more fight she had put up than Jerry Lynn Dean.

He was able to do what Karla was not. He lodged the blade in the woman's shoulder.

When Deborah Thornton begged for death, saying she couldn't take any more—Karla later said her last words were, "Oh God, it hurts, if you're going to kill me, please do it now"—Danny Garrett obliged by kicking her in the chin, knocking her flat on her back. Then with brute force so efficient that it must have seemed clinical in its execution, he took aim and swung the pickax into her chest. When police found Deborah Thornton the next morning, the weapon was sitting upright, its business end buried seven inches deep.

For good measure, Danny Garrett and Karla loaded the last of the motorcycle parts—the frame—into the bed of Jerry's El Camino. (Jimmy Leibrandt had already disappeared with the Ranchero.) They stole a few smaller items, including both the victims' wallets, and made off with his vehicle.

When daylight came and they had left behind this bloody mess, and the pickax too, the radio was still going, loud. That music, and the overhead light, were the only signs of life inside apartment #2313.

At about ten minutes shy of seven in the morning, a man named Gregory Travers showed up at the door of Jerry Lynn Dean's apartment. Gregory Travers was twenty-six. He lived in Windtree apartments, too. Jerry had been supposed to pick up Travers, a friend of his, for work. They had a gig together installing burglar alarms with

a security company and they were scheduled to clock in at seven. When he failed to show by twenty till, Travers thought maybe his buddy JD had overslept, so he toted his favorite coffee cup—the one with an American flag on it—the short distance to Jerry's place. He found that his ride to work—Jerry's El Camino—was nowhere in sight. The hell? Had Jerry left without him? It wasn't like Jerry to just take off and leave him hanging like this. The apartment door was ajar. He rapped on it.
No response.
He called Jerry's name.
No response.
Then he went on in.
The first thing Gregory Travers noted was loud music. Rock 'n' roll. "Maybe Lynyrd Skynyrd or something like that," he later recalled. Or maybe something like Loverboy's "Hot Girls in Love" or Billy Idol's "White Wedding," both of which were Power Plays on Top 40 radio that week. He noticed that Jerry's bike was gone from the living room, that his TV had been moved to the floor. He moved toward the music, following its trail, drifting deeper into the apartment, toward the bedroom in the back where the racket seemed to be coming from. Those were likely some slow steps he took.

Finally he passed through the door. Piles of dirty laundry lay about the room. Garden tools were strewn about. Boxes and boxes of stuff. Streaks of red on the walls.

And then there is Jerry Lynn Dean: naked, his long hair over his face, his body riddled with holes. Travers doesn't take time to count, but the stab and puncture wounds in Jerry's body will total twenty-eight. Next to Jerry, well, here are Gregory Travers's words: "I seen the girl with a pickax in her heart."

He backed out of the room, kept backing almost to the door of the apartment, only stopping long enough to set his coffee cup with the American flag on the kitchen counter. "I tried to run back to my apartment, but I couldn't catch my breath," he said.

Then Gregory Travers did the next natural thing when walking into a nightmare such as this one. He called the police.

In the coming months and years, he would struggle to sleep at night and get the image of what he had seen out of his head. But right now, he had more pressing and immediate concerns. As law enforcement made their way to the scene, he sat down on the curb outside Jerry Lynn Dean's apartment and tried to breathe.

Chapter 4

EVANGEL

It is September of 1987, and Reverend Jerry Falwell is about to take a trip down a water slide. It's not just any slide, mind you, it's the Killer Typhoon—a 163-foot straight drop that, if he stays in the good graces of his God, will deposit Falwell safely into a pool of sparkling chlorinated water in four seconds flat. The Killer Typhoon is the feature ride at Heritage USA, a 2,300-acre theme park advertised as the Christian Disney World, at Fort Mill, South Carolina. If you're standing on the ground, squinting up at its peak fifty-three feet high, it must look like a waterfall spilling out of heaven. But if you're up there at the top, as Falwell is, it likely doesn't feel like heaven, because we all know there's no fear in heaven. Worried the current will sweep him down the slide before he's prayed up and ready, Falwell clings to a metal bar as though it's salvation itself. Way down there at the bottom, in what no doubt seems like another zip code, the Rock Hill, South Carolina, rescue squad and the pool lifeguards wait for the good reverend to take the plunge. Falwell asks who put the piranhas down there. He jokes about being a lamb led to the slaughter. He complains about how cold the water is. "Twenty-two million dollars," he says. "Was it worth it? I don't know."

Reverend Jerry Falwell is here to prove to you he's a man of his word. He's making good on a vow. The PTL club—standing for Praise the Lord, or People that Love, or (to its critics) Pass the Loot—is $68 million in the hole, but Falwell has orchestrated what he calls a "summer of survival" campaign. He has promised that if PTL can raise

$20 million during a fundraising drive, he'll hit the skids of the Killer Typhoon. One thousand people donating $1,000 each by Labor Day, that's all he asked—how clean and tidy his request—and sure enough, the people have come through. When he announced that the goal had been met, Falwell told viewers, "I may break my fool neck, but I'm going down that water slide . . . I invite you to watch this idiot do it." He added that those special donors would receive an autographed copy of his life story, which would be published in October.

But to really understand what's gotten into the reverend and how he's come to find himself in this predicament is to wind through the history of American evangelicalism, from our emergence from religious slumber during the Great Awakening of the 1700s to the moment Falwell perched his 245-pound frame at the top of that slide, said his prayers, and shoved off. To my mind, the spectacle surrounding this stunt also tells us a lot about the peculiar elixir of cultural forces that led to the rise of men like Falwell and Pat Robertson and ultimately provided a platform for Karla Faye Tucker to cause America to reckon anew with the death penalty.

A poster fashioned for the occasion quips, *Don't Backslide, Jerry.* He's wearing a sticker on his back that reads, *Farewell Falwell.* He recites the Lord's Prayer and the twenty-third Psalm. He crosses himself, then crosses his legs. He assumes the posture of a man in a coffin, about to be laid to rest—and perhaps he is. But first, before he pushes off, we must observe this salient detail: Reverend Jerry Falwell is wearing his Sunday suit. It's a blue suit, with a white dress shirt, red tie, and suspenders. Along with the Lord's Prayer, it's likely that he utters a brief but silent appeal to his Heavenly Father that these suspenders will be sturdy enough to endure the Newtonian force that this type of concentrated velocity can exert.

Evangel means "gospel," or simply "good news." It's a Greek word that conceivably could apply to all Christians, but during the early 1700s, when the First Great Awakening spread religious revival across America and democratized faith through an appeal to a thoroughly individual and deeply personal relationship with Christ, the term came to fit Protestants in an enduring manner. "Evangelists" like George Whitefield—who brought the gospel to field workers on a voice that was said to carry a mile—and Jonathan Edwards—who relied upon the frightening imagery of a "God that holds you over the pit of Hell, much as one holds a spider" to startle worshippers from their complacency—aimed to convert the masses one by one to the faith. In a tradition that so emphasized your unique relationship to the Almighty, there was room for disagreement about creeds, but the faith coalesced around a select few beliefs that came to define the doctrine of these people: the Bible was the inerrant word of God and the final authority; you were born a sinner, but you could be "born again" via a profession of faith that Jesus had died on the cross to atone for your sins; and it is your duty as a believer to carry out the Great Commission by spreading the word of Christ's death, burial, and resurrection to unbelievers so that they too might be transformed same as you were. Though the Great Awakening generated a marketplace of diverse sects of Protestantism, you could be a member of virtually any branch—everything from Baptist to Pentecostal to Methodist to Dutch Reformed—and still be welcome among the evangelicals.

The Second Great Awakening would arrive in the early 1800s, leading to a further diversification of sects and a series of reform movements. As one of these movements, abolitionism, gained momentum and the Civil War drew closer, slavery became the fulcrum that divided the evangelical world and, in particular, gave different expressions to it in North and South. My denomination, the Southern Baptists, actually became a distinct sect by breaking ties with their northern brethren over the issue of human bondage. As abolitionist sentiment grew in the North after 1830, and William Lloyd Garrison and his ilk started circulating pamphlets advocating emancipation throughout the southern states, slaveholders felt their way of life was under assault. Some northern ministers went as far as to call for their excommunication from the church.

In 1844, the Baptist General Convention announced it would not acknowledge and support any missionary who was not committed to emancipation. The following year, at Augusta, Georgia, southern Baptists retaliated by officially splitting from their northern brethren and forming the Southern Baptist Convention. Their founding document was silent on the issue of slavery, declaring their formation was "for the purpose of carrying into effect the benevolent intentions of our constituents," but those constituents recently had made clear their "benevolent intentions" in a test case by nominating one James Reeve as a missionary. That Reeve was a slaveholder was no accident.

In the aftermath of the 1845 formation of the SBC, religious southerners reconceived of their identity and their relation to the rest of the US. By their estimation, the South was God's country; the North was the world—the secular, godless, crass, materialistic, worldly world. The southern way of life had to be protected and preserved, and a first step was for slaveholders to resort to the ultimate defense of their practice of slavery. They told abolitionists that if they had a problem with the peculiar institution, they shouldn't complain to them—they should take it up with the Almighty.

Read your Bible, they advised. It's there in black and white, the natural order of things. Look at Ephesians 6:5: "Servants, be obedient to them that are your masters according to the flesh, with fear and trembling, in singleness of your heart, as unto Christ." Or Titus 2:9: "Exhort servants to be obedient unto their own masters, and to please them well in all things; not answering again." Or Colossians 3:22: "Servants, obey in all things your masters according to the flesh; not with eye service, as men pleasers; but in singleness of heart, fearing God."

Remember, it was the North that had served as home to America's first protestant dissidents, the Puritans. Since the origins of European settlement in the New World, the North had been God's territory—home not only to the Puritans but also religious groups like Quakers and Catholics who ran afoul of their strict laws. The North had John Winthrop, the governor of the Massachusetts Bay colony, whose 1629 sermon *Model of Christian Charity* outlines clear religious motives for life in America:

First of all, true Christians are of one body in Christ (1 Cor. 12). Ye are the body of Christ and members of their part. All the parts of this body being thus united are made so contiguous in a special relation as they must needs partake of each other's strength and infirmity; joy and sorrow, weal and woe. If one member suffers, all suffer with it, if one be in honor, all rejoice with it.

The South, by comparison, was a veritable Babylon. It had the Virginia Cavalier William Byrd, an Anglican planter who infamously kept a diary recording his daily activities.

October 6. I rose at 6 o'clock and said my prayers and ate milk for breakfast. Then I proceeded to Williamsburg, where I found all well. I went to the capitol where I sent for the wench to clean my room and when I came I kissed her and felt her . . . About 10 o'clock I went to my lodgings. I had good health but wicked thoughts. God forgive me.

But the fact that southerners had structured their whole economic system around the engine of forced labor meant they and northerners would reverse their original religious identities. If manumission were granted, Thomas Jefferson's doomsday prediction in *Notes on the State of Virginia*—that "considering numbers, nature, and natural means only, a revolution of the wheel of fortune, an exchange of situation, is among possible events"—would become manifest. In other words, insurrection and anarchy could reverse the social order and make the white man subject to his former slave. And so it was that southerners became literal interpreters of scripture. Slavery, they argued, was sanctioned and protected by God's word.

A distinct and recognizable South, then, emerged. A clear line of division was drawn between it and the North. It was not simply a location directionally below the North; it was, simply put, Beulah Land. Now a separate future was not only imaginable but practically visible.

Of course, we know what that led to, and how it turned out.

It wouldn't be until 1995, on the occasion of the Sesquicentennial meeting of the Southern Baptist Convention in Atlanta, that the organization officially adopted a resolution in which it renounced its racist roots and apologized for its historical defense of white supremacy. Early on, the statement acknowledges that "our relationship to African-Americans has been hindered from the beginning by the role that slavery played in the formation of the Southern Baptist Convention" and that "racism profoundly distorts our understanding of Christian morality, leading some Southern Baptists to believe that racial prejudice and discrimination are compatible with the Gospel." Then the document shifts to a litany of resolutions, among them the claim that every human is made in God's image and that through Christ, all are united as one. "We lament and repudiate historic acts of evil such as slavery from which we continue to reap a bitter harvest," the statement claims, "and we recognize that the racism which yet plagues our culture today is inextricably tied to the past." An apology is extended to all African Americans, an offer of repentance is made, and a request for forgiveness is tendered. It's a fine resolution, all things considered. It was even accompanied by a piece of cultural theater. Reverend Gary Frost of Youngstown, Ohio, who was the first African American to be elected to second vice president of the SBC, made a grand acceptance of the apology on behalf of his race and extended forgiveness in the name of Jesus Christ. Just like that, 150 years of white supremacy within the Southern Baptist church was magically atoned for.

Shortly after this announcement, I made a rare appearance at the church I had grown up in, where my father was still a deacon. I suppose I was in search of some discernible change that the SBC's statement had generated in our congregation.

Maybe the reckoning was inward, invisible to the casual onlooker. It was impossible to know.

Every face in the building was white.

With the rise of industrialism and the destruction wrought by World War I, early twentieth-century evangelicalism centered around a fundamentalist rebellion against everything "modern": speakeasies, jazz, the Charleston, women's bobbed hair, and virtually any kind of change. President Warren Harding seemed to capture the evangelical desire for a return to foundational principles when he claimed, "America's present need is not heroics but healing; not nostrums but normalcy; not revolution but restoration . . . not surgery but serenity." It was the Scopes Trial of 1925 that dramatized the rivalry between fundamentalism and modernity—and ultimately illustrated how little cultural capital evangelicals actually possessed.

It was as much sideshow as court proceeding, as the tiny town of Dayton in East Tennessee became, for a time, the center of the universe. Science and religion were squaring off in the Trial of the Century, which became the first courtroom proceeding to be broadcast over national radio. Local schoolteacher John T. Scopes had the unmitigated gall to teach evolution, which violated the laws against such practice in the state. (Three students had testified against him at the grand jury, one of whom afterward told reporters, "I believe in part of evolution, but I don't believe in the monkey business.") In came Clarence Darrow, a bigshot lawyer and avowed agnostic, to defend Scopes. A fundamentalist politician, William Jennings Bryan, led the prosecution. From as far away as London, two hundred reporters descended on Dayton, and brought with them an atmosphere that can only be described as carnival-like. Monkeys, monkeys everywhere: pictured on billboards and in shop windows. You could even pay to get your picture made with a live chimpanzee.

Of course, fundamentalists celebrated the verdict when, after only eight minutes of jury deliberation, John Scopes was convicted of teaching evolution in a high school science class. He was fined a hundred dollars. But the trial's defining moment—both at the time and historically—was defense lawyer Darrow's scathing examination of prosecutor Bryan on the stand. For two hours, Darrow relentlessly grilled Bryan as an expert witness on the Bible. He queried Bryan as to whether Eve was indeed created from Adam's rib and where in the world Cain found his wife and how about that whale that swallowed Jonah whole—anything that scrutinized whether Biblical stories could square with even a remotely rational perspective on human life. Darrow told Bryan, "You insult every man of science and learning in the world because he does not believe your fool religion." It was all grand amusement to a crowd so big that proceedings had to be moved from the courtroom to the courthouse lawn because officials feared the floor would collapse (and indoors was hot as Hades too). But the trial's impact on the public's regard for fundamentalists particularly and evangelicals generally went far beyond the small town of Dayton, Tennessee. It resigned them to the margins of society, where everybody thought they would remain forever. The journalist and critic H. L. Mencken provided an apt summation of Bryan and the South, dismissing both in one fell swoop as a "tin pot pope in the Coca-Cola belt." The fundamentalists had won the case, but lost in the court of public opinion. Similar to the Civil War, where the North gained victory but lost the narrative as the United Daughters of the Confederacy persuaded generations of southerners to embrace Lost Cause mythology, the fundamentalists won the case but looked absurd to much of America.

For his part, Bryan himself got the worst of it. He died five days later during an afternoon nap.

Things did not go well for us evangelicals for a good long while. For the first time in US history, Protestantism's cultural dominance was challenged. By and large, evangelicals retreated into their own subculture and isolated themselves from mainstream America. They were not politically engaged; many were not even registered to vote. The emergence of revivalist Billy Graham in the late 1940s helped keep the faith afloat in public consciousness, particularly his brand of neoevangelicalism that rejected narrow fundamentalism, but the increasing secularization of American society was becoming evident in almost every respect. Perhaps the low point for believers came in 1962, when the Supreme Court barred religious instruction from public schools and outlawed school-sponsored prayer. Atheist Madalyn Murray O'Hair named her son as plaintiff in a lawsuit against the Baltimore school system. (Her son William later became a Christian and a Baptist minister, prompting O'Hair to say,

"I repudiate him entirely and completely for now and all times. He is beyond human forgiveness.") The 1971 case *Green v. Connally* only fueled the fire. In the aftermath of *Brown v. Board*, so-called segregation academies (including Jerry Falwell's Lynchburg Christian School in Virginia) had responded by exercising what they believed was their God-given right to exclude Black students. But *Green v. Connally* declared that segregated private schools were ineligible for tax-exempt status. Then came the nadir, *Roe v. Wade*, in 1973. Falwell described reading about the decision in the newspaper: "I sat there staring at the Roe v. Wade story, growing more and more fearful of the consequences of the Supreme Court's act and wondering why so few voices had been raised against it." In total, this collection of court decisions served as a series of dominoes that evangelicals watched fall with a feeling of desperation and a realization that they were drowning in a secular culture that threatened to drive them to extinction. But this helplessness was short-lived, because ultimately this conviction—that they were being persecuted in the land that God had set aside for them as His chosen people—galvanized them.

They were about to make their presence felt again in a way nobody could deny.

In 1976, the year I turned eight, Jimmy Carter ran for president. Jimmy was a Georgian like us, a peanut farmer from Plains, down in Sumter County, and we heard our voices in his accent. He was Southern Baptist too, devout, vocal, and outspoken about his beliefs. Two-thirds of Georgians voted for Jimmy as he won the election over Gerald Ford. He carried all 159 counties in the state. Four years earlier, Nixon had run the table in every Georgia county, so the election of this homegrown boy with the pearly teeth completely overturned the recent past. Jimmy proudly carried the title of America's first "born again" president.

The election of a devout believer like Carter set the mainstream media and the pollsters on a mad scramble to identify exactly who these evangelicals were. One moment we were regarded as a fringe group, adrift like so much deadwood amid the tide of secularism—the next a force to be reckoned with, capable of engineering a shift in the zeitgeist. Gallup estimated that the number of born-again Christians in America exceeded some fifty million—almost a quarter of the US population. To arrive at this number, Gallup asked a straightforward question: "Would you say that you have been 'born again' or have had a 'born again' experience—that is, a turning point in your life when you committed yourself to Christ?" In other words, have you had your Before and After? Thirty-four percent of respondents said yes.

But what the national media failed to ascertain is that the evangelical community was more eclectic, diverse, and unpredictable than anyone suspected. My father portended the real changes to come. He did not vote for our fellow Georgian Jimmy Carter. Evangelicals would become instrumental players in national politics, all right, but Carter's brand of progressive faith was short-lived. They unexpectedly shifted their allegiances to the right.

Four years later, in the run-up to the 1980 election, evangelical leaders orchestrated what became a monumental rally in Dallas. Texas televangelist James Robison served as the event's lead organizer. Over seventeen thousand Born Againers filled Reunion Arena. The list of speakers constituted a who's who of evangelical heavyweights—First Baptist Dallas pastor W. A. Criswell, future Southern Baptist Convention president Adrian Rogers, First Baptist Atlanta pastor Charles Stanley, and current Convention president Bailey Smith (who incidentally almost singlehandedly undercut all the momentum generated by the rally when he made an off-the-cuff remark that "God Almighty does not hear the prayer of a Jew"). Perhaps other presidential candidates were leery of the optics; maybe they weren't extended as hearty a welcome. In any case, only one accepted an invitation to take the stage: Ronald Reagan.

James Robison offered Reagan some advice. "I looked at Mr. Reagan," Robison recalled. "I said, 'We really like you; we really like you. We like the principles that you espouse. But you need to understand something about the nature of this group that you'll speak to tonight and those of us in this room. We're not partisan; we're not pro-party;

we're not pro-personality. We're pro-principle. If you stand by the principles that you say you believe, we'll be the greatest friends you'll ever have.' But I said, 'If you turn against those principles, we'll be your worst nightmare.'"

Reagan navigated all of it with precision and aplomb. He spoke last, just after Robison, his appearance serving as the climax of the event. And he wasted no time bonding with the room. He opened with words that have been dubbed "the most famous lines in the Age of Evangelicalism." Standing at the podium, in a setting awash with red, white, and blue, Reagan trotted out all the folksy vernacular that became one of his trademarks. "I know you can't endorse me," he told the crowd, "but . . . I want you to know that I endorse you and what you are doing."

During his address, he said everything his audience came to hear: we need to get rid of pornography, drugs, and street crime, and restore the rule of law; we need to make America an economic powerhouse again so that nobody becomes "a perpetual ward of the state"; we need a return to "that old time religion and that old time Constitution." He told them about the supremacy of the Ten Commandments. He claimed traditional values were under assault in a secular culture. He told them that, as persecuted, oppressed, and marginalized victims of a Godless state, their religious dissent linked them to a tradition going back to Roger Williams that *made* them American. He said, "Under the pretense of separation of Church and State, religious beliefs cannot be advocated in many of our public institutions—but atheism can. You know, I've often had a fantasy: I've thought of serving an atheist a delicious gourmet dinner and then asking he or she whether they believed there was a cook." Applause and shouts of support interrupted Reagan frequently, forcing him to stop and wait out the praise. He held them in the palm of his hand.

It must be said that this seemed an unlikely pairing—Reagan and these evangelicals. Reagan's background showed that he was a divorced movie star, had signed legislation to expand abortion rights during his tenure as governor of California, and almost never went to church. The story goes that during the 1976 primaries, he was asked if he was born again—and he seemed to have no idea what the term meant. But tonight, surrounded by thousands of voters who defined themselves precisely that way, he wanted them to know he was one of them. Toward the end, he seized this moment to ally with evangelicals everywhere. Maybe it was calculated and contrived, but Reagan knew his audience: if he were trapped on an island with just one book, he told them, he'd take the Bible. Like them, he was someone who looked to the Scriptures for "fulfillment and guidance."

"We gave him a ten-minute standing ovation," Paul Weyrich, the coiner of the term "the moral majority," recalled. "I've never seen anything like it. The whole movement was snowballing by then."

In November of 1980, Jimmy won Georgia again, garnering 55 percent of the vote, but our state was one of only six that supported him. Reagan won the national election in a landslide, earning over eight million more votes than the incumbent and 82 percent of the evangelical tally. The Republican tide was so strong that even the Senate went red, for the first time since 1954. Carter had suffered his share of troubles both domestic and international—record inflation, gas lines stretching forever, hostages in Iran—that could have threatened any bid for reelection, but he had also left evangelicals underwhelmed. He'd been teaching Sunday school classes in Plains since his high school years, but many believers felt he left those lessons in the classroom. He was blamed for the government rescinding tax-exempt status from those so-called "segregation academies," including the evangelical Bob Jones University. And they believed he waffled on abortion. In contrast, a vital piece of Reagan's success had been his ability to enlist Jerry Falwell, Pat Robertson, and conservative Southern Baptists leaders to rally people like my father to enlist in a crusade against what they called "secular humanism." Abortion, gay rights, the ERA, the banning of school prayer: this was the battleground in an emerging holy war. Pro-lifers began publishing photos of aborted fetuses in jars. Anita Bryant, of orange-juice commercial fame, became the spokeswoman for Save Our Children, an antigay crusade. To combat NOW, Beverly LaHaye founded Concerned Women for America, a movement based on the conviction that "the feminists' anti-God, anti-family rhetoric" did not represent the majority of American women that Betty Friedan and others claimed to speak for. Public schools started instituting a moment of silence to replace the missing prayers. Falwell and his brethren had convinced the masses that, if they didn't show up at the ballot booth, America would fall, just like mankind had fallen in the Garden of Eden—and it would never again be the great Christian nation it once had been. It made for so persuasive a jeremiad that evangelicals flocked to the polls in record numbers. Carter himself acknowledged the success of Falwell's tactics: he claimed the Moral Majority had "purchased $10 million in radio commercials on southern radio and TV to brand me as a traitor to the South and no longer a Christian."

More than any president before him, Reagan made the phrase "God bless America" a commonplace statement in his addresses. He appointed C. Everett Koop, whose movie *Whatever Happened to the Human Race?* argued that abortion was infanticide, as Surgeon General. He declared 1983 the "Year of the Bible." The White House released an "issue alert" that described the numerous ways voluntary student prayers could be included in the school day. And Reagan continued to receive praise from evangelical leaders. Falwell called him "the greatest thing that has happened to our country in my lifetime." Robertson called him "probably the most evangelical president we have had since the founding fathers."

But by the end of Reagan's second term in the late eighties, the Moral Majority had started to wane, in part because Falwell hadn't persuaded Reagan to enact any of the "pro-family" legislation evangelicals had been promoting since long before the candidate's appearance in Dallas. Maybe out of frustration, Falwell passed the baton to Pat Robertson, son of a former US senator from Virginia named Absalom, initiating a second wave of the Christian right and a rebirth of the culture wars.

Robertson seemed bred for success in most any field. He possessed a family tree going back as far as Jamestown, a patrician private-school upbringing, a magna cum laude diploma from Washington and Lee, a degree from Yale Law, and he had held a lieutenant position during the Korean War. But then he failed the New York State bar exam. He secretly married a Yale nursing student who birthed their first child just ten weeks later. He started a company that sold, of all things, electrostatic loudspeakers, which promptly went belly-up.

Then, thanks to more than a little intervention from his fundamentalist mother, Robertson became a born-again Christian. He enrolled in seminary in New York. After graduation and a move with his family to Portsmouth, Virginia, in 1960, he bought an out-of-business UHF television station in a gutted building with a weak signal. He called his new venture the Christian Broadcasting Network, or CBN. Originally, the station aired sitcoms, westerns, kids shows, and a couple of religious broadcasts—none of which attracted what might be called a reliable audience. To keep his company going, Robertson needed money, badly, so in 1963 he held a telethon. He prayed that seven hundred watchers—*just seven hundred, friends!*—would reach deep into their pockets and contribute ten bucks per month. He made it clear that the future of the station depended on the generosity of the viewers, if there were any out there.

Here's where you probably think the miracle happened. You figure money started flooding in. You think this was the moment that God, human gullibility, new technology, or maybe sheer luck allowed Robertson to begin assembling an empire that would one day give Karla Faye Tucker the kind of platform that just might save her life.

That's not what happened. No windfall resulted. But Robertson did have a show title: *The 700 Club*. And years later, it would be that show that brought Karla Faye Tucker's face to the American public's attention.

Chapter 5

FISH AND KETCHUP

On the morning of June 14, 1983, the *Houston Post* ran a headline about funding for the Hardy Toll Road. The *Houston Chronicle*'s front page featured a story about a five-alarm hotel fire in Fort Worth. And on page fifteen of the *Chronicle*, tucked away far from the big stories of the day almost as an afterthought, was an article about two of the 556 homicides committed in Houston in 1983: a man and a woman had been hacked to death in a northwest apartment. The article ran only a few paragraphs in length.

"We had killings like that all the time—big, gruesome, horrible, bloody," said *Chronicle* reporter Eric Hanson, who covered police news for the paper throughout the decade. "Other than the pick ax, it wasn't that unusual, two people dead in an apartment. You'd think the pick ax would have gotten a lot of attention, but it didn't, which tells you a lot about Houston in the early '80s." Television news covered the story, including the standard footage of two covered bodies wheeled out on gurneys, but the incident merited no special attention otherwise.

Two years earlier, in 1981, Houston had endured an all-time high of 701 homicides, but now those numbers were dropping, and there was the general sense that violence was trending downward in the city. That trend, in fact, would continue throughout the decade. And overall, Houston at the time seemed like a good place to be, or at least a better one than the homicide rate suggested. You of course had NASA, big oil, and the "eighth wonder of the world," the Astrodome. Crude prices had begun to fall amidst a decline in demand, but the bust in the economy's sole industry was still a couple years away. The "Luv Ya Blue" era of Oiler football was in the rearview, but Earl Campbell, a Heisman trophy winner with the UT Longhorns and owner of thighs the size of tree trunks, was still toting the pigskin and punishing would-be tacklers. And the city was still reveling in the spotlight of *Urban Cowboy*, the 1980 movie set in Houston that had featured perhaps Hollywood's most bankable star in John Travolta and kicked off the mechanical bull craze.

Urban Cowboy showcased a heretofore underpublicized side of Texas that was straight-up Houston: the New West. In place of sunset mesas and open ranges, you had oil refineries and concrete and a honky-tonk based on Gilley's. In place of outlaw country music icons like Waylon Jennings, you got dance fads like "Cotton Eye Joe" and a soundtrack of polite country like Johnny Lee's "Looking for Love." You had Texas chic—new denim and bolo ties and felt ten-gallons and diamond-beaded hatbands and boots shined bright enough to reflect the neon lights. All in all, despite its utter lack of curb appeal, Houston, Texas seemed like a setting slap-full of rugged individualism and equal opportunity. A crass and sometimes crude meritocracy. A place where you could climb on the back of that mechanical bull, this New West's version of the bucking bronco, and ride it till you fell off. Who was in your family tree didn't matter so much—as long as you could hold on to the rope. All of which served as a distraction from the deaths of two people in a northwest apartment.

"As far as the actual crime scene, I don't remember it at all," reporter Eric Hanson continued. "I don't remember anyone even talking about it. It just sort of slipped through the cracks somehow."

They ditched Jerry Lynn Dean's El Camino in a parking lot near the Astrodome and burned the title papers. They threw his motorcycle parts into the Brazos River. You would think their next move would be skipping town in a panic, flooring the pedal of Danny Garrett's Ranchero and squeezing the wheel until their knuckles turned white as bone, but instead they made a curious move: they simply returned to 2205 McKean with a war story and absolute certainty there would be no repercussions to pay. What they had done did not even seem to register with Karla. "I was so spaced out on drugs all the time," she later told CNN's Larry King, "that it didn't seem real to me." And she didn't feel immediate remorse. "I not only didn't walk around with any guilt, I was proud of thinking that I had finally measured up to the big boys."

Later, Karla's ex-husband, Stephen Griffith, would insist this turn of events was simply the fulfillment of the destiny Karla herself had prophesied long ago. "She always said that someday she would be famous," he claimed. Now they were. Or maybe not Karla and Danny Garrett—not yet—but what they had done. All the media knew was the gristly mess they had left behind. The perpetrators of the crime were still a mystery.

That night, June 13, 1983, Karla and Danny Garrett were watching television news when a story about the murders came on the screen. It was a mind-bending moment for them, sitting back and seeing the world scramble to make sense of what they'd done without knowing who'd done it. The whole thing struck them as funny and more than a little absurd, and they giggled and laughed aloud like schoolkids at the futility of law enforcement's first bumbling attempts to formulate a strategy for their apprehension. I picture the two of them reveling in their deed Bonnie and Clyde-style, sitting side by side on the couch, their faces bathed in the blue screen light of the TV, marveling at how two people with their kind of background could suddenly find anything they did the subject of widespread attention. They had done something that moved the needle. Maybe never, in their whole lives, had they felt this kind of power. Never had other people taken this kind of time to care about anything they'd ever done. They were having so much fun, these two, maybe they should go find somebody else to off.

For the next five weeks, between June 13 and July 20, they were desperadoes—brazen, shameless, and full of undiluted adrenaline and braggadocio. Simply put, there was a lot of chest-thumping going on. For her part, Karla especially liked to tell friends she had an orgasm every time she swung that pickax. "Got a nut" was the way she liked to put it. The very depravity of the phrase brought her no little satisfaction. It seemed to be her favorite part of the story, the detail she never forgot to mention when regaling visitors with lurid tales of that night.

Meanwhile, investigators searched in vain for any clue that would lead them to the killers, sifting through suspects (including Karla, Danny, and everybody else who ever had beef with Jerry Lynn Dean) like cards in a deck. At first, they were mystified. There must have been a lot of head scratching going on. They seemed at a loss about what to do next.

Until finally they received a break in the case.

It came from, of all people, Doug Garrett. Danny's brother. He contacted Houston police. Doug and Tucker's sister Kari had been scared, scared. Kari in particular was becoming so nervous and paranoid that she couldn't sit still. They were worried about their role in the murders—the fact that they had known about them from the beginning but were sitting on the information. Creeping into the forefront of their consciousness was the persistent fear that Tucker and Garrett might get a notion to off *them*. Since the murders, they'd moved out of 2205 McKean in order to put some distance between themselves and all that trouble, and became something of a couple. (They would marry, eventually.) They took one of the pit bulls and struck out for safer environs. Now they were living together—an arrangement just like their brother and sister, Danny and Karla. But distance didn't bring them peace. Doug Garrett and Kari Tucker were taking turns sleeping, the waking one standing guard over the other with a shotgun. Now that their siblings had crossed over into homicide, who knew what they were capable of? Police were coming around, asking questions, showing them pictures of the crime scene, poking around. Maybe they were setting a trap for Doug and Kari. So they called up HPD homicide detective J. C. Mosier, who just happened to be a friend of Doug's, and told him what they knew.

It sounds like a cable TV movie, but that's the upshot: brother and sister called the law on brother and sister. Soon they went down to the police station and spent two hours spilling the details to detective Mosier in a formal report.

Eventually, on July 20, law enforcement would wire Doug Garrett with a recording device and, despite the Texas heat, send him in a long-sleeve black shirt to 2205 McKean, where during a conversation lasting little more than an hour, the killers gave police everything they would need to arm prosecution during the trial. Unexpectedly, maybe downright miraculously, while they were chatting something too fortuitous to possibly happen, happened. Their accomplice Jimmy Leibrandt, the third wheel, just happened to drop by. He hadn't been around for days. Doug Garrett probably could hardly contain the excitement he felt, knowing all three of the characters who rode over to 4000 Watango in the middle of the night were here, where a little one-stop shopping on behalf of the police force could round up all the bad guys in one fell swoop. No doubt, the detectives from HPD in an unmarked police van parked along a nearby side street felt the same thrill as they monitored the conversation and hoped Doug would execute his duty, which amounted by and large to simply keeping his mouth shut and letting Karla and Danny Garrett say all the magic words.

Doug Garrett played his role first-rate. He deflected questions about his long sleeve shirt on such a hot day by explaining he was just wearing his only clean one. He drank a beer and tried to act casual and asked the questions he'd been coached by law enforcement to ask. Did they plan to kill Jerry? No, they just "freaked." Why did they use the pickax? Because "it was there." Did Karla "get a nut" from the murders? "Well, hell yes," she said. Doug waited for a moment when he might need to say "Jesus Christ" and signal the guys in the truck that he was in trouble, but the moment never came. He just got the hell out of the way and let Karla and Danny Garrett do the rest. In an interview with Larry King, Karla described it this way: "[Danny's] brother came in," she said, "and he had a wire on him and he sat down on the bed, and he asked us about the crime.

And we shared detail for detail every step from what happened that night, what made us decide to go over there all the way through to when everything was over. And as soon as he got all of that, he left out of the house."

Karla told Doug Garrett goodbye, watched him climb on his motorcycle and ride away, then went to the refrigerator to rummage for a bite to eat—a piece of leftover fish and some ketchup.

Danny Garrett and Jimmy Leibrandt left out, drove away too—Danny to work and Jimmy to a nearby storage shed, where he planned to grab something or other before he went to a party. Law enforcement went into action immediately. At 6:30 p.m., Jimmy Leibrandt was unlocking a padlock in the parking lot of the storage facility when suddenly he found himself surrounded by policemen, guns drawn. They told him he had the right to remain silent; they told him he had the right to an attorney, and if he could not afford to hire an attorney, one would be provided for him. Minutes later, at 6:44, a squadron of police circled Danny Garrett as he drove to work in his blue Ranchero. He offered no resistance when police approached his vehicle.

Back at 2205 McKean, nobody knows that both Jimmy Leibrandt and Danny Garrett have been read Miranda and are in custody.

So it's only a few moments later, then, that Karla Faye Tucker's sitting on the couch dipping her fish into her ketchup, and the police bust in. Shouts and brandished weapons and demands to get their hands up, goddammit, *up*! They spill throughout the rooms. Riled up by the racket, the dog behind a closed bedroom door barks like gunfire. Everybody in the house scatters. One guy leaps out a window in the back, naked but for a robe. Karla's off the couch, in the hallway, stumbling around in circles in snakeskin cowboy boots, blue jeans, and a spaghetti-strap shirt and still clinging to her plate of fish. Before she can process what's happening, they're kicking her feet apart and planting her face against the wall and pressing a gun against her head.

The fish winds up somewhere on the floor. The ketchup splatters everywhere, like blood.

In the police cruiser, on the way to jail, she is chatty, gossipy about people she knows that detective J. C. Mosier also knows—as though it does not register with her what is going down here. She seems oblivious as to why she's being arrested. Maybe she's indeed that clueless; or maybe it's an ill-fated attempt to use whatever charm she can muster to orchestrate a better ending than this one. Likely she's just too drug addled to process exactly what's happening, the sheer weight of this moment, the world tipping on its axis in such a way that nothing will ever be the same for her. In any case, she's not up to speed yet, but she will be soon enough, because let's make it clear: as long as she lives, Karla Faye Tucker will never gulp a breath of free air again.

Chapter 6

PUPPET SHOW

Karla Faye Tucker was most certainly her mother's daughter. Carolyn Tucker was born in Houston, a Texas girl through and through. She married in '56, gave birth to three girls: Kathi in '57, Kari in '58, and Karla in November of '59. When the daughters were young the family did okay for themselves, had some money coming in, made a gradual climb into neighborhoods each slightly better than the last, kept a dog named Ladybug. They even got a bay house and a boat on a lake an hour from Houston. You look at pics of Karla from those days and she seems for all the world like a poster child for Americana.

Then who knows what precisely shifted in Carolyn's head and heart, but when the sixties hit in full force she decided she wasn't cut out anymore for the prim and proper. All those rigid and clear-cut June Cleaver-type expectations of what a woman should be and do suddenly seemed to fit like a knock-off Christian Dior dress she'd hopelessly outgrown. She developed, in particular, a liking for men who seemed as far away from convention as possible. Stable ones like her husband Larry held no sway with her. And by the time Karla was eight, Carolyn Tucker was already escorting her youngest daughter into the world of drugs, teaching her how to roll the perfect joint, because if you're gonna do it, girl, you might as well do it right.

By ten, Karla was injecting heroin—she loved the sensation of the needle piercing her skin almost as much as she loved the dope coursing through her veins. And she was ten when Carolyn divorced

Karla's father, Larry Tucker. But it was in the divorce proceedings that Karla discovered that the man she had always known as Dad was in fact not her biological father at all. Karla instead was the offspring of an extramarital affair. She'd always looked different from her sisters—darker of skin and hair and eyes, wiry and hard—but she had never imagined that her ties to the family could be any less rock-solid than the bond the rest shared with each other. She was her mother's daughter, all right, but not her father's—not biologically anyway.

Carolyn Tucker's descent must have been steep and visible to anybody with eyes, because after the divorce, the court awarded custody of the three girls to their father. In comparison with his ex-wife, Larry Tucker was fixed and solid. He was a longshoreman on the Houston ship channel, toiling through odd hours and plenty of shift work but with a steady income and a reliable future. He was also a distant man both physically and emotionally, not given to hugs or soul-baring conversations. He was in no way prepared to deal with the responsibilities he inherited.

As the Tucker girls grew older, their father became increasingly unable to exert any control or authority over their behavior. When Kathi and Kari became teens and old enough to decide where they wanted to live, they chose to go to their mother, leaving Karla alone with her father. On the rare occasion Karla's mind was actually clear enough of drugs to decide to do things with her father—go out to eat, say, or maybe throw the football—she enjoyed those couple of years. Ultimately, though, Larry Tucker forfeited custody of Karla because the ship channel was far away, the hours were long, and Karla, it must be said, was so wild he didn't know what to do with her. She was shooting up, getting high, dropping acid, screwing boys, failing school, fighting anybody who crossed her. And she wasn't even a teenager yet. Larry Tucker simply could not manage her and keep a paycheck coming in too. If he had any mind to try, Carolyn put an end to the attempt. She told Larry that if he ever laid a hand on the girls or tried to control them in any way, she'd have him jailed.

Whether she had that kind of sway didn't seem to matter. What mattered is she had the audacity to make the threat.

But when Karla went to stay with her mother, she found herself living in a bona fide den of iniquity. Carolyn Tucker was working a day job and turning tricks at night. A considerable amount of her time was spent inserting needles in her arm. She had also become something of a rock groupie, following around bands like Dr. Hook and the Allman Brothers, and soon enough Karla was on the road too. By this time she had failed seventh grade twice, gotten kicked out of school early the next year, and had nothing better to do than to start road tripping. She flat-out loved it. She and her best girlfriend Shawn (later Shawn Dean, Jerry's wife), in particular, spent the next couple of years partying with bands for weeks at a time, sleeping with marginal band members and helping themselves to whichever drugs were making the rounds. All of this when Karla wasn't yet even old enough to get a driver's license.

When Karla did turn sixteen, she surprised everybody by getting married. Her husband, Stephen Griffith, was nineteen. He wasn't in a band. He worked carpentry. How she went from groupie to bride in such a short time is hard to untangle, but perhaps it amounted to two disparate but related manifestations of a deep and intense desire to rebel. Stephen Griffith described how he and Karla got acquainted: "I had a Harley Davidson, worked six months a year, and made $20,000," he told the *Houston Chronicle*. "I thought I was on top of the world. Me and a bunch of buddies pulled into a local park. We were hanging out and partying. Karla Faye and one of her friends were over there smoking a fat, pink joint. I hollered over and introduced myself. That's how we met." They married about a year later, and remained wed for the next six years.

Not that those years were always smooth going. "We got along fairly well," Griffith said. "We fist-fought a lot. I've never had men hit me as hard as she did. Whenever I went into a bar, I didn't have to worry because she had my back covered. She was tough." Nevertheless, he envisioned a bright future ahead with Karla. "I saw things in her that no one else did," Griffith said. "That girl had so much potential. She could talk to someone and make them feel at ease. She was charismatic. Even when she was on drugs and could hardly walk, she was beautiful." Overall, Griffith viewed Karla as a "pretty good wife" who kept up with the cooking and cleaning. She got him up and off to work each day. But when she announced she was leaving him, he feared the worst. "When we split, I told my friend she was going to get killed or kill somebody."

By the time Karla's marriage was nearing its end, her mother was having bouts of hepatitis. All those needles had caught up to her, and now she was frail, washed up. Carolyn Tucker died a painful death on Christmas Eve, 1979, when she was only forty-three years old. Karla was twenty. If there was any lingering doubt about whether to divorce her husband, it was gone now. She told Stephen Griffith in no uncertain terms that she had to work out her wild streak. When the paperwork was finalized, she got back her birth name and again became Karla Faye Tucker, her mother's daughter, once and for all.

Those with even a smidgen of compassion for Karla point to her upbringing as the time when the seeds of her destruction were planted. They paint Carolyn Tucker as the unmistakable villain—a mother so preoccupied with her own selfish indulgences that she didn't even realize she was dooming her daughter's future, or perhaps didn't care. How can a mere child who's taught to roll blunts and turn tricks grow up to be anything but trouble? But Karla never bought that narrative—she never saw herself as a victim of Carolyn's indiscretions. Karla loved her mother. She, in her words, "idolized" her, and was fiercely protective of her. While Karla's defenders excoriate Carolyn Tucker and lay virtually all blame at her feet, Karla's version of her life story diverged from what she regarded as a too easy explanation of a girl gone astray. Instead of drawing a line from Karla's youth to Jerry Lynn Dean's apartment, Karla herself pointed to a different place on the timeline. "I don't think any of this would have happened," she said, "if my mother hadn't died."

It's a fool's errand to hazard a guess about where and when a seed gets planted that sprouts into such foul bloom. But I guess I'm that fool. I believe Karla. Remember, if you're inclined to forget it, that the most logical explanation for why she got in Danny Garrett's Ranchero and rode over to Watonga that night—the *reason*, if there can ever be one for such a decision—was that he had stabbed a picture of Carolyn Ann Moore Tucker full of holes. Everything flows inexorably forward from that moment. *That* was the event she'd be able to trace forward to the darkest hours of a June night in 1983, when she followed Danny Garrett into a Houston apartment.

But then there's the question of how Jerry Lynn Dean ever managed to get his hands on the photograph in the first place. This time I'm empty of conjecture. Lord only knows. Some things, I suppose, just occur. You can search for the reasons, but in the end a thing just happens and nobody will really know how or why.

Karla was the baby of the family, but after her mother's death she assumed her mother's role of caretaker—which in this particular family meant she was the ringleader of a gang of girls. When Carolyn Tucker was alive, she had taught her daughters the domestic arts, because a woman had her duties after all, but also how to roll joints; she had worked as a prostitute, a true *call girl* in the sense she had made her arrangements over the phone, and had passed johns on to Kari, who in turn passed them on to Karla; and she had dispensed a stubborn pride into each and every one of them that gave the Tucker girls an *identity*. In her absence, now, Karla took over organization of the gang, and included her best girlfriend Shawn, who would eventually marry Jerry Lynn Dean, as a de facto sister and honorary member of the Tucker clan. "Siamese twins," was the way Karla described their relationship. Once a month Karla and Kari went to a hotel in Midland for a week, where they sold their bodies to oil field workers and raked in enough folding money to get them through the rest of the month. Like their mother, they also fielded calls at home on a line set up specifically for the purpose. A red telephone no one else was allowed to answer. They had a list of regulars, especially while the oil business was rolling along. The depth of her immersion in prostitution during this time would suggest that a romantic relationship with some degree of emotional reciprocity was the farthest thing from her mind.

But here it was. She met Danny Garrett in January of 1983, six months before the murders, in the waiting room of what she called their "pill doctor"—a physician who swapped prescriptions for cash. For Karla, the attraction seems to have been based on her desire to prove herself rowdy enough to run with the big dogs. Danny Garrett, older, ex-military, a badass biker, was the proverbial bad boy who showed her where the line lay and downright dared her to cross it. He was a drug more illicit than any she had ever done, and he gave her a feeling of power. So almost immediately they rented the three-bedroom house at 2205 McKean, next to a sand pit filled with water where Karla liked to go swimming. They got a couple of pit bulls, bitches they called Tessa and Tooter. By all accounts, Danny Garrett was in love with Karla. He wanted to marry her. Stay in it for the long haul. She'd been down that road, though, and wasn't sure right just yet. She was still young—fourteen years younger than Danny Garrett—and she knew she had too much wild in her to settle down again. She kept fielding calls from johns because business was business and had nothing to do with a woman's heart. Danny Garrett didn't always agree with this logic, but he went along, figuring she'd get a real job that required her to keep her clothes on, eventually.

For his part, Danny Garrett always held a real job, of one kind or another. "He'd once been a high-class bartender," Karla said, "making drinks at bars like the one on the roof of the Galleria, inside a fancy hotel." People would actually stand back and admire his sheer artistry when he mixed drinks. "He had been good," she said, "but he had gone down." Now he had a gig at a slimy swinger's bar. But he was helping make rent and apparently paying off his Ranchero—taking care of business in ways Karla knew men could not always be counted on to do. By Karla's standards, he had much to recommend him. He knew Harleys and Vietnam and how to wear a pair of jeans. He had an animal instinct about him, too he could walk through the pitch-black night and see as though it were day.

He was thirty-seven and had witnessed way more of the world than Karla had ever laid eyes on.

He was, in the world Karla Faye Tucker lived in, the kind of man you want to impress. Daniel Ryan Garrett was the kind who, when he grabs a piece of paper and starts drawing the floor plan of a house and says y'all can go case the joint and maybe steal some motorcycle parts, well, you'd follow that man to hell.

All of which is to say, from Karla Faye Tucker's perspective, in order to die she wouldn't need a lethal injection of chemicals administered by the state of Texas. She took care of that herself. She put the old Karla to death by her own hand and was, to her way of thinking, reborn. "The other Karla no longer exists," she would eventually tell *60 Minutes*. "I'm so far removed from the person that I used to be out there." "Out there," of course, referred to the world beyond the prison gates; but undoubtedly it also applied to a state of being that, in retrospect, she imagined lying on the threadbare edges of the universe, far removed from any kind of safety or security or dependability.

Prior to her trial, at Harris County Jail in Houston, Tucker found God. In a televised interview with Larry King of CNN, she told the story of her conversion. "A ministry came to that jail to do a service, a puppet show, one night," she said, "and everybody in my tank was going out to the puppet show." Never a regular churchgoer, Tucker nonetheless joined the others, more out of boredom than any genuine curiosity. "I didn't want to stay alone in my tank, so I decided to go with them and socialize in church." But at the show she kept to herself, aloof and apart from the crowd. Probably savoring the chance to see something a little different, but bound and determined not to buy whatever these Jesus folks were selling.

At some point, though, she proceeded to do the thing that would transform her life: "I stole this Bible, not realizing Bibles were given out free in jail." Whether propelled by spiritual curiosity or the familiar enticement of larceny, Karla never said. But she carried the Good Book with her back to her cell. Because she didn't want to be perceived as weak for reading a Bible, she hid in the corner of her cell so no one would see her. It was here that Karla fell under the spell of what she was reading and ended up on her knees with a prayer for forgiveness on her tongue. "At the time I didn't understand how the Holy Spirit works," she said. "I just remember the whole weight of everything I had done suddenly became a reality. Two precious lives were gone because of me."

Jailhouse conversions are of course common—an almost expected part of the narrative. They are part of the plan: the term penitentiary after all derives from the Latin *paenitentia*, meaning "repentance." Prisons are a place for penitents to dwell on their sins. I suppose it would have come as a surprise if she *didn't* have some kind of spiritual reckoning. Famed prosecutor Joe Freeman Britt, called "America's Deadliest DA," liked to say, "I probably brought more people to the Lord than Billy Graham." People are justifiably skeptical of these public professions of faith from inmates. Karla knew folks would question the authenticity of her conversion. "I don't try and convince people of that," she told Larry King. "For me, if you can't look at me and see it, then nothing I can say to you is going to convince you. I just live it every day and I reach out to people and it's up to them to receive from the Lord the same way I did when somebody came to me. And then there are fruits in people's life. There is evidence, consistent evidence, in a person's life."

It's these "fruits" that in fact seemed to distinguish the Damascus-type transformation of Karla's character. Starting with that October 1983 conversion, she began leading the Bible studies, crocheting the handiwork, offering a hand to fellow inmates. This once surly, distrustful, and vindictive woman who claimed no greater pride than how handy she was with her fists and how she could pleasure a man became a confidante to other female inmates. The woman that Danny Garrett's prosecutor called "the personification of evil" was now, according to that selfsame man, Charley Davidson, doing some pretty redemptive work behind bars. And Davidson wasn't alone. He was one of a whole host of folks in the legal or prison system who'd seen this Born Again business too many times to count but, in Karla's case, grew convinced she was a different woman from the one who took up that pickax.

In the interview with Larry King, Karla would describe her transformation this way: "The things that were in me when I did that 14 1/2 years ago, I guess I would say it this way—that God reached down inside of me and just literally uprooted all of that stuff and took it out, and poured himself in."

Karla now believed she had something that would do nothing less than revolutionize her life. It could not change what she had done, but it could change its significance. A month before her scheduled death, in that interview with King, she gave name to it: "It's called the joy of the Lord . . . I know what real love is. I know what forgiveness is, even when I did something so horrible. I know that because God forgave me and I accepted what Jesus did on the cross. When I leave here, I am going to go be with him."

All that remained, now, was to learn how much longer she had before she met up with her Jesus.

My father no doubt recognized the rhetoric. The exact words that Karla Faye Tucker was speaking he'd uttered many times over, and her story of sin and salvation was roughly his too, minus the drugs and gore and pickax. It's the narrative arc every evangelical Christian since the Apostle Paul has applied to his life, like a transparency you lay over your history. You knead around the circumstances of your past until they conform to the overarching plotline, namely *I once was lost but now I'm found*. Those lyrics from "Amazing Grace" that Kelly Gissendaner sang at her execution dramatize the story structure that builds toward conversion. That *I'm found* moment is the climax, the turning point—and it's easy to name because it's the moment you accept the saving grace of our Lord Jesus Christ and, in our Baptist tradition, pray the Sinner's Prayer. You tell God you're a sinner, that you understand the wages of sin are death; you say you know Jesus Christ died on the cross for your sins; and you accept the grace freely offered through the sacrifice of his innocent blood. You're born again. It's the Before and After moment. The more sordid and regrettable your Before, the more transformative your After, the more impactful your personal testimony of how it all went down. Hence the power Karla Faye Tucker had over my father. She had a personal testimony few can compete with.

His wasn't a tepid story either. He was a Depression-era kid, raised on 125 stubborn acres of land in the North Georgia mountains, poor as the dirt he and his two older brothers plowed and harrowed behind a mule. His father needed farmhands more than sons, and treated them like hired labor, even pulling them out of school when the crops necessitated it. In the unlikely event my grandfather felt any ambivalence about compromising the boys' education, ultimately my father one day made it easier on him. He did something or other on the school premises—something apparently involving matches and fire—that got him expelled and made him now readily available for labor whenever the occasion rose. Dad did return to school the next year—chastened appropriately, I suppose, because the record shows he behaved himself long enough to graduate. (His parents didn't attend the ceremony.) It was then that Uncle Sam came calling and whisked him off in the first airplane he'd ever boarded to a foreign land in a hostile and distant corner of the world called Korea. There, he spent nine months freezing in foxholes, took up cigarettes, and became a master sergeant. I once asked him, with all the bloodthirsty tact of a nine-year-old boy, whether he'd killed anybody. "We're not going to talk about that," he said. And indeed we never did.

Upon his return home to the States, he promptly picked the beggar lice from his overalls and moved to Atlanta, where he took a job at the Sears-Roebuck plant right across Ponce de Leon from the Atlanta Crackers baseball park. There the stock boy met a girl named Norma Fay who filled catalog orders. A courtship ensued. Soon he got up the gumption to say, "I'm thinking we ought to get married," and she responded, "Well, I think so too." Sure enough, they exchanged their I do's before the justice of the peace, signed the paperwork to make it all legal, and officially became husband and wife. My brother was born soon after, in 1954; they called him David, after the Old Testament king, and the family settled into a rental home on Atlanta's east side. But one evening my father attended a union meeting—just to get a look-see at the possibilities—and when he arrived at work the next morning at Sears, he found a pink slip in his mailbox.

Eventually he got hired on at the post office—a blessing that arrived in no small part, according to my mother, because she had prayed him to a passing score on the civil-service exam.

It was around this time that Dad's Before and After arrived. Some visitors from a local church dropped by the house for what they called visitation. They laid out for him God's plan for salvation and soon Dad was on his knees in his own living room, following through. He said the words, the deacons laid hands on him and prayed over him, and then he rose to his feet, a brand new creature.

His first act as a Christian was to give up cigarettes, cold turkey, because a church member had complained of the smell. And on his postal route one frigid morning that winter he stumbled upon a boy in the streets without any shoes. The next time Dad came around with the family's mail, he also brought with him a pair of new sneakers. And he filled the offering plate on Sunday mornings with ten percent of his paycheck, and the lint from his pocket too. Mom tells me money was tight in those days, but he gave anyway, because he insisted that whatever you give to the cause of the Lord never fails to come back to you many times over.

Through the coming years, Dad's life revolved around his faith. This was my father: he was a postman in the city of Atlanta five days a week; a deer hunter on Saturday; a Southern Baptist deacon on Sunday; and a devout evangelical Christian every day of the week. He kept a pocket-sized New Testament nearby at all times—in the glove compartment of his Ford, his locker at the post office, his orange vest when he shimmied up a tree and sat in a deer stand thirty feet up, with a tin of Vienna sausages, a thermos of coffee, and his 30.06 in the crook of his arm. God's Word kept him steadfast company while he waited for a big buck to come loping down the ravine in his direction.

Dad was, in the words of his Baptist brethren, "on fire for God." He was in a state where everything seemed invested with holiness. He must have felt like the meaning of pretty much all of it had opened up and been laid bare for his examination.

Like all fires, his flickered from time to time, the flame gone ragged against heavy winds. But it never, ever went out.

Chapter 7

AND THAT'S THE WAY WITH JESUS

Pat Robertson had his show title, *The 700 Club*, but that's not when the miracle happened. The miracle came in 1965 when Robertson hired a husband-and-wife team, Jim and Tammy Faye Bakker, to do a children's show. The world seemed a happier place when Jim preached, Tammy sang, and they performed puppet shows for kids. Using the caps of bubble-bath bottles, they created Susie Moppet and Allie Alligator, and Jim served as the front man while Tammy hunkered down behind the props and alternated between her little Susie Moppet voice and her gruff Allie Alligator one. Relying on unscripted banter, they played off each other well, Jim the straight man, Tammy the silly one, and together they made for a peculiar but enticing brand of must-see TV.

There was a heavy comedic element to their bit, but occasionally they relied on straight pathos. The most (in)famous example would be the 1965 telethon, when late in the evening, after Robertson's fundraising goals appeared unattainable and all seemed lost, Jim joined Pat on set and, to put it mildly, *lost it*. He began crying—not mild sniffles that caused him to dab his eyes, mind you, but great, heaving, body-convulsing sobs that convinced viewers far and wide that, yes, something really was at stake, something was about to be lost, forever. "Listen, people," Jim pleaded. "It's all over. Everything's gone. Christian television will be no more. The only Christian television is gone, unless you provide us with the money to operate it." A "move of the spirit," as it came to be called, was transpiring live on television screens across America.

Sure enough, telephone lines started crackling. Pledges came rolling in. The telethon ran past its 11:00 p.m. signoff into the wee hours of the morning, finally concluding at 2:30 a.m. But the pledges still kept coming, day after day. Some callers who couldn't get through actually drove to the studio to hand deliver their donations. Thanks to Jim Bakker's unscripted emotional outburst, Robertson's network was solvent for the next year at least. More importantly, though, he had hit upon a method that would secure CBN's financial security for years to come. Heading into the future, "a move of the spirit" became the rallying cry, the stated goal the network was trying to achieve through all its religious programming.

To capitalize on his role in this shift in methods, Bakker proposed to Robertson a Johnny Carson-style talk show that would invite viewers to call in and help inspire "the move of the spirit" on a nightly basis. Audiences would share their need for salvation, healing, or encouragement in their Christian walk. There'd be a monologue, guest interviews, sketch comedy, and a live band. Robertson gave the green light, and *The 700 Club* was born, officially, in 1966. Initially Robertson hosted frequently, but the spirit seemed to move more freely when Bakker hosted, if fundraising donations were any indicator of divine locomotion.

Bakker recognized as much. After years of tension between him and Robertson, much of it related to the question of who controlled the spotlight, the Bakkers quit CBN in 1972 and headed for the up-and-coming city of Charlotte, North Carolina. There Jim eventually formed his own network, PTL, in a former furniture store; and with a meager six employees on staff, he commenced following much of Robertson's blueprint toward success.

"It's not listed in the Bible," Bakker told *Christianity Today*, "but my spiritual gift, my specific calling from God, is to be a television-show host." Indeed, the network's feature show, the PTL Club (*Club* made it sound exclusive) was again modeled after the *Tonight Show* and Bakker was its Johnny. It was unscripted, and completely contrived. The set was classic seventies camp, with lots of handclapping, leisure suits, gold medallion necklaces, and deep plush carpeting. His wife Tammy proved a particular asset, too, as she possessed an uncanny ability to cry on cue—at the slightest provocation, tears pooled around her false eyelashes and mascara flooded her inch-thick makeup. Together, they challenged viewers to give to God, and guaranteed that in return he would bless them in ways unimaginable. They referred frequently to the "abundant life" and material "blessings." Simply put, God wanted you to be rich, and the more you supported the PTL ministry, the richer you'd become. Jim Bakker quoted Luke 6:38 on the regular: "Give, and it shall be given unto you; good measure, pressed down, and shaken together, and running over, shall men give into your bosom. For with the same measure that ye mete withal it shall be measure to you again." And Bakker made it clear that there were consequences if you didn't fulfill your side of the bargain. "If you don't give," he warned viewers, "you'll not receive. It's God's fixed law." Cameras fixed on operators waiting for a call; in fact, there'd likely be a wait to get through, because other callers were already burning through the phone lines. Dozens of operators—men and women, Black and white, young and old—perched over telephones, receivers cradled between their shoulders and ears, scribbling donation amounts while men in suits and ties circulated constantly around the room collecting pledge slips. The audience responded with checks, cash, jewelry, mink coats, and even property deeds, and the Bakkers themselves became walking exemplars of how God would reward those who answered his call faithfully. Jim insisted he was not the proverbial rich man whose wealth prevents him entry into heaven, because he did not put money first; it was only a byproduct of his and Tammy's devotion. You could do it same as they did.

Yet the Bakkers mastered the art of conspicuous consumption. They owned three resort homes, matching Rolls-Royces, a private jet, and a $570 shower curtain. And then there was the air-conditioned doghouse, almost as tall as a man, for their pup Snuggles, which would become the most frequently cited symbol of their excesses. None of this plenitude shamed them; their theology was the very essence of prosperity gospel. "If you pray for a camper," Jim advised viewers, "tell God what color. Otherwise, you're asking God to do your shopping for you."

The Bakkers repeatedly vowed they made no money from their audience. All donations to PTL, they said, went straight to the ministry. Yet it was clear that they were living lavish lifestyles, and that money was coming from somewhere. Tammy admitted that she enjoyed shopping—"It's kind of a hobby to help my nerves," she said—but she assured viewers she was a "bargain hunter" and that her hobby was "better than a psychiatrist."

Eventually it was revealed that from 1984 to 1987, the Bakkers personally received over $4 million dollars. Yet among supporters of PTL, the general consensus seemed to be that, given the amount of money they generated for the ministry, this kind of compensation was only appropriate. Despite the luxuries, they somehow came across as modest Midwesterners, Jim the son of a machinist from Muskegon, Michigan, and Tammy the product of an International Falls, Minnesota, house with no refrigerator and an outhouse in the back.

Ever the innovator, Jim Bakker brought broadcast satellites to Christian television. "From this moment on," he announced, "the PTL television network plans to broadcast 24 hours per day until the second coming of Jesus Christ." The talk show became the centerpiece of a network that was becoming more powerful, influential, and downright rich than anyone—likely even Jim and Tammy—imagined it could be. They welcomed guests from a broad spectrum of American life—everyone from religious figures like Billy Graham, to boxers like George Foreman, to pitchmen like Colonel Sanders, to actors like Gavin MacLeod, captain of *The Love Boat*. And at the end of every episode, Jim looked directly at the camera and signed off with his standard parting line: "God loves you—He really, really does!"

The success of the satellite network made possible what many saw as the crown jewel of Jim and Tammy's empire. In Fort Mill, South Carolina, right on the border separating the Carolinas, PTL ministries built Heritage USA, a Christian Disney World sprawling across 2,300 acres, hosting six million annual visitors, dramatizing the passion play in an outdoor amphitheater, and showcasing a water park featuring what Bakker called the first Christian wave pool and the gargantuan waterslide they christened the Killer Typhoon. The wave pool spread across a crystal blue expanse the size of a football field; the waterslide hurtled riders up to thirty miles per hour down a 163-foot drop. The Lazy River gently transported riders around the area at a more leisurely pace. In total, the pools contained 1.6 million gallons of water. "The Bible says we're fishers of men," Bakker declared. "This is the *bait*." There was a railroad, paddleboats, antique cars, bicycle rentals, putt-putt, tennis courts, horse stables, a carousel, and a petting zoo. There was a main street that led toward the King's Castle, which bore an eerie resemblance to Cinderella's but actually housed a go-kart track and an arcade. There was a Heavenly Fudge Factory. A Noah's Toy Shop that trafficked in Bible-themed toys and disciple action figures. A store that featured Tammy's line of makeup. Ye Old Bookstore, Perry's Jewelry Emporium, the Shutterbug Shoppe, Designer Bags and Accessories, Copeland Drugs, and Goosebumps Handcrafted Gifts, among others. Billy Graham's actual childhood home was saved from demolition in Charlotte and transplanted to the grounds. There were plans to spend $1.2 million to build the world's largest Wendy's restaurant, designed to look like a sand castle with a ten-story turret.

The people came, in droves. After Disney Land and Disney World, Heritage USA became the third most popular theme park in America. It was said that this Christian-themed park was like heaven on earth. But if this was in fact Jim Bakker's City Upon a Hill, and he its John Winthrop, it was a curiously secular one that represented the confluence of faith and materialism that had been merging for decades in America.

To complement Heritage USA, Bakker decided to build a giant, five-hundred-room hotel he called the Heritage Grand. And before it was even finished, he ordered the building of a second tower also containing five hundred rooms. To raise funds, Bakker offered PTL visitors an unheard-of bargain: for a one-time donation of $1,000, they would receive a special membership card entitling them to stay in the Heritage Grand for four days and three nights, every year for *the rest of their lives*. Bakker knew his market—he sold more than sixty-six thousand lifetime partnerships. Which would have been impressive indeed, except for the fact that the hotel didn't have enough rooms to accommodate all the donors.

In the midst of Jim and Tammy's rise to unprecedented levels of power within televangelism, Tammy occasionally broke script with the rest of the evangelical world. That was the thing with Tammy—she had no script. What people found refreshing about her was her lack of guile—her utter refusal to stand on ceremony. She said what came to mind whether anybody approved or not. Never were her candor and independence on greater display than in 1985, when she interviewed a man with AIDS via satellite. This was on her show, *Tammy's House Party*, an offshoot of her regular gig alongside Jim. Her guest, Steve Pieters, was a devout Christian. He was also an uncloseted gay man who insisted his sexuality came as natural to him as any heterosexual's, which of course in the mid-eighties would have got him summarily dismissed from any other Christian media outlet in America.

But not Tammy's show. Tammy acts as a stand-in for countless Americans as she peppers him with questions: "At what time in your life did you feel that you were different?" "Did you try to be around girls a lot and everything, so that no one would think anything?" "Did girls make you nervous, Steve?" She is a gracious host, deeply engaged in the conversation—not in a strictly professional way, but as one genuinely curious person clearly inspired by the humanity in another. It's when he tells her about his parents' reaction—how his father told him he was his son no matter what, that nothing could separate him from his love—that Tammy seems to begin to think about gay people in a new and surprising way. You can almost see wheels turning in her mind as she processes the story Steve Pieters is sharing with her.

When she arrives at her epiphany, she seizes the opportunity to address the audience and share it with viewers. "Thank God for a mom and dad who will stand with a young person!" she says. "You know, I think it's very important, because no matter what happens to a young person in life, they're still your boy! They're still your girl!" And it's when she says these words that the conversation clearly takes a meaningful turn for Tammy. She gets a lump in her throat. Suddenly things get intensely personal for her. "And that's the way with Jesus, you know—Jesus loves us through anything. And that's the wonderful thing about Jesus, you know!" She admits this is an emotional experience for her, this interview, and she wants to reach across the satellite divide and put her arm around Steve Pieters.

Maybe it's this intimacy that she feels toward him that accounts for where she goes next as she continues her questions. "Steve, have you ever had a sexual experience with a woman?" When he answers no, she asks, "Do you think it's just that you haven't given women a fair try?" Moments later, she asks, "What made you think that you were homosexual—did you feel feminine inside? A lot of time, you know, in the gay community, some of them—you know, some men look like a homosexual. Other men do not—*you do not*! You do not look effeminate at all. And there are a lot of macho guys that are in the gay community. What made you feel that there was no hope for you to be straight?" It's a cringe-worthy line of questioning, to be sure, if you forget the zeitgeist of the time, especially within the context of the evangelical world. But when you remember those things, you see how downright transgressive the interview actually is. She's perfectly aware that the most vocal members of the evangelical community see AIDS as God's just punishment for sinful behavior. She's perfectly aware that many of her viewers are turned off by the sight of a gay man on their TV screen. She's aware—as she and Jim were aware, always—that what she says will affect PTL's bottom line.

Yet she tells Steve Pieters about a television program that she and Jim watched recently about a young man with AIDS. She recounts how, in the show, the man faces a litany of obstacles resulting from his illness, the most painful of which is his parents' fear of touching him. Tammy again gets the lump in her throat. Through tears, the mascara starts running, and she proceeds to deliver what very well might be the most genuine declaration of Christian love in all of 1980s televangelism. Listen to her: "How sad that we as Christians, who are to be the salt of the earth, and we who are supposed to be able to love everyone, are afraid so badly of an AIDS patient that we will not go up and put our arm around them and tell them that we care. But Steve, I just wanna tell you something. . . . I know that you were sick, and that's the only reason we didn't have you come and sit in the studio next to us, 'cause you have your chemotherapy treatments, and you needed to get home quickly so you wouldn't miss them. But I wanna tell you, there's a lot of Christians here who love you and who wouldn't be afraid to put their arm around you and tell you that we love you and that we care." There's polite applause in the studio. "We're all just people," she continues. "Somehow it seems like when a person gets a disease, it *separates* you somehow from just an ordinary person—and we don't change! You know, we get a disease, we get cancer, that doesn't change us—we're still the same person—I'm still Tammy Bakker, you're still Steve Pieters!"

Then, in January 1987, Tammy Faye Bakker had a breakdown. It was revealed that she had developed a prescription drug addiction—Ativan, likely—and she entered the Betty Ford Center, in Palm Springs, California. In March, she and Jim appeared on the air, with their son and daughter in tow, to publicly confirm that she was being treated for long-term addiction. Jim did most of the talking. He told viewers, "We had to face some . . . realities . . . that Tammy Faye had been taking a lot of medications for a long time."

Toward the end of the broadcast, he added, "Seven years ago Tammy and I went through a very severe marriage problem. Our marriage collapsed, our lives collapsed. During that time . . . we both made terrible mistakes. But we're so thankful that we serve a God who forgives and forgets."

When and how Tammy's addiction began was murky, but it's almost certain that her breakdown was triggered by the vague and cryptic marital "problem" to which Jim was referring in his closing remarks. In retrospect, it's easy to read his words as preemptive damage control, because the revelation of a long-buried secret was about to go public. It was during Tammy's treatment that news of a December 1980 incident in Room 538 of a hotel in Clearwater Beach, Florida, made national news. It had been kept shushed for seven years, perhaps even from Tammy. Now the world was about to be in on the secret.

You probably know this part of the story. Jim Bakker had sex with a woman named Jessica Hahn. Hahn was twenty-one, a church secretary from Long Island and regular viewer of PTL who idolized Bakker. The story goes that she sent fifteen dollars a month to the ministry and bought her first black-and-white TV just so she could watch the show every day. She'd been enticed to travel from her home on Long Island to Florida by John Wesley Fletcher, who was a frequent guest on Bakker's show. She'd done some babysitting for Fletcher and was told she might do the same for Bakker. Bakker and Fletcher were doing a telethon together. Hahn later would claim she was a virgin and had no idea of the true nature of this visit until she found herself in a Sheraton Sand Key hotel room with Bakker. "I went with the intention of being in the presence of some people I had admired my whole Christian life," she said.

Bakker called the act consensual. Hahn never accused Bakker of rape, but she insisted this was not what she wanted to occur. "It just happened," she later told John Wigger, author of a book about PTL, "it just suddenly happened and I didn't run out of the room because I felt, to be honest with you, that this guy was like my idol and I didn't know what to do. I just thought I should go through with this because it's Jim Bakker. I can't call it rape. I just can't. Everybody else does, though, and it bothers me for some reason." She saved most of her wrath for John Wesley Fletcher, going so far as to suggest that both she and Bakker were victims of his manipulation.

Afterward, a mixture of fear and confusion convinced her that she should keep the episode to herself. "I thought this was going to be my secret for the rest of my life," she said, "and that I should never speak of this, ever." Indeed, she accepted a hush money payment of $265,000—from PTL funds, of course. To cover it up, there were phony invoices for the Passion play performances at Heritage USA.

PTL battened down the hatches and went into self-preservation mode. The organization needed a fellow televangelist with a widespread following who might take the helm and see it through these storms until Jim Bakker could resume leadership. Bakker feared Jimmy Swaggart would take over his ministry in his absence—Swaggart had gotten wind of Jim's sexual misconduct and attempted to launch a church investigation into the matter—so he needed to arrange a safe transfer of power, and quick. On March 19, 1987, he officially resigned and appointed his successor. He handed the reins to Jerry Falwell.

Those outside the evangelical faith might assume that substituting one televangelist for another was an apple-for-apple transaction. It was not. Bakker and Falwell were not cut from the same clerical cloth. Bakker was part of the Pentecostal movement, a believer in ecstatic worship in the Charismatic style, a preacher of a feel-good theology that emphasized the fruits of a generous spirit and the rewards of an open wallet. Falwell, in contrast, was a fundamentalist, and his fire and brimstone brand of preaching was full of warnings about the eternal torment that awaited sinners if they didn't comply with the Moral Majority's "pro-life, pro-traditional family, pro-moral, and pro-American" agenda. In a moment of both self-deprecation and candor, Falwell once distinguished his fellow fundamentalists from other Protestants, defining a fundamentalist as "an evangelical who is mad about something." Founder of Thomas Road Baptist Church, Liberty University, and the *Old-Time Gospel Hour* TV show, Falwell was expert at rallying Christians behind his conservative values; he was not expert at spreading rainbows and unicorns. He generally regarded Pentecostals like Bakker with disdain; he thought their campy style lacked integrity and a genuine commitment to the faith.

The two, in fact, had never met face-to-face until Bakker asked Falwell to visit him in Palm Springs on March 17 and discuss the future of PTL. According to Falwell, in that meeting Bakker told him that Tammy had fallen in love with another man. In order to make her jealous and win her back, he made a request of John Wesley Fletcher that he arrange for Jessica Hahn to come to Florida.

Bakker respected Falwell's longstanding reputation and admired his ability to raise money. So perhaps out of desperation as much as anything else, he gave over PTL to Falwell until the scandal died down. "You're the only preacher I trust right now," Bakker told Falwell. Already he was envisioning a campaign titled "Forgiven": he would confess his sins, receive pardon both from his God and from his audience, and be redeemed. He would return to his Heritage USA and live out the rest of his days as a walking exemplar of God's tremendous grace. In their goodbye appearance on PTL, Jim assured viewers that he and his wife someday would be helping people once more and Tammy sang a twangy, rousing rendition of "The Sun Will Shine Again" while Jim stroked their pet cat. This farewell was filmed on location from their home and beamed via satellite to a live audience in the PTL studios.

When Tammy sings "your midnight is almost over, and thank God the sun is gonna shine again!" she offers a pump of her tiny fist and the studio audience erupts into a standing ovation. The people can't help themselves—they break into expressions of pure glee and their applause almost drowns out the swelling music that's piped in through the speakers. They see themselves on the monitor, which prompts them to only clap harder. You know there's probably some crew member orchestrating every moment of it, some off-camera grunt exhorting the crowd with APPLAUSE signs. But when you look at the expressions on these people's faces, you get how PTL became such a force in the evangelical world, and maybe you even believe in redemption and resurrection and you think maybe the sun really will shine again on the faces of Jim and Tammy Faye Bakker, sure enough.

Except things did not proceed according to Bakker's plan. On April 28, a little over a month after assuming leadership of the organization, Falwell barred Bakker from returning to PTL.

On May 27, he gave America a disturbing explanation of why he had resorted to such extreme measures. Standing at a podium in Bakker's Heritage Grand Hotel, he told a roomful of reporters all that he had learned about the depths of Bakker's depravity since taking over PTL. He began by holding aloft a piece of correspondence, dated May 6, he had received from the desk of Tammy, on her letterhead. Then he read aloud the list of things she and Jim were asking to receive as part of their severance from PTL. Among their requests: Jim's salary at $300,000 annually for lifetime; Tammy's salary at $100,000 for lifetime; their house on the lake and the furniture in it; two cars; and a maid for one year. "I don't see any repentance there," Falwell concluded. "I see the greed, I see the self-centeredness, I see the avarice that brought them down." It's a public takedown, a clear sign that he's taking the gloves off in this battle for power and control, but what he does next takes things to a whole new level. Jim Bakker is nowhere near his Heritage Grand, but Falwell continues recounting the story in second person, as though he's speaking directly to his fallen colleague and the rest of us are just bystanders to the tongue-lashing. "Jim, since that time, I have learned that not only did you have sex with Jessica Hahn, so did your associate John Wesley Fletcher, and a third person, a member of your team, went in with the intention of having sex with her, and she was prostrate on the floor and unable to respond and could not accommodate him. And I've learned, Jim, that two weeks after that, in Hawaii, you went to that person and asked the question, 'Did you get her too?'

And, Jim, *that made my blood boil.*" Falwell goes on to tell Bakker he's learned that he's made a number of homosexual advances to men within PTL and that the organization is drowning in debt—$65 million and bleeding at a rate of $2 million a month. "Jim, I must tell you that I would be doing a disservice to God, as much as I love you and care for you and will pray for you—I would be doing a disservice to God and to the church at large to allow you to come back here, now or ever."

Falwell's press conference is straight-up gangster, rhetorically—and devastating in its impact. He plays it as though he and Bakker are having an intimate conversation, man to man, but of course the rest of America is listening in, eavesdropping on all the lurid details. Falwell's measured tone and stern demeanor give everything he says an air of incontrovertible fact. This is not merely one man's version of events; it is what Falwell has always believed he is in possession of: the unassailable Truth.

That evening Jim and Tammy appeared on *Nightline* with Ted Koppel, in what turned out to be the show's highest rated episode ever. It drew twenty million viewers. From the beginning of the broadcast, sitting hip to hip on a sofa in their home, Jim's arm draped over Tammy's shoulder, they seem keenly aware of what's at stake. Lacking the platform of their TV show, this is a rare opportunity to reach their audience and try to restore the people's faith in Jim and Tammy.

They do what they can, invoking Jesus's words against casting stones in order to condemn Falwell's tactics and referencing scripture at every available opportunity. Koppel doesn't bully the couple, but neither does he go easy on them. He asks Jim why he doesn't sue Falwell if what he says isn't true—he could "wreck" Falwell and his ministry and Liberty University in one fell swoop—and Jim responds that it is unscriptural to return evil for evil. Tammy vouches for her husband's heterosexuality. She's been married to him for almost three decades and knows better, she says. But they seem to understand their kingdom is collapsing and they can do nothing to stop it. As the interview proceeds and Koppel delves into the couple's financial malfeasance, citing figures that the Bakkers seem to have no knowledge of, Tammy's eyes start glistening and she occasionally dabs at her mascara. If there's a single surprise in the whole hour-long exchange, it's that Tammy doesn't end up shedding the bucketful of tears all of America expects to see. But when Koppel signs off and ABC goes to commercial, extant footage will show that Tammy buries her face in her hands and cries inconsolably.

At PTL, Falwell cleaned house, literally, auctioning off sundry personal items that had belonged to the Bakkers, including a mini go-kart, Jim and Tammy's bed, and the infamous air-conditioned doghouse. He called Bakker "probably the greatest scab and cancer on the face of Christianity in 2,000 years of church history." He also committed to raising $20 million for PTL and vowed to ride the Killer Typhoon if viewers came through with the money. They did, and he did.

That September of 1987, fifty-four-year-old Jerry Falwell recited the Lord's Prayer, then folded his arms and crossed his legs, looking for all the world like a corpse, and took his four-second plunge down the slide in his Sunday suit. Some have interpreted his attire as an expression of his fundamentalism—after all, he'd already announced plans to put a stop to skimpy bathing suits in the water park and enforce a stricter dress code. But I suspect his navy-blue suit said more about his intentions to maintain his dignity as head of an organization that had lost all dignity. Like Christians in their earthly realm, he was in it but not of it, obligated to do this thing he did not want to do and trying to grin and bear it with some finesse in the meantime.

In any case, when he splashes into the pool at the bottom, he at first goes socks up. Then Jerry Falwell staggers to his feet with his eyes shut tightly and his hair pasted to his head, his arms flailing around wildly in a desperate search for a helping hand, like a man waiting for somebody to save him.

Ultimately, $20 million wasn't enough. Falwell couldn't pull PTL out of bankruptcy. A month later, in October 1987, he resigned leadership.

And for Jim Bakker, the worst was still to come, because the financial turmoil led to legal charges. In 1988 he was indicted on twenty-four total counts of fraud and conspiracy, and the ensuing trial carried an air of inevitability. The presiding federal judge was Robert Potter, whose nickname was "Maximum Bob." (Interestingly, no charges were brought against Tammy. Somebody must have decided being married to Jim Bakker was punishment enough.)

The trial was a national spectacle, and often Bakker did not play the leading role with grace or aplomb, especially as the evidence grew more damning. During testimony, there was the expected description of his excesses. (One curious anecdote even asserted that the Bakkers kept $100 worth of cinnamon rolls in Jim's office simply because they enjoyed the smell. An assistant heated the rolls in the microwave each morning to trigger the scent. A few days later, they threw them away without eating a single bite.) Perhaps the low point, though, came when Bakker failed to show up for day four of his trial. His attorney told Judge Potter his client had become irrational, suffering from hallucinations of giant ants in the courtroom, and needed immediate mental intervention. Bakker's psychiatrist testified that, just that morning, Bakker had wedged his body under the couch in his attorney's office and assumed the fetal position. Bakker wanted to be treated in a local private hospital, but Potter committed him to a federal prison psychiatric ward. The resulting diagnosis was that Bakker had suffered a panic attack brought on by extreme stress. He had a mild personality disorder but was competent to stand trial.

As with so much of Jim Bakker's public life, whether you see his breakdown as what Jessica Hahn would call a "sympathy stunt" or a pitiful plea for mercy is a matter of interpretation. For her part, Tammy tearfully told the media that her husband had been "manhandled, strip searched . . . paraded . . . and treated like a freak at a carnival show."

By the time the jury—active church members, each and every one—found him guilty on all counts and "Maximum Bob" Potter sentenced him to forty-five years in prison, adding that "those of us who do have a religion are sick of being saps for money grubbing preachers," the only ones who seemed surprised by the outcome were Jim and Tammy. In his final words to the jury, Bakker acknowledged he had sinned but insisted he never attempted to defraud.

Tammy again came to his defense, and declared the story was not finished. Surrounded by reporters outside the courthouse, she announced, "I have a song for ya!" and launched into a rendition of "On Christ the Solid Rock I Stand" so bright and cheerful that even her red dress and polka-dot turtleneck paled in comparison. By now, it was becoming clear that this was a defense mechanism of Tammy's, this belting out a song whenever she was under duress. Many a southern choir director has exhorted their charges with the admonition, "If you can't sing good, sing loud," and by this measure Tammy possessed a remarkable voice. What she lacked in timbre she made up for in gusto. It was as though whatever sorrow came knocking on her door could not come inside as long as she was lost in song. She had a lot to sing about these days.

Then, she mustered enough confidence and perhaps self-deception to smile broadly and proclaim, simply, "It's not over—till it's over."

But it was over—not just Jim's trial but the Bakkers' marriage, too. Jim ended up filing an appeal, and he served just shy of five years. It was time enough, though, for Tammy to decide she could not wait. She divorced Jim, fell in love with a man named Roe Messner, who had been Jim's partner in building Heritage USA, and remarried. (Unfortunately for Tammy, she had a habit of marrying felons, because Roe Messner, too, ended up going to prison for bankruptcy fraud during the fallout at PTL.)

In 1996, she was diagnosed with colon cancer. She beat it once, but during the next decade it returned. By 2007, when she was sixty-five-years-old, it was clear that she would not beat it again. In July, she made what turned out to be one final television appearance on CNN with Larry King and acknowledged the cancer had spread to her lungs.

It's a hard video to watch. Tammy looks hideous; she looks like, well, death. At first, if you're like me, you watch the clip and all you can manage to do is pity her. It feels utterly inappropriate to watch her in the interview. You're looking at this emaciated woman who's clearly knocking on heaven's door, and you feel that you're witnessing something that only her immediate family should see. You think that even in this condition she's seeing her life as a performance piece, a tawdry reality show in which she makes a final appeal for validation. It's as though even here at the end, Tammy is doing what she's always done, making a too-desperate sentimental appeal to our heartstrings, breaching all standards of decorum. Once again, she can't tell the difference between the effect she thinks she's creating and the one she is actually creating.

Yet as I continue watching, I can't help myself—almost against my will, a strange kind of empathy invades me. It's been said that Tammy Faye Bakker wore her makeup like a mask, concealing her true identity from the world. She was anxious and fearful, and all the mascara and heavy rouge protected her. Tammy disputed this interpretation, once saying in an interview with the *Washington Post*, "I wish people could look beyond the mascara and see my heart. I think it's really sad when people only look on the outside when there's so much underneath." But then, fearing the conversation had gotten too deep, which wasn't Tammy's style, she resorted to jokes: "Oh, I don't care what people think . . . I'm going to Heaven in this stuff—God won't know me when I get there if I don't have it on!" In any case, here she is, sixty-five pounds, her voice barely a whisper, her body racked with pain and laced with morphine. She is as honest and vulnerable and open about what's happening to her as it's possible to be. *This is what death looks like.* Maybe for the first time we're seeing what Tammy sees when she looks at herself in the mirror. Her husband, Roe Messner, sits beside her. Later he will explain Tammy's decision to appear tonight as an attempt to say goodbye to all her friends.

She died before the sun rose the next morning. Roe Messner described it this way: "Well, about a quarter till 4:00 Tammy said she was hungry, and so we put her in the wheelchair, took her out to the kitchen, and she wanted to eat some Frosted Flakes, and so we made her a bowl of Frosted Flakes, and she tried to eat them and she couldn't eat them and she loved peanut butter, and she said, Roe, 'Take a spoon and give me some peanut butter.' She loved to take it just out of the jar, you know, and so she tried to eat some peanut butter and she couldn't swallow it, and so we took her back to the bedroom and she laid down, and in just a matter of two or three minutes she died. She just..."

"Just like went to sleep," Larry King added.

"She sort of gasped for breath one time and then she was gone," Messner said.

By this time, Tammy had somewhat rehabilitated her reputation. Over the previous decade, she had starred in a couple of secular TV shows and became an icon within the gay community, many of whom revered her as the ultimate drag queen. Jessica Hahn, for her part, got breast implants, posed for *Playboy* three times, and writhed around on the floor in various stages of undress while joining comedian Sam Kinison and the popular hair bands of the day in a thoroughly abhorrent music video of "Wild Thing." Tammy saw it as vindication. "It showed me what kind of girl she was," she said. "And it showed other people too. I mean, she didn't even have boobs." And while all of this was transpiring, evangelicals tried to rescue a woman named Karla Faye Tucker who had murdered two people with a pickax from the death penalty.

It was the nineties. We were coming up on the dawn of a new millennium, or maybe the End Times. I, for one, wasn't quite sure which.

Watching this spectacle unfold on a national stage throughout my twenties created in me more than a little personal discomfort. So much of what was transpiring would have seemed laughable—and certainly was for many—if it weren't for the deep resentment of and hostility for evangelicals that these shenanigans were engendering in much of the American public. Many onlookers were taking great satisfaction in watching the pathetic fall of the Bakkers and the humiliating decline of the religious right. America, it seemed, had been waiting impatiently for this bomb to go off.

The optics, I knew, were bad. But I wasn't particularly embarrassed by the media coverage of the latest sordid detail of Gospelgate. After all, I knew that Christianity had always operated under a wide umbrella, and that a whole spectrum of people claimed the appellation even if they appeared to share little in common. But the last couple of decades of American Christianity, which coincided with my adolescence and young adulthood, had left me asking questions of a much more personal variety. I suppose they could be summed up in one overarching query: who *were* these people? I was wondering who I was as a Christian and what I meant when I called myself by the same name that Jim Bakker answered to. This shameless circus was triggering in me what can only be called a private reckoning.

I found myself bound in the sump and morass of a state the Baptists I grew up among called *backsliding*. Usually this would mean I'd taken to drink or carousing with women of ill repute, or maybe committed a series of misdemeanors that ended me up in the hoosegow. I hadn't fallen prey to these vices that they for time immemorial had preached against, but instead had drifted into what might be termed a circumstance more dire and threatening to the status of my eternal soul. I was seriously questioning whether fidelity to the tenets I had grown up with was actually sustainable in the long run. My soul was in a funk not due to worldly temptation, but due to the suspicion that all I had once thought true might not be so bona fide after all.

I suppose the kind of shift in perspective I'm describing is unsettling for anyone. For the young Christian, though, it's seismic. It prompts a dizzying set of questions that culminates in nothing short of an identity crisis. By my estimation, I wasn't becoming an apostate, because an apostate finds enough certitude in his newfound self to make the trade-off seem worthwhile. I was finding no such recompense. I was too Christ-haunted to get free and clear of all I was brought up to be. I wasn't lost, but something almost as troublesome: someone who, in the eyes of the people who loved me, looked as though I was.

For his part, Pat Robertson had gone on to assemble nothing short of an empire in television, staying remarkably ahead of the curve as the industry moved toward cable, and capitalizing on it when the cable movement exploded outright. Robertson deftly mixed religious programming with sports, children's programming, and reruns of *Leave It to Beaver*. By the mid-eighties, CBN was the third largest satellite network in America, behind only HBO and Turner Broadcasting. In short, Jesus's Great Commission to "go ye therefore, and teach all nations" had always motivated evangelicals to adopt new technologies and invent new methods for getting the word out, Robertson merely perfected the art.

Maybe because ratings demanded it, or maybe because, as he suggested, Robertson sincerely believed he wanted to bring people from all walks of life to the Gospel, *The 700 Club* gradually became more secular in subject matter. But Robertson kept his show mostly free of politics and was happy to defer to Jerry Falwell in merging faith and policy. He largely stayed the course with this intention until 1987—when he announced that a conversation with God had interrupted his thinking and his plans. "I had everything you could ask for," Robertson explained, "but . . . I heard the Lord saying, 'I have something else for you to do. I want you to run for president of the United States.'"

It was not the ideal time for Robertson to declare his presidency. The newspapers at the time were full of the misdeeds of televangelists. Jim Bakker's was only the start. Oral Roberts had just climbed his prayer tower and declared God would "call him home" if his followers didn't produce eight million bucks of support. As if this weren't enough, Jimmy Swaggart was soon photographed escorting a prostitute into a New Orleans hotel room.

Nevertheless, Robertson forfeited his ties to CBN, resigned his ordination as a minister, and promoted himself to the American people as a businessman and a military veteran—most definitely *not* a televangelist. But to compound his efforts, video clips depicting him pleading for God to spare believers of everything from hurricanes to hemorrhoids circulated far and wide. And his past forays into politics—rare as they had been—were often resurrected. Reporters wanted to know how his religious beliefs would affect his political decisions. They wanted to know if he believed he could pray away Soviet missiles. Robertson responded by developing an antagonistic relationship with many journalists, calling them bigots who scorned religion and promoted the agenda of the liberal press.

Though he received very few endorsements, especially from the biggest names in the evangelical community, Robertson did moderately well early on—finishing second to Kansan Bob Dole in Iowa. But Vice President George H. W. Bush swept all nine primaries on Super Tuesday and soon became the Republican nominee.

Robertson's candidacy ended, but his foray into politics did not. After the 1988 election, he returned to CBN, and his show *The 700 Club* became his platform for spreading his political ideology. He found his favorites, took up his share of causes. But one would be hard-pressed to find a political cause he became more committed to than the pending execution of one Karla Faye Tucker.

It was Robertson who introduced America and my father to this death-row inmate, which in turn accounted for why I was trying to save her life with my words.

Chapter 8

WELL, HELL YES

Karla Faye Tucker was tried for Jerry Lynn Dean's murder, Danny Garrett for Deborah Thornton's. You might think they'd each be tried for both deaths, but there was a logic to it: Karla had been the first to take the pickax to Jerry; Danny Garrett had left it in Deborah Thornton's heart. Prosecutors were betting they'd have a stronger case if they paired each defendant with only one victim. And besides, each could be tried for the other's murder too, if it came down to that. The fact that Karla went up on trial before Danny Garrett says more about judicial logistics than culpability. The luck of the draw, literally. A lottery system was used to determine which judge got whose case. Somebody plucked a ping-pong ball from a machine, marked with a judge's name.

The tumble of Ping-Pong balls resulted in Judge Patricia Lykos presiding over Karla's trial. Some suggest this fate made Karla quite unlucky indeed. To say that attorneys were not particularly fond of Judge Lykos would be a gross understatement. Almost without exception they regarded her as somewhere on the spectrum between annoyingly abrasive and downright tyrannical.

But initially at least, Lykos made decisions that could benefit Karla. She anticipated the kind of attention this trial would draw, so she appointed Mack Arnold and Henry Oncken, two attorneys with sterling reputations, to defend Karla. Arnold was more theatrical in the courtroom, Oncken more measured, controlled. Their personalities and dispositions would dictate a synchronized working relationship, a way of playing off one another during the trial. Arnold would be the stage performer, Oncken the behind-the-scenes director. Notably, Arnold and Oncken both had spent more time serving as prosecutors than defense attorneys, which struck some observers as peculiar—but in any case, they were certainly better lawyers than Karla could have found on her own.

At first Oncken did not take kindly to this appointment. He was unimpressed by his new charge. "The day I was appointed to represent her," he said, "I could have pulled the switch myself and not blinked an eye."

Charley Davidson, the attorney who would later prosecute Danny Garrett, concurred: "I just remember when she first came into court—her attitude and the way she looked and everything about her was the personification of evil. When she was in court at first, you didn't even want to turn your back. It was just kind of an invisible cloud surrounding her so you could look at her and she looked bad." Oncken and Davidson were not unique in their first perception of Karla. Almost everybody who had any kind of interaction with her during that time characterized her in the same way. It probably would not be overstatement to say many people downright feared Karla. She seemed uninterested in courting any other perception.

On April 11, 1984, the case of *State of Texas v. Karla Faye Tucker* commenced. First came the culpability phase. On the advice of her lawyers, Tucker pled innocent of capital murder, claiming it wasn't premeditated—she hadn't gone to Jerry Lynn Dean's apartment with the intention of killing him. Years later, in a letter to Governor George Bush, she would reflect on this decision and explain her plea this way: "I was advised by my attorneys to plead not guilty and I was trusting their legal expertise. They knew I murdered Jerry and Deborah. I did not lie to them about it. I am, in fact, guilty. Very guilty." She had no prior convictions, but from the outset it was clear how the trial would go.

In his opening statement, prosecutor Joe Magliolo laid out the chronology of events and established the state's version of the story. Magliolo was a physical dynamo, aggressive and constantly moving about—it was his first capital case and he was deeply motivated. Over and over, he kept coming back to the image of Karla wriggling the weapon free from Dean's body, grinning, hoisting it over her head, and plunging it down again. He favored graphic descriptions, the coarser the better. "Hacked to death" was his favorite phrase, the one he used repeatedly to describe the events of that night. He wanted the jurors to imagine it, visualize it in their heads, then go home and have nightmares when they couldn't shake it from their mind's eye.

Prosecutors rolled in evidence, the pickax, the shotgun, the motorcycle parts—one damning piece after another. And the graphic pics: the defense objected to their introduction, but Judge Lykos permitted the prosecutors to show many of them, including several of the pickax buried in Deborah Thornton's chest. Magliolo led the jury through the photos like a kind of macabre tour guide, starting outside Apartment 2313, a parking lot shot, then gradually leading us inside, through the rooms, under that low ceiling, pulling us down the hallway, toward the back, building anticipation and milking suspense as though we don't know what we'll discover, toward where that rock 'n' roll music is coming from, passing first into one bedroom and then the last, where now, as though for the first time, we see Jerry Lynn Dean lying half-on, half-off the mattress, his head bloody, his body mutilated, and to his left, on her side, is Deborah Thornton with a pickax in her chest. Magliolo lingered on the carnage. It must have been like watching a horror flick.

Curiously, though, one item that was not admitted as evidence was the hammer Danny Garrett used to slug Jerry Lynn Dean into unconsciousness. The hammer in fact was never found.

All along, Karla maintained it was a hammer, a ball-peen hammer. But according to the Houston medical examiner's expert opinion, the weapon used to bludgeon Jerry Lynn Dean's head was likely more blunt—the handle of the pickax, maybe, or possibly the butt end of Danny Garrett's shotgun. Or maybe, they conjectured, conceivably, it *was* a hammer. Karla claimed she chunked the bloody tool into the sand pit near the house on McKean Street: a pit filled with water deep enough to swim in, its bottom a slurpy ooze so far down and so thick there's no telling what all might be buried in the muck. There was never any chance of fishing it out. The hammer might still be there, as far as anybody knows.

There was crime scene video too, in color. HPD had filmed the gruesome footage in case they needed it. Joe Magliolo kept it on hand, like an ace up his sleeve just in case circumstance ever necessitated its use, but he never played that card. You have to exercise judgment, because you can never tell how a jury will react, whether they'll think you're resorting to sensationalism. In the end, he didn't need it.

When their turn came, the defense tried to argue that Karla was only an accessory to the murders, that it was Danny Garrett's blows to the head with the hammer that led directly to Dean's death. But the medical examiner testified that it indeed was the pickax that caused the death of the victims. Detective J. C. Mosier came to the stand; then third wheel Jimmy Leibrandt, who was indicted for mere burglary rather than armed robbery; then Kari Tucker, who told the jurors that her sister had bragged she "got a nut" every time she "picked" Dean and that "the girl was a tough motherfucker to kill"; then Doug Garrett, who said Karla phrased it this way to him: "I picked him. I come with every stroke."

That kind of talk did serious damage. This linking of sex and violence—from a woman, no less—surely sealed the verdict as much as anything. In the March 9, 1998, issue of the *National Review*, writer Florence King proposed a retrospective theory about all this provocative chatter. "The murder occurred in 1983 when the multiple-orgasm phase was going full-tilt," King wrote, "when it was impossible to turn on the TV without hearing feminists talking about the female's 'superior capacity,' or read *Cosmopolitan* without finding an article on the mighty G-spot. I would bet anything that enough of this pop carnality filtered through to Karla Faye to inspire the trendy lie that sealed her doom."

In any case, this guilt phase of the trial lasted a mere two weeks and was relatively empty of highlights. The real substantive debate was over when Jerry Lynn Dean expired, and who directly caused it. Regardless, the defense never called a witness. Karla never took the stand. Which would not have helped her anyway. Onlookers claimed she looked out of it, start to finish. She just sat there, impassive, her head still fogged by the residue of all the drugs that had passed through her system. Her attorneys, Arnold and Oncken, had instructed her to try to appear calm and dignified, but her demeanor was interpreted instead as cold and remorseless. In his closing statement Mack Arnold even conceded Karla's guilt. "The evidence is overwhelming," he told jurors, "that my client is guilty of capital murder, and I think it would be an injustice for you to arrive at any other verdict." This admission was a tactical decision. He was already looking ahead to the sentencing phase, trying to get some credibility ahead of time. Trying to save his client's life with brutal honesty. No use at this point denying the obvious. He and Oncken must have felt like they were fighting a grizzly bear with a peashooter.

After only seventy minutes of deliberation, eight women and four men rendered the predictable verdict. They determined that Karla Faye Tucker did indeed "intentionally cause the death of the complainant by striking and stabbing the complainant with a mattock."

Or, what's more commonly called, a pickax.

Old Testament law prescribes death for any number of offenses, including but not limited to: murder, incest, adultery, bestiality, homosexuality, blasphemy, perjury, insubordination, kidnapping, witchcraft, disobeying parents, working on the Sabbath, lying about a woman's virginity at the time of her marriage, and failing to confine a bull that has a habit of goring people—in which case both the bull and its owner must be put to death. Some Biblical executions are easily recalled. Lot's wife is turned into a pillar of salt when she casts a glance back over her shoulder at the ruins of Sodom and Gomorrah. John the Baptist is beheaded because the daughter of Herodias requests it on a platter. And of course, Jesus's crucifixion stands as the most well-known case of capital punishment in history.

Others we need reminding of. Tamar plays the harlot, gets pregnant, and is burned to death. Abihu and Nadab go down for bringing their "strange fire" to the altar. Uzzah is offed for carrying the Ark of the Covenant inappropriately. Onan is killed for failing to fulfill his duty to impregnate his dead brother's widow. (Well, perhaps his more regrettable punishment is becoming the namesake of the practice of onanism.) Hananiah, Nabal, Jeroboam, Phinehas, Hophni, Jehoram: throughout the Old Testament, people are stoned, burned, impaled, given bowel diseases, or simply struck down for their transgressions, sometimes by a wrathful Jehovah, other times by their fellow man.

There are some noteworthy exceptions. Mercy sometimes seems to prevail over vengeance. The Bible's first recorded homicide, for example—Cain's murder of his brother Abel—results in Cain being banished to the land called Nod, where he wears the original scarlet letter—a mark that simultaneously identifies him as a lawbreaker and protects him from being killed by others. Also, premeditation matters; if the victim's death is accidental, the punishment is typically exile.

In the New Testament, Jesus of course says nothing directly about the death penalty—or about most of the sins for which the law prescribes it as punishment. He claims to fulfill the spirit of the law but rejects the whole eye-for-an-eye retribution plan. Which makes things tricky for Christians who claim belief in an "inerrant" word of God. Which Old Testament passages require strict adherence? Which are excused by grace? Perhaps the most famous case study focuses on an adulteress. You know it well: a crowd is gathered round with rocks in their hands. Jesus invites anyone without sin to cast the first stone. Everybody drops theirs and slinks away. Left alone, Jesus and the woman work it out amongst themselves. "Go and sin no more," he tells her.

During the guilt phase, Joe Maglioli claimed Karla had killed deliberately and posed an ongoing threat to society. The state's first witness, Karla's sister Kari, had testified she was afraid that Karla and Danny Garrett would murder her and that they had talked about killing others. If they had not been arrested, they might have murdered someone else. But now, in the sentencing phase in November 1984, Karla's lawyers knew the prosecution was going for the death penalty. So they suspected she could more likely avoid the death sentence—maybe it was her only chance—if she testified. She could tell her story. She could work to humanize herself, because of course it's so easy to condemn a monster, but it's a hard, hard thing to send a woman to her death. During the guilt phase, the question had been simple: did she commit the crime? But the punishment phase of a capital case was another thing altogether. Death is different. That's the way the Supreme Court has long put it—"death is different," Justice William Brennan concurred in *Furman v. Georgia* in 1972—because what's done can't be undone. The punishment is irreversible, so the standards for death must be higher. As a result of this difference, in the punishment phase the defendant could present mitigating factors. Life history, mental health evaluations, meaningful context. Karla could tell of finding Jesus, and the positive influence she had on her fellow inmates, and the pretty things she made for the prison dayroom. She could make them see she had indeed been transformed. "I wanted to tell the truth," she said. "I wanted the real story to be told. I had to do something about how sick-minded we must have been to think about something like this."

When her turn came to take the stand, she wore a white plastic cross and told the jurors how she was only eight or nine when she started smoking dope, how her mother had insisted she learn to do it right, to roll the papers just so—how she and her mother had been so close that they "used to share drugs like lipstick." She told them about shooting heroin at ten, losing her virginity with a grown man at eleven or twelve, flunking seventh grade twice, getting a hysterectomy at fifteen, marrying at sixteen, watching her mother die of hepatitis at twenty, divorcing her husband, turning tricks—the whole sordid tale. And she told these jurors that she had spent practically every moment of it all—save maybe two weeks when she kicked everything shortly after she got hitched to Stephen Griffith—helplessly and hopelessly strung out on drugs.

She also told the jury that Danny Garrett had actually been the one to kill both Jerry Lynn Dean and Deborah Thornton. He had taken that hammer to Jerry's head and struck the particular blow that killed Deborah with the pickax. She said she made up all the talk about taking sexual satisfaction in swinging the weapon. "I've hurt a lot of people," she said, "and I wish I could take the hurt out of everybody and put it on myself. I sometimes don't think enough could be done to me to really be justice." Magliolo asked her if she thought she deserved death for what she'd done. She said she didn't know.

Her defense team called in a psychiatrist who testified to the effects of Karla's long history of addiction—how she conceivably could have been in a drug-induced psychosis and therefore incapable of processing her actions or understanding their impact. The psychiatrist said Karla was too small to even heft a pickax without the assistance of speed. And as for her claims of sexual gratification? People who get that high, the psychiatrist said, don't get those kinds of kicks.

Karla's lawyers, Arnold and Oncken, called a handful of character witnesses as well—Karla's father ("I have not heard one cuss word from her"), a jailhouse deputy, a drug and alcohol counselor, and a chaplain who said Karla had been participating in Bible studies and wasn't just "playing church." All of them agreed that she was somehow a different woman than the one who had committed the crime.

But the prosecutor planted seeds of doubt about all of it. In addition to poking at Karla by repeatedly calling her by her married name "Mrs. Griffith," Joe Magliolo got witnesses so flustered and muddle-headed that no one was quite sure how many drugs Karla had taken or what their effect might possibly have been. In his cross-examination of the psychiatrist, he even persuaded her to acknowledge the fact that, okay, maybe in some cases people *do* get pleasure from all manner of sexual perversity.

From start to finish Magliolo hammered home the two things that even today most people remember about her trial—the pickax and the nut. When he offered his closing argument, he advocated the death penalty as a deterrent. "If she had known she was going to be sitting right here before she swung that ax," he told jurors, "it never would have got swung. If she knew she was going to receive death for killing those two people and taking their property, she would have never even gotten in that car and gone over to that apartment." Then when he asked jurors whether Tucker should be sentenced to death, he used a snippet from Doug Garrett's secretly recorded tape of Tucker.

Playing up the courtroom histrionics, Magliolo told the jury to listen to Tucker's own words. She'll tell you herself whether she deserves the death penalty. "Should Karla Faye Tucker be executed?" he asked the jury.

He let the question hang in the air for a moment. Then, on cue, Magliolo pressed play on the tape recorder.

Well, hell yes, Karla answered, her voice slurring the words.

Magliolo let the recording of Karla's voice sit there, boring into the consciousness of each of the twelve jurors. Then, "I think that says it all, ladies and gentlemen," Magliolo told the courtroom.

Turns out Magliolo was playing loose with the facts. What Karla was answering yes to on the recording was whether she "got a nut" when she wielded her pickax. She was talking about orgasm, not execution.

It hardly mattered. Judgment again was swift. After three hours of deliberation, the jury found Karla guilty of capital murder and sentenced her to death by lethal injection.

For the record, Danny Garrett's trial began in early October 1984, shortly before Karla's sentencing phase. Prosecutors Rusty Hardin and Charley Davidson asked Karla to testify in his trial. For a capital punishment defendant to testify against a codefendant is virtually unheard of. The likelihood of incriminating herself with her own testimony would seem reason enough to avoid the stand.

But she agreed. Danny Garrett's attorney, Ray Bass, insisted she testified only because she hoped the prosecutors would write letters to officials noting her participation—which might eventually help her in her quest to have her sentence commuted to life—but Karla insisted it was simply the right thing to do.

Ray Bass, a diminutive man who often wore a bow tie, performed his share of courtroom theatrics, which might explain why Danny Garrett's trial lasted considerably longer than Karla's, containing ten thousand pages in transcripts. But in the end, it only delayed the inevitable for him too.

In concluding his argument against Danny Garrett, prosecutor Rusty Hardin resorted to video evidence—he showed jurors a clip of Jerry Lynn Dean's bedroom, including a graphic view of both victims. The pickax was still embedded in Deborah Thornton's torso.

Those brutal images pretty much sealed the deal. In late November of '84, Danny Garrett too was sentenced to death via the needle.

Suspense pertaining to the story of Karla Faye Tucker and Danny Garrett was dwindling. What remained of it boiled down to a single question: who would die first?

Chapter 9

THE THING IS QUICKLY ENOUGH DONE

The nature of Karla's crime was so brutal that, if she had committed it, say, during the eighteenth-century, the consequence likely would have been worse than death. Quite possibly she would have been gibbeted, which is to say, after hanging her in the gallows, officials would have coated her body with tallow or pitch to delay decomposition, encased her in an iron cage called a gibbet, and showcased her corpse for public viewing in a setting with foot traffic aplenty. She'd have been denied a customary burial and would've instead served as a "spectacle for warning to others." Subjected to all manner of weather, pestilence, and avian interference, her corpse would have signaled disgrace to all onlookers.

Revolutionary War hero Paul Revere gives us a sense of how memorable an act of gibbeting could be in a community. In 1755, in Charlestown, Massachusetts, a slave named Mark was hanged and gibbeted for poisoning his master. Two decades later, Revere made his famous ride through Charlestown. Two decades after *that*—forty-three years after the enslaved man died—Revere made clear that the lurid showcase of the gibbet had indeed made its desired impact on the locals: "After I had passed Charlestown Neck & got nearly opposite where Mark was hung in chains, I saw two men on Horse Back under a Tree."

CHAPTER 9

Julius Mount Bleyer liked that lethal injection was cheaper than hanging. It was quicker, too, and infinitely more humane. This was 1888. A New York physician, Bleyer was the first American to propose the method. In a medical journal article, "Best Method of Executing Criminals," he laments the fact that America has inherited hanging as its method of choice—the "bungling and barbarous method of capital execution in use from time immemorial in England." He concedes that hanging is "sometimes sudden, painless, and as free from hideous display as such a process well can be." But occasionally, he claims, things go awry. The rope breaks, for example. The victim falls to the ground, only to be picked up and returned to the scaffold for a do-over. In such scenarios, the integrity of the act is compromised beyond all remedy. And then there's the problem of estimating the proper length of the drop. It all depends on the offender's weight; the rope must be of proper length to ensure a quick death. A perfect drop fractures the neck and severs the spinal cord instantly, leaving the offender "dangling between heaven and earth," as the saying went in those days. A perfect drop, however, was hard to come by. Sometimes it was a matter of variables: the position of the knot; the give of the rope; the weight of the offender and the condition of his neck muscles; the weather; and of course the skill of the hangman. (It must be said there was an art to the practice, as with any skill.) Other times, the perfect drop was a matter of distance. Too short of a drop could result in slow strangulation in which the prisoner writhes and gasps and convulses in what newspaper reporters called the "dance of death" for as long as forty-five minutes. The mouth and nose turn dark purple, the tongue lolls outside the mouth, eyes bulge and pop from their sockets, the bowels loose, and arms and legs flail violently. It's a wholly regrettable thing to witness. Too long a drop, on the other hand, can end in decapitation, "and we have the bloodiness of the guillotine," Bleyer says, "without its grim decorousness." In other words, we don't get a show to gussy up the tragedy and make it palatable to onlookers. We just get the tragedy.

Not that Bleyer favored going back to the guillotine, mind you. Whatever problems beset hanging, he had no nostalgia for the method that gave capital punishment its title in the first place—*capitalis* in Latin translates to "of the head." In another article, "Instant Death by Decapitation an Impossibility According to Biological Analysis" (1898), Bleyer tells us the guillotine didn't cause instantaneous death either. To onlookers, the deed looked like it was done and over with in no time. But Bleyer claimed we were missing something: there was the problem of consciousness to consider. He built his research on the father of electrocution, Dr. Cinel of Paris, who according to Bleyer, made claim that death does not follow beheading for several hours, "on account of the fact that the brain finds nourishment for an hour after decapitation. Also during this time the head of the victim retains the sense of feeling, hearing, smell and sight . . . Dr. Cinel lays much stress upon a point in connection with the blood supply to the brain, long after the head has fallen into the basket."

Bleyer said we need to be thinking about consciousness—namely what the devil it is, and what it has to do with decapitation. The problem is, once the guillotine drops, we can't detect consciousness. Unlike light or electricity, we can't measure it. Bleyer writes, "I concede that consciousness, soon after decapitation, must cease; how soon, no one can exactly explain, as all experiments are too coarse to give us any positive reliance." Then, the good doctor can't contain his impulse to launch into metaphor: "After all," he writes, "there must remain a certain class of conscious state which such a person lapses into, which will remain forever to us a closed book, and an abyss too deep for us ever to fathom." Kittens snap at the air when they are decapitated, he notes. Tortoises too. He suggests it is possible for a brain cell "to receive impressions still, after immediate decapitation, and hold them firm for some time." To corroborate this finding, in 1905 a French physician, Dr. Gabriel Beaurieux, experimented with the guillotined head of prisoner Henri Languille. Beaurieux called Languille's name, to which the prisoner responded at first by lifting his eyebrows as though in acknowledgment, and then fixed Beaurieux in his gaze. "I was not, then, dealing with the sort of vague dull look without any expression, that can be observed any day in dying people to whom one speaks," said Dr. Beaurieux. "I was dealing with undeniably living eyes which were looking at me."

Bleyer praises Dr. Cinel's new, revolutionary method of electrocution, deeming it "decorous, involving no brutal or barbarous intervention of the executioner." He says the electrical spark performs its deadly errand before the nervous system knows what hit it. "Life is undoubtedly extinct" before we feel a thing. We don't know we've been pricked by a pin "instantly," he says. A man who cuts off his finger with a saw feels no pain "at the instant."

Bleyer seems positively giddy as he describes how we could borrow electric wires from the main circuits connecting with a city's streets lights—well concealed and guarded, of course, lest criminals or their friends gain access to them! We'll run the first electrode to a little wooden house, where the condemned will stand barefooted on a metal plate; then we'll run a second one through the roof of the hut to touch the top of the criminal's closely shaved head. The sheriff, his deputy—or whoever we appoint—then pushes a button, and "before bystanders have consciousness of the act . . . all is over."

Bleyer says he's performed these experiments on animals. A large dog never made a move or uttered a sound. Same outcome with rabbits. And as an added bonus, he notes an "incidental advantage" he hadn't anticipated: "Decomposition proceeds with extreme rapidity." With electrocution, you wouldn't need to go through the "customary wake over the criminal's carcass." Death is swift via this method of execution.

But for Julius Mount Bleyer, there was only one problem. Electrocution was Dr. Cinel's method. His predecessor had already made too much headway with the research. So if Bleyer were to contribute anything to the conversation about the death penalty, it fell to him to offer an alternative method. Enter lethal injection. He claims this method is "equally painless" and "eminently suitable" to executions. Again, Bleyer describes a hypothetical execution in as clean and orderly a fashion as imaginable. At the appointed time, he says, the sheriff comes into the prisoner's cell, where the condemned is lying on a couch as though in a state of tranquil repose, and "administers six grains of sulphate of morphine" into his arm. In mere moments, the prisoner becomes drowsy and falls asleep, at which point the sheriff repeats the dosage. If necessary, the shot can be repeated multiple times. Within a half-hour, the man is dead. "The thing is quickly enough done," says Bleyer, "when it is well enough done." Again, the whole event is speedy, painless, and this time "the man simply goes to sleep, never to awake." It's all very low-key and void of theatrics. Here in the privacy of his cell, the condemned will be subjected to none of the spectacle—Bleyer calls it the "dying game"—that was common when Hanging Day drew crowds sometimes numbering in the thousands. There are no processions from the jail to the gallows, no grand orations filled with rhetorical flourish, no zealous sermons about the consequences of sin, no children looking on nearby. And none of the drunkenness, fisticuffs, gambling, and general debauchery that often broke out among spectators in the carnival atmosphere—what Dickens called "the brutal mirth"—of public execution.

In the nineteenth century, when Bleyer was writing, it was becoming of increasing concern that women were turning out in droves, especially genteel women. At stake was nothing less than the culture's moral standing, evinced through threats to its steadiest barometer, feminine delicacy. In 1826, Hanging Day in Lenox, Massachusetts, elicited this criticism in the *Berkshire American*: "What a group appeared at Lenox! . . . There were high (not high-minded) and low, rich and poor, old men and young, black and white . . . and to crown the whole, women! Yes, gracious heaven! Soft, delicate, tender-hearted females who would faint at the killing of a chicken went fifteen miles to see a fellow creature put to death!" An 1841 St. Louis hanging of four men drew similar concerns from the local newspaper: "The place and occasion seemed to us to be one at which no female should have appeared. Nevertheless, judging from the equipage and dress which we saw, we supposed that some who rank high in fashion were present." In 1858, the *New York Times* reported that a middle-class woman "made strenuous efforts" to obtain a ticket to see her husband's murderer hanged. According to the *Times*, "She importuned the Sheriff, and for a long time would take no denial. It was not till the Sheriff told her that her request was highly improper that she withdrew from his office, evidently disappointed at the result of her interview." The victim's brother, on the other hand, requested an admission ticket, and was granted it without question. In 1871, when John Ware was hanged in Camden, New Jersey, the *Times* reported that 150 people gathered for the spectacle enclosed by "a high wooden fence," and "the only unseemly portion of the proceedings" was "the appearance of several women at one of the windows." (Just to clarify, I'll note what you've undoubtedly recognized already: in all this verbiage, the concern lies only with the spectators. There's absolutely zero consideration that the criminal might be female.)

And Bleyer lists yet another advantage of lethal injection—there'd be no sympathy for the criminals. No malefactors dying as if they were martyrs, taken from the gallows to glory. Plus, compared to constructing a scaffold, or even preparing an electrocution, lethal injection is cost-effective. The syringe and morphine are a pittance. And perhaps best of all, by all appearances, lethal injection *looks* like a medical procedure.

As the US moved toward almost exclusive use of lethal injection in the 1980s, all Bleyer's reasons—the painlessness, the efficiency, the privacy, the cost—contributed to the conviction that lethal injection was indeed the most civilized method of capital punishment ever devised.

Two weeks before her own date with the three-drug cocktail, Karla Faye Tucker was asked whether, under the circumstances, she thought it was a serviceable procedure.

"I think that for capital punishment, if there's a way it must be done, I think that's a humane way," she told Larry King. "I don't agree with it, but I guess if we're going to have it in this society, it's a humane way. Is there any humane way to kill a person?"

But Julius Mount Bleyer would have to wait for lethal injection to become America's preferred method of killing criminals. First, Dr. Cinel's method of execution would win out for the next hundred years. Alfred Southwick, a Buffalo, New York, dentist, originated the electric chair in 1881. He had heard tell of (or maybe witnessed) a drunk man touching a live electric wire and dying instantly and, apparently, painlessly. Initially, Southwick intended his invention to euthanize stray dogs, but soon he was proposing it as a more progressive form of capital punishment. As a dentist, Southwick treated his patients in chairs, so he adapted his invention for use upon a man who was seated. After a series of botched hangings, the governor of New York state charged a committee with developing a more advanced method, and selected Southwick to join the three-member team. They wanted to improve upon primitive forms of capital punishment that inflicted agony on the criminal and institute a new practice that would be efficient, certain, and humane. An electric shock of sufficient force would be ideal—as ideal as any means of putting a man to death can be. "The velocity of the electric current," the committee posed, "is so great that the brain is paralyzed; is indeed dead before the nerves can communicate any shock." In 1890, they did a test run on a horse, which promptly fell over. The next day, August 6, William Kemmler, who had killed his common-law wife with a hatchet, became the first criminal appointed to die via the chair.

At Auburn Prison, twenty-five witnesses gathered in a dimly lit room to watch officials attach one electrode to the base of Kemmler's spine and another to a metal cap tied onto his head. "Gentlemen, I wish you all good luck," Kemmler told the crowd. "I believe I am going to a good place, and I am ready to go." He added a special instruction for the warden: "Take your time and do it right." The warden assured Kemmler he'd feel no pain, told him goodbye, and instructed an employee to pull the switch. With that, one thousand volts surged through Kemmler for seventeen seconds. His mouth "twisted into a ghastly grin" and he clenched his fists so tightly that his fingernail sliced his palm and "blood trickled out onto the arm of the chair." An attending physician pronounced him dead.

There was a problem, though. Kemmler wasn't dead. He was still breathing.

A "purplish foam" oozed from Kemmler's mouth. The man began fidgeting and moaning in the chair. The doctor immediately ordered a second charge—"quick, no delay"—of two thousand volts. The voltmeter, though, had dropped to zero, and the current had to rebuild. Meanwhile, Kemmler wheezed and gasped for breath; his head started smoking and the back of his coat caught fire.

Once the current again began surging through Kemmler, this time they kept it going for more than a minute. The *New York Times* described what happened next thusly: "An awful odor began to permeate the death chamber, and then, as though to cap the climax of this fearful sight, it was seen that the hair under and around the electrode on the head and the flesh under and around the electrode at the base of the spine was singeing. The stench was unbearable." The capillaries in Kemmler's face ruptured. Blood popped from his features like beads of sweat. Kemmler then was examined a second time, and pronounced dead for a second time.

Eight minutes had passed since the first charge. As Kemmler remained in the chair, his body cooling, the witnesses filed out in misery. "It had nauseated all but a few of them," the *Times* reported, "and the sick ones had to be looked out for." The New York deputy coroner concluded he'd rather see ten hangings than one execution the likes of this. George Westinghouse, an inventor who specialized in electricity, commented, "They would have done better with an ax."

But the chair's inventor, the dentist Alfred Southwick, watched the whole thing unfold, and was satisfied. "There is the culmination of ten years work and study!" he proclaimed. "We live in a higher civilization from this day."

The *New York World* opined, "The first experiment in electricity should be the last." Yet within a year, in 1891, four more murderers were electrocuted on a single day at Sing Sing Prison. Less than two hours passed between the entrance of the first offender, James Slocum, and the exit of the final one, Shibaya Jugiro. This time, the procedure seemed to unfold according to plan, each man appearing to die instantly and his corpse evincing no damage. One witness, Dr. Samuel Ward, called it "regular, methodical, and dignified." By the early twentieth century, then, one state after another—Ohio, Massachusetts, New Jersey, Virginia, North Carolina—approved the chair. In total, between 1888 and 1913, fifteen states adopted the chair as their primary means of execution. Though further incidents occurred—chief among them a botched 1903 incident in which the offender was pronounced dead but found to be breathing again in the autopsy room—it was generally regarded as a more orderly, swift, and certain method than hanging. Pop culture even reflected the trend. In early talkies, movie gangsters were often sentenced to "fry" or "sit in the hot seat."

In 1928, the process did undergo serious scrutiny when a reporter smuggled a camera into the execution of Ruth Snyder and published the picture on the cover of the *New York Daily News* the next morning. Tom Howard strapped a camera to his right ankle, under the cuff of his pants leg, and navigated his way through security into the execution chamber where photography was strictly forbidden. He'd been hired from the *Chicago Tribune*, because unlike New York's beat reporters, he was unknown to the guards. At the precise moment that the executioner started the voltage, Howard pointed his toe at Snyder and squeezed a bulb that triggered a wired shutter release running down his leg. The resulting image is tilted and blurry, but it captures Snyder, wearing a dress, sensible shoes, and a mask, seemingly in motion as electricity courses through her body. Her fingers grip the arms of the chair. There, too, are the legs of the prison guard, which were cropped for the newspaper's front page.

The headline the next morning read, simply but sensationally, "DEAD!"

In the mid-1940s, two separate cases involving African American boys invited scrutiny about use of the electric chair. The first was

George Stinney, who was only fourteen when he was electrocuted—the youngest child executed in America in the modern age. The story went that in 1944, two white girls, eleven and seven, were sharing a bicycle as they headed out on a springtime hunt for maypops, the fruit of a wildflower. They were passing the lumber mill in their small South Carolina town when up ahead they saw a Black boy, a seventh grader named George Stinney, who alongside his younger sister had taken their family's cow out to graze. The two girls, Betty June and Mary Emma, asked the Black children where they might find some maypops. George and his sister Amie didn't know. What happened next has been a mystery for more than seventy years.

In the version of events that would send George Stinney to the chair, he follows them down the road and bludgeons them to death, singlehandedly, with a railroad spike. He leaves the girls' bodies in a shallow ditch in the woods, lying on their backs, their bicycle nearby with its front wheel gone from its frame. His handiwork is gruesome: Mary Emma is in possession of a two-inch laceration above her eye and a hole boring through her forehead into her skull. Betty June bears the marks of at least seven blows to her head, the damage so remarkable that the back of her skull is, in the words of one Dr. Asbury Cecil Bozard, who conducted her autopsy, "nothing but a mass of crushed bones."

The sheriff told newspapers that within forty minutes of the arrest of George Stinney, the boy had confessed to the murders. He claimed that George had killed the girls after they had resisted his sexual advances and threatened to tell their parents. But as the execution neared, protestors began contacting Governor Olin Johnston, urging him to consider George's age and commute his sentence to life imprisonment. When support for George reached a fever pitch, Governor Johnston responded with a letter defending his refusal to wield his authority in George's favor. "I have just talked with the officer who made the arrest in this case," he wrote. "It may be interesting for you to know that Stinney killed the smaller girl to rape the larger one. Then he killed the larger girl and raped her dead body. Twenty minutes later he returned and attempted to rape her again, but her body was too cold. All of this he admitted himself."

In the weeks between his arrest and trial, law enforcement detained George in a place no one knew, far away from both marauding bands of angry whites in search of vigilante justice and his parents too. The Stinneys were prohibited from speaking with him, and fears of a white mob prevented them from showing up at his trial. Fifteen hundred people did attend, too many to crowd into the courthouse. But there wasn't much to see, as it turns out. Stinney's court-appointed attorney chose not to cross-examine any witnesses and offered no evidence of his own. How does a five-foot-one, ninety-five-pound boy beat two girls to death at once when one of the girls is bigger than he is? How does he drag them into the woods at three o'clock in the afternoon in the Jim Crow South without anybody taking notice? Nobody asked. After three hours of testimony, a jury of white men convicted George with no recommendation of mercy. The judge sentenced him to die by electrocution.

Another version of the story, though, describes the girls stopping by the house of a prominent white family of the town, to see if the wife of the mill boss might accompany them in their quest to locate the flowers. The wife declines the invitation, because her grandbaby is napping inside the house, but her son drives up in his logging truck and offers to help the girls find their maypops. They throw their bike in the back and climb in. No one sees the girls alive again.

But when their bodies are found, nobody goes looking for a white killer. Nobody investigates Dr. Asbury Cecil Bozard's written conclusion that "a round instrument about the size of the head of a hammer," not a railroad spike, caused the fractures on the girls' skulls either. Instead, someone fingers George, and he is promptly taken away to jail, where he confesses to the crime. Or so the story goes. The problem is, there's no written record of the confession, or trial transcripts either. And nobody can agree on exactly what kind of boy George Stinney was. He was characterized as everything from a quiet, withdrawn child who loved to draw and maintained an endless fascination with airplanes, to a bully with a temper who once scratched a girl with a knife. All that remains for certain are the graves of three children and a mystery that will likely live on in the little sawmill town of Alcolu, South Carolina, eighty miles north of Charleston, forever.

In any case, on June 16, 1944, at 7:30 a.m., George Stinney Jr., toting a Bible under his arm, was escorted to the electric chair at the state penitentiary in Columbia. The fathers of the two murdered girls were in attendance, along with about fifty witnesses. His small build made it difficult for law enforcement to strap him into the chair. It was especially hard to attach an electrode to his right leg. It's been claimed, but remains unsubstantiated, that he was asked to sit atop his Bible in order to compensate for his slight frame. This much, though, we know: the death mask he wore was manufactured for an adult, so when the first current of 2,400 volts shot through his body, the mask slipped off. The witnesses got a glimpse of George's tear-streaked face, saliva foaming around his mouth; and four minutes later, after three separate jolts of electricity, his skin took on a bluish tint and "wisps of smoke and a brief shower of sparks" rose from his body. The boy slumped in the chair in his striped jump suit, like a scarecrow that had lost its filling. Throughout the death house came the smell of burning flesh.

Another incident involving an African American boy threatened the chair's use in 1946, when the state of Louisiana attempted to electrocute seventeen-year-old Willie Francis and failed. Two drunken executioners did a slipshod job of rigging up "Gruesome Gertie," a portable chair weighing three hundred pounds that had already killed twenty-two people (including a woman) and eventually would be used to kill eighty-seven over half a century. Moments after the switch was thrown, the boy was heard calling from behind his leather mask, "Take it off—take it off! Let me breathe! I am n-n-not dying!" Willie Francis strained and kicked so much that Gruesome Gertie's legs jumped six inches off the ground and the chair made a full quarter turn before coming to rest. They unstrapped the boy from the chair and led him back to his cell. His head was still buzzing and he was a little disoriented—"It seemed like they were in an awful hurry to get me out of that chair so they could bury me," he said—but otherwise unharmed. No burn marks or singed flesh, just a quickened pulse. The sheriff offered some food and a chance to venture outside for a breath of fresh air, but the boy only wanted to rest on the cot in his cell. Willie Francis was virtually illiterate and known to speak with a stutter, but he later described his trip to the chair in perhaps the most poetic language ever uttered by a death-row prisoner. He said getting electrocuted was like having "a mouth full of cold peanut butter, and you see little blue and pink and green speckles, the kind that shines in a rooster's tail."

Some saw Willie Francis's survival as divine intervention, a blessing from God. Mothers, in particular, reached out to offer solace and wish the boy well, calling him "son" in their letters. His lawyers appealed to the Supreme Court, claiming cruel and unusual punishment, but alas, this was Jim Crow Louisiana. Willie Francis understood as much. From the outset, he had seemed resigned to his fate with greater certainty than those around him. "I'm right interested to find out if I can die like the man I thought I was," Willie told a reporter. "I always sort of wondered if I was a brave man. Now I guess maybe I'm gonna find out the hard way, Boss, so there won't be no doubt in my mind when I leave. A lot of men never find out. A lot of men die still wondering if they was the man they thought they was." He wiled away his time in the New Iberia Parish jail, eating candy, reading comic books, and practicing his enunciation by use of a booklet that promised a cure for stuttering. But in the run up to his second execution, he told a reporter he was prepared to meet his maker with "my Sunday pants and my Sunday heart . . . Ain't going to wear no beat-up pants to see the Lord. Been busy walking my way into heaven for this past year. Them folks expecting me to come in style." Indeed, two days later he strode to the death chamber wearing dark formal pinstripe slacks, a white shirt, and dress shoes instead of the prison uniform he'd worn a year ago. He was now eighteen. Onlookers noted how he had grown considerably taller over the past twelve months.

This time, the chair worked.

Like the guillotine and the gallows, the electric chair would fall out of favor too, and for the same reason. Starting in the 1920s, gas became a popular alternative. Firing squads, too, were permitted in Utah and Nevada, states with heavy Mormon populations who supported the doctrine of blood atonement. When *Gregg v. Georgia* reversed *Furman* and reinstated the death penalty in 1976, Gary Gilmore elected to die six months later, in 1977, by firing squad in Utah. Whether by gas or by bullet, executions, as Julius Bleyer had promised, became private events administered by the state, behind closed doors or gates—meaning that deterrence became less of a persuasive reason for continuing the practice. Unlike those public spectacles that accompanied hangings and the guillotine, now there was virtually no chance a person who might fit the description of the kind that executions were supposed to deter would actually witness one. The media became the place where we go for the oft-sensationalized story of how a man, in some remote space in some remote prison, was put to death. An important ethical shift occurred: the state, not the people, played the role of executioner.

Then, in 1982, Karla Faye Tucker's state of Texas was the first to employ lethal injection when Charles Brooks, Jr. was executed. Though ceremony surrounding execution had changed dramatically since the era of Hanging Day, the scaffold speech, now called a final statement, remained intact (The heart of Brooks's last words: "I, at this very moment, have absolutely no fear of what may happen to this body. My fear is for Allah, God only, who has at this moment the only power to determine if I should live or die"). By the mid-eighties, the three-drug cocktail became the preferred method of execution in most states. First, sodium thiopental renders you unconscious within ten seconds; then comes pancuronium bromide, a total muscle relaxant that paralyzes your lungs and diaphragm and stops your breathing in fifteen to thirty seconds; and finally, potassium chloride stops your heart's electrical functioning and induces cardiac arrest. The American Medical Association prohibited physicians from actually administering the drugs—the Hippocratic Oath, you'll recall, stipulates that doctors "abstain from intentional wrong-doing and harm"—so the responsibility usually fell to prison employees, often through a machine. Still, the whole procedure usually went smoothly. Doctors did the bookend jobs—providing sedatives beforehand and performing the autopsy afterward.

Maybe Julius Mount Bleyer would've been proud. He had lobbied long and hard for lethal injection to become the preferred method of putting people to death. But he wasn't around to celebrate the legacy of his research. Bleyer himself had died long ago in 1915, at age fifty-five, at his home in New York City.

Chapter 10

HERE AND HAPPY

In December 1984, law enforcement drove Karla two hundred miles from Houston and delivered her and her two garbage bags of belongings to the Mountain View Unit of the Texas Department of Corrections in Gatesville, about an hour west of Waco. Gatesville was a town of a little over eleven thousand people, a locale full of pickup trucks, feed depots, and barbecue joints, surrounded by sprawling ranches far as the eye could see (but, curiously, Mountain View lacked any view of mountains). Over eight thousand adult offenders lived confined behind coils of razor-wire circling the six correctional facilities that made up the prison industrial complex. Over six hundred women were incarcerated on the ninety-seven-acre compound, but those on death row were separated from the rest of the population by a crash gate locked with a six-inch-long skeleton key.

Karla's small cell was equipped with a bunk, a small bookshelf, a sink, a commode, a chest of drawers, a chair, and a radio. The floor: concrete. The windows: paned with frosted glass and sealed with bars. The lone television: in the day room, across from the cells. She would take her meals at a table in that day room too. Breakfast arrived at 4:30 a.m. She was given twenty minutes to eat before her tray was removed. At 10:30 a.m., she received lunch, which sometimes featured sausage links from pigs bred and slaughtered on site. When she showered, she stripped naked in her cell while a guard watched. For a while she was the only woman on death row.

Because death row is a wait station where inmates prepare to die, the state makes no attempt to "rehabilitate" them and prepare them for a return to civilization. They are separated from the general population of inmates and live segregated from the daily activity of the larger prison facility. The state regards these prisoners as, quite simply, beyond redemption.

But Karla did not sit morosely in her six-by-fourteen-foot cell, waiting for her summons from the Grim Reaper. The same woman who had thrice repeated seventh grade took high school classes, earned her diploma, and began taking college classes by correspondence. "I knew there were things I could do and achieve," she said, "and I hadn't done it. The more little things I did, the better I felt about myself, and the better I felt, the more I felt I needed to do to feel better, and on and on." She read Tolkien—*The Hobbit* and *Lord of the Rings*. She taught herself sign language, "so I could take these two hands that used to hurt and let them help." She wrote antidrug letters to teens. She exercised, gardened, cooked, prayed, ate ice cream, read her Bible, threw birthday parties for her fellow inmates once any joined her, and spent six hours per day making stuffed dolls with dimpled knees and rosy cheeks called Parole Pals. Prison employees ordered the dolls according to certain specifications of gender, skin tone, eye and hair color. Girl dolls wore ruffled pinafores, boys patched overalls. Like any seamstress, Karla was allowed to use scissors and other sharp instruments because prison officials trusted her.

And she grew deeper in her faith. The solitary time gave her plenty of opportunity for reflection. "I lay in my bed and cry and think about what I've done," she said. "I would never take my own life, but sometimes I think, if [the victims' families] could, maybe that would just take care of it all, and I wouldn't have to worry about it no more, and they'd feel good about it." The impossibility of ever balancing the scales again made her wonder if redemption were even possible. "God helps me deal with it. Sometimes I feel like I need to hurt for it. If they execute me then it's going to be over. In the long run here, alive, that's just how long it's going to stay in my head. You can't just forget it unless you're just really sick. And, whereas before I really didn't think about what it did to everybody, now I do. I mean, do I really deserve to be here and happy?" There were no easy answers, but at least she could think more clearly, now that her brain was no longer clouded with narcotics. "When you're drug-free," she said, "your mind is clearer to think things out. . . . I have a better grasp on things, maybe because I want to, maybe because my mind's free of drugs, and it allows me to."

Over time other women joined her on death row: Pamela Perillo, who'd strangled two hitchhikers using their own ropes; Betty Lou Beets, who'd killed her fifth husband and buried him under a wishing well in her front yard for retirement and insurance payoffs; and Frances Newton, who killed her husband and two children for $100,000 in insurance benefits. Of the four of them, two had confessed their crimes, two claimed innocence. Perillo had actually been sentenced to death before Karla, but she was in Houston, appearing before a judge, when Karla arrived. The women's cells were unlocked at 6:30 each morning, when they were allowed to mill about the day room decorated with afghans they'd crocheted and draped over benches or around an outdoor recreation yard. At 10:30 p.m. they returned to their cells—1:30 a.m. on the weekends.

These women created a kind of sorority no one wanted to join, but it became their community and provided a sense of comfort and belonging. Death-row women have a reputation among prison guards for complaining and just generally talking nonstop, but they rarely resort to violence against each other or the guards and, as a result, they're given leeway that men don't often enjoy. So Karla and the other women cooked meals together, typically adding cream cheese, no matter the dish or the recipe. They celebrated each other's birthdays and holidays with parties, exchanged gifts they'd made by hand, and played silly games like pin the tail on the donkey. They did knitting, crocheting, needlepoint—they created clothing for the others to wear to their next appearance in court. They cut each other's hair. They rallied around whichever one had fallen into a funk and endeavored to raise her spirits, often with talk about Jesus—maybe because the only other people allowed inside the space with them were prison mission programs with a Christian message. Some of these programs taught interpretive dances that conveyed spiritual themes. Some of them led clay sculpting seminars. All of them featured personal testimonies from visitors aimed at laying out a plan of salvation. The women prayed, they sang, they recited scripture. Occasionally visitors from the mission programs would anoint the inmates' bodies with oil. They would get caught up in the spirit. They would swoon in each other's arms.

Within these first few years, Karla seemed to make peace with her situation. "I'm not going to say that being in prison makes me happy," she said. "But, what I'm doing for myself makes me feel good inside. . . . Instead of being at a standstill, I'm moving ahead." One Christmas day, her former attorney Henry Oncken brought his wife and daughter to visit Karla, who knitted him a sweater for a present. The same woman Oncken couldn't tolerate when he was appointed to defend her now regarded her as, in his words, a "caring person. That's hard for people to understand, given what she did. She genuinely cares about other people, is genuinely interested in improving the quality of her life at this point. She is someone I've developed a liking for, a fondness for." Now he and Karla were frequently exchanging letters. Likewise, a member of the jury that called for her execution noted her transformation. "I'm not saying that at the time it was wrong to give her the death penalty; she did deserve it at the time," juror Paul Ward said. "But things have changed. She has changed." When Karla spoke about her transformation, she phrased it as though she were recalling a long-ago acquaintance. "The other Karla," she said, "no longer exists."

Even prosecutor Joe Magliolo softened his view of Karla, a bit. "I think she is different now," he acknowledged. "And if there was some way to sentence to death the person who hacked those people, and take the present Karla Faye Tucker and sentence her to something else, I would be happy with that. But even though she is different, the person who hacked those people to death is Karla Faye Tucker." He felt the die was cast, unfortunately, early on in Karla's life. "If she is executed, I'll be a little sad but really sad for society almost more than for Karla. We allowed Karla to get into the predicament that she was in. She was a child when she started going down the path. Somebody should have noticed that and cared enough about her to help her."

It was around this time that Pat Robertson first featured Karla on *The 700 Club*. It was on his show that Robertson began to shape the narrative that would compel many Americans to see Karla as a new woman, deserving of mercy. "When we sent a reporter down to talk to her [in 1992]," Robertson said, "we didn't find some wild-eyed hippie, we found the most beautiful Christian woman we had ever encountered . . . sublime, if I can use that term, a lovely spirit. The person who had committed those crimes really wasn't there anymore. She was like a different person, and when we interviewed her and showed her testimony on television, and others did the same thing, they found a person who was absolutely radiant." And as a result of this narrative, it was George Bush's predecessor, Governor Ann Richards (the last Democrat to hold the office in Texas), who began receiving the first wave of letters from Robertson's viewers, pleading for clemency.

Despite the perceptions of many people who had spent time with Karla, public opinion, even in light of these recent events, stayed consistent. In response to a "beautiful picture" of Karla on the front page of the *Houston Chronicle*, a reader commented, "The first thing a criminal learns when he or she is put on death row is to become a born-again Christian. Life is very cheap with these people until of course theirs is at stake. Then they will use any and every trick in the book to beat the punishment. I say give this lady the needle. If she is truly a convert to Jesus, He will see that she has everlasting life."

In early 1993, Danny Garrett was granted a new trial, because it was determined that almost a decade ago prosecutors had improperly dismissed a potential juror.

He never made it that far.

In June of 1993, the news came that Danny Garrett was dead. Cirrhosis of the liver. He was forty-seven.

It's impossible to know precisely how Karla responded to the news, deep down inside. She hadn't corresponded with him through letters. She probably knew he had basically cut himself off from family—especially his brother Doug Garrett, with whom he'd had no contact since Doug showed up at 2205 McKean with a black shirt hiding a recording device—and how he didn't receive visitors or respond to their letters. But she probably took some time to think. Likely she spent at least a few minutes moving backward in her mind, to that day in January of 1983 when she met him at the pill doctor, and that night when he had taken her slow dancing at the Diamondback saloon, and how they had taken a shine to one another and moved into together almost instantly. And no doubt she reflected on the night six months later, in June, when she unlocked that door to Jerry Lynn Dean's apartment and followed Danny Garrett inside, and the carnage that had ensued. Maybe she felt one more time that pride that had lit her up inside like a white-hot bulb when she reckoned how her actions that night showed once and for all how tough she was.

But maybe she was too far past all that to look back. When asked about it, Karen Gill, a Christian prison counselor with Family Life Training Center who had known Karla since 1983, offered a different hypothesis. Gill had witnessed Karla's transformation from drug-addled murderer to spirit-filled believer. She said news of Danny Garrett's death would likely sadden Karla for a different reason. "From what I know of Karla," Gill said, "what she would want from him is to find peace with God and peace with man through Jesus Christ. I know she will hope that he already achieved this before he passed away. That would be her main concern."

Two more women joined Karla and the others on death row in 1995. In April, Erica Yvonne Sheppard arrived. She had robbed and murdered a Houston woman who was carrying clothing from her car into an apartment. In June, Cathy Lynn Henderson came aboard. She had abducted and murdered a three-month-old boy she babysat.

And then a strange thing happened. It was in the midst of the whirlwind of stays and execution dates that Karla became a June bride. In 1995, she married Rev. Dana Brown, a prison chaplain with Mike Barber Ministries. She wasn't in attendance at the ceremony, of course—it was conducted with a proxy bride saying "I do" in her stead. In a separate ceremony, a fellow inmate walked Karla down the aisle while another read from the Bible. Karla was well aware of the optics of the whole thing. "It sounds silly," she said, "but it was beautiful."

Afterward Dana Brown visited the Gatesville prison in a vehicle decorated for a honeymoon. It was all pomp and circumstance though. Death-row prisoners are forbidden physical contact with visitors, so Karla and her husband never even kissed, never mind fully consummated their union. Dana Brown would be asked by Larry King why he would marry a woman he could not touch. "I was drawn to the spirit inside of her," he answered, "the spirit of Christ."

Ironically, marriage meant Dana Brown was likely limiting his physical access to his thirty-five-year-old bride, because ministers are permitted proximity to inmates that spouses and fiancées are not. Until now, they had possessed something resembling privacy, but their new status meant they faced scrutiny of every interaction. "We let everyone know upfront and immediately when we started writing letters to one another," Karla said. "Since we didn't let the physical relationship get in the way, we have a totally spiritual relationship that's so deep, a lot of people wouldn't understand."

Then in February of '97, Darlie Routier—who, despite her claims of innocence, was convicted of killing her five-year-old son—joined them. Now the women on Texas's death row numbered seven.

As 1997 drew to a close, the Supreme Court rejected Karla's final appeal, clearing the way for her execution. On December 18, thirteen and a half years after her original trial commenced, state district judge Debbie Mantooth Stricklin set a date of February 3, 1998, for her execution. Karla was now thirty-eight years old. She must have understood the import of this turn of events. Upon learning of the court's decision, she requested withdrawal from the prison's work program and separation from the other women on death row in order to read the Bible and spend more time in prayer. Her request was granted.

There remained, though, options. If Governor George W. Bush received a recommendation from the Board of Pardons and Paroles, he could commute the death sentence to life in prison. Otherwise, his only authority in a death penalty case was to grant a one-time, thirty-day reprieve.

In his three years in office, fifty-nine men had been executed in Texas. Not one had received this temporary reprieve.

Chapter 11

UNTIL SHE BE DEAD

Three weeks before her February 3 execution, Karla Faye Tucker told CNN's Larry King, "There is something inside of us, either bred in there or naturally, that we grow up wanting to protect women and children, and yet, there's the issue of, if women can do it just like men can do it, then they need to pay for it too, so I—it just..."

"You don't see it as a woman's issue?" King asked.

"I don't. I really don't."

Some agreed, and wanted to see it applied in Karla's case. Janice Sager, founder of Texans for Equal Justice, offered what might be interpreted as a condemnation of Karla, a subtle critique of the feminist movement, *and* a feminist statement—all in one fell swoop: "For years, women's groups have been screaming equal rights, so if you do the crime, you deserve equal punishment," Sager said. "She should be accountable. It doesn't matter if she is a woman. Her victims won't get a second chance."

Watt Espy, director of the Capital Punishment Research Project at the University of Alabama Law Center, saw a correlation between equal rights and capital punishment. "Women have been placed on pedestals, especially here in the South," he said. "I would suspect that as women become more liberated, we'll see more women receive the death penalty."

Historically in America, capital punishment most certainly has been a woman's issue. Going back to the colonial era, less than 3 percent of executions involved female offenders, the earliest being the hanging of Virginian Jane Champion in 1632 for killing a child she had conceived out of wedlock. (It's worth noting, too, the youngest person to be legally executed in America was twelve-year-old Hannah Ocuish, a Pequot girl in Connecticut who was charged with beating a six-year-old white girl to death in a quarrel over strawberries. On the day of her hanging in 1786, Rev. Henry Channing delivered a sermon warning the masses of the "natural consequences of too great parental indulgence" and exhorted Hannah to repentance: "You must consider that after death you must undergo another trial, infinitely more solemn and awful than what you have here passed through, before that God against whom you have offended; at whose bar the deceased child will appear as a swift witness against you—And you will be condemned and consigned to an everlasting punishment, unless you now obtain a pardon, by confessing and sincerely repenting of your sins, and applying to his sovereign grace, through the merits of his son, Jesus Christ, for mercy." The *Hartford Courant* reported that Hannah Ocuish "thanked the Sheriff for his kindness, and launched into the eternal world.") In the twentieth century, the percentage of female executions dropped to well below 1 percent. And in the twenty-five years of what was known as the current era of the death penalty—that is, when new statutes were established in 1973—only one (0.002 percent) of the 434 executions had been female. In 1998, the year Karla Faye Tucker was scheduled to die, statistics showed that women committed one in eight murders, but only one in seventy death-row inmates was female.

"When it comes to the death penalty, in both the sentencing and the actual carrying out of the execution, I think women have an advantage," said Victor Streib, a law professor who has spent most of his career studying women and capital punishment. "I think there is a sexism factor.... Women are unlikely to be arrested for murder, extremely unlikely to be sentenced to death, and almost never executed." He claimed that women are screened out of the judicial process at almost every turn; prosecutors are reluctant to charge women with capital crimes, and jurors more easily believe that women experience emotional duress or some other mitigating circumstance when committing a crime. Simply put, women don't just kill—not the way that men sometimes seem to. Streib later asserted that "if it was Karl Tucker instead of Karla Tucker, I don't think we'd be having this conversation. Nobody says it, because it's not politically correct, but there is a gender bias in the system—a double standard for women and men."

When it came to the very real possibility that Karla would be executed, many in fact saw her gender as a crucial aspect of her case. Houston defense attorney Brian Wice predicted that Texans "are going to be totally horrified and unnerved by a woman stretched out on that antiseptic table with a needle full of poison shoved in her arm."

Not a single Texan had ever witnessed such an event. The last woman executed in the state, Chipita Rodriguez, was hanged during the Civil War in 1863. This lonely fact remains one of the few known about Rodriguez. Where the truth ends and the legend begins is difficult to discern, and her story has taken on all the mythic qualities of folklore. We know Rodriguez moved with her father from Mexico to San Patricio, in the southern part of the state near the Gulf, where for many years after her father's death she operated a makeshift inn by furnishing travelers with food and a cot on the porch of her shack on the Nueces River.

We know, too, that in August of 1863, she gave lodging to a man named John Savage, a horse trader who sold mustangs and mules to the Confederate army in San Antonio. Legends vary, but around that time a small girl picking up firewood alongside the river, or maybe it was two Negro women, glimpsed a burlap bag floating in the river. Inside the bag was a male corpse: John Savage. He'd been murdered with, of all things, an ax (though not a pickax), presumably for $600 in gold. His head was split open. Authorities found blood on the porch of Chipita Rodriguez's inn.

The idea that Rodriguez could be responsible came into question, though, when the gold for which she'd allegedly done the killing was found. Some claim it was in the river, near where Savage's body floated. Others say it was secured in Savage's saddlebags.

In any case, Chipita Rodriguez, who was likely in her sixties at the time, and a man named Juan Silvera, who was rumored to be her illegitimate son, were indicted for John Savage's robbery and murder. Sheriff William Means made the arrest. Almost all court records were destroyed, but apparently the foreman of the grand jury was the same sheriff who arrested Rodriguez. What's more, Sheriff Means also appointed all the other men who served on the jury. They were a strange mixture of county employees and alleged felons who were awaiting their own trials. Rodriguez had little legal representation, and her only defense was her words, "No soy culpable." Due to her advanced age and the circumstantial evidence, the jury recommended mercy.

But the judge, Benjamin Neal, overrode the jury; he found Rodriguez guilty of first-degree murder. Judge Neal ordered thusly: "She will be taken to the place of execution and there between the hour of eleven o'clock and sunset of said day she will be executed according to the law by hanging by the neck until she be dead." Until that date Rodriguez was bound in leg irons and chained to a wall in the San Patricio courthouse, where local children brought her cookies and candy and corn shucks for rolling cigarettes. Her alleged accomplice, Juan Silvera, who was considered (in the parlance of the time) touched in the head, was found guilty of second-degree murder for disposing of John Savage's body and was sentenced to five years of hard labor.

Many claimed Rodriguez was protecting her illegitimate son. Others insisted she may have been involved in gathering information to influence the state in deciding which side to join in the Civil War.

Whatever their motives, on November 13, 1863, Chipita Rodriguez rode side saddle on a horse to the designated place of her execution, a mesquite tree. Or maybe she rode in a wagon that the hangman, John Gilpin, had borrowed from a townsperson, Betty McCumber, who had initially tried to run Gilpin off with a stick before relinquishing her wagon, probably with some prodding from the sheriff's deputies. Again, accounts differ. Some claimed they spied

Rodriguez sitting atop her newly carved cypress coffin, smoking a cigarette as the wagon carried her and her box toward the mesquite tree. And maybe it wasn't a mesquite tree, because some assert there were no mesquites in San Palacio in 1863. One woman, Geraldine McGlain of Corpus Christi, even claimed Rodriguez wore her great-grandmother's special dress for the occasion. "She didn't have a decent dress for her hanging, so my great-grandmother gave her her wedding dress." In any case, a whole gaggle of townspeople followed Rodriguez as she rode toward her eternal fate and were there to bear witness to the grim event. The noose was looped around her neck and Rodriguez spoke her last words—again claiming, "No soy culpable"—then the horse was led away from under her. Or, if you like, the oxen started up and pulled the wagon away, leaving Rodriguez dangling at the end of the rope. It was such a gruesome sight that a woman screamed and a boy ran home full speed and didn't stop till he was in his bed with a pillow over his head.

It was the hangman's job to cut her down, lay her out in the coffin, and put her to rest. None of the townspeople offered their assistance. The hangman, Gilpin, buried her beside the river in an unmarked grave that has never been found. (The story goes that lightning struck the tree and it was soon split for kindling.) At least one bystander claimed to hear a moan—a long, slow, bone-chilling moan—coming from her coffin as it was lowered into the earth.

Time has been sympathetic to Chipita Rodriguez. Over a century later, a couple of years after Karla Faye Tucker pickaxed two victims to death, state senator Carlos Truan of Corpus Christi appealed to the Texas legislature to absolve her of murder. Her trial had been unfair, he said. The sixty-ninth legislature passed the resolution, and on June 13, 1985, Governor Mark White signed the paperwork and made it all official.

But she nevertheless is said to haunt the San Patricio area. When a woman is scheduled to be executed anywhere in Texas, she lets loose a chilling moan and appears as a specter with a noose around her neck. She clutches the other end of the rope and roams the river bottoms, alone.

In 1949, when a Black woman, Emma Oliver, was condemned to die in the state for knifing a "well developed and well nourished colored man" to death in a dispute over three dollars, Chipita Rodriguez could be heard in the distance. But when Oliver's sentence was commuted, no one heard from ol' Chipita again until 1959, when another Black woman, Maggie Morgan, was sentenced to the electric chair. But her sentence, too, was commuted, and Chipita's ghost went silent once more. In 1978, Mary Lou Anderson went on trial for the murder of her father and stepmother, but her sentence was reduced when she testified against her accomplice. Then in 1979, Linda Burnett was sent to death row for the murder of a three-year-old boy, one of a family of five who were abducted, bound, shot, and buried in a pre-dug grave near Beaumont. But her conviction was overturned due to inadmissible evidence; she was retried, found guilty, and sentenced to life imprisonment. As all these condemned women came near to execution but never were actually put to death, the mythology around Chipita Rodriguez grew. The idea was that she would not abide the state-sanctioned death of another female. She became a personal guardian of each and every woman who had been sentenced to Texas's death row.

Since Linda Burnett's stay of execution in '79, Chipita Rodriguez had been silent and no one claimed to know her whereabouts. But now, with Karla's date drawing nigh, she was again starting to stir. The river bottoms were echoing with the eerie sound of her moans.

Karla would be the first female to be executed anywhere in the US since 1984, when fifty-two-year-old North Carolinian Velma Barfield was put to death for poisoning her fiancée, Stuart Taylor. Barfield had put ant and roach poison in his beer. Afterward, she accompanied him to an evangelical rally, where he became ill. "I didn't mean to kill him," she told law enforcement when she was arrested. "I only meant to make him sick." Though she also confessed to the fatal poisoning of her mother and two elderly people for whom she had been hired as a caregiver, she was not tried for those slayings. Stuart Taylor had been her only victim since the new death penalty statute was enacted.

Barfield's appearance seemed wholly incompatible with her actions, which is why she was nicknamed "Death Row Granny." Indeed, in the words of Mara Bovsun of the *New York Daily News*, Barfield "had a shy smile, rosy cheeks, and the gentle rounded figure that would seem at home spooning out comfort foods at church suppers. She was the kind of lady you'd expect to see bouncing her grandchildren on her knee at Easter, giving them gifts of hand-knit fluffy bunnies."

When Velma Barfield took the stand during her trial, though, the prosecutor, Joe Freeman Britt, a blustery and brazen DA who the *Guinness Book of World Records* had listed as the deadliest prosecutor in America, became aggressive and hostile with her, and she responded in kind. As Britt, standing six foot six and possessing a booming baritone voice, gave his final summation to the jury, Barfield took it upon herself to offer sarcastic silent applause. This gesture did not go over well with the jury, and after only an hour of deliberation, they sentenced her to death.

In addition to being the first woman to be executed in the US since 1962, Barfield also was the first to die by lethal injection. Like Tucker, she had become a Christian on death row. On the day of her execution, she told a family member that the death chamber was "my gateway to heaven." And like Tucker's case, Barfield's attracted widespread attention and many claims that she had been of great assistance to other inmates behind bars, particularly female prisoners, whom she counseled regularly. She often wrote letters on behalf of illiterate inmates. Once, a fifteen-year-old girl who had been convicted as an accessory to murder was put in the cell next to hers. Barfield reached her hand through the bars, clasped the girl's, and prayed aloud for her. It was this type of gesture that inspired even the likes of evangelist Billy Graham to regard her as a sister in Christ and express public solidarity with her.

Prison officials offered a specially prepared last meal, but Barfield declined. Instead, she chose a twelve-ounce Coca-Cola and Cheez Doodles.

Outside, just beyond the reach of the prison floodlights, three hundred opponents of capital punishment stood silent vigil as they waited for news of Velma Barfield's death. They gathered around a sign that spelled out HOPE in tiny lights.

Inside, where thirty-nine more prisoners were awaiting their own executions, inmates banged out a steady rhythm on the Plexiglas windows of their cells.

For her 2:00 a.m. execution, Barfield wore pink pajamas embroidered with flowers and blue house slippers. She accepted a sleep-inducing drug. As the drugs surged through her veins, she wet her lips and appeared to utter a prayer. Her color drained from pink to gray. Sixteen people watched her die, none of them family. One witness, Ramona Jones, a reporter with the *Raleigh Times*, said, "I didn't notice any type of suffering. She just seemed to relax."

When the moment of Barfield's execution passed and her *hope* was extinguished, those standing vigil outside the building blew out the candles.

Even as her date of execution drew nearer, Karla remained optimistic. In a televised interview with Larry King on CNN on January 14, 1998, about three weeks before she was set to die, she confessed to feeling "a little tired sometimes but not down." As her case drew more and more national attention, she felt like she was playing a small but vital role in an event so spiritually revolutionary that it could leave thousands of redeemed souls in its wake. "It gets a little more exciting every day," she said. "Just to see how God is unfolding everything. Every day something new comes up and it's exciting to be part of it because there's a lot going on, and it's going to affect a lot of people. And it's a blessing to be part of it, and it's exciting to know that God has a plan for this."

With such broad shifts taking place in the zeitgeist, Karla was hesitant to talk with King about the details of her crime, often offering only curt summaries ("Bad choices, drugs") or repeating King's words ("Bad boyfriend"). When he specifically asked her to recount what happened on "that terrible day," Karla initially avoided the conversation altogether. "The details of what happened that night," she said, "I don't share. I mean, that's the worst night of my life, and . . . with how I feel now, I don't relive that night."

But knowing his viewers' craving for gruesome specifics, King persisted. "For the facts, for the benefit of the audience . . . two people were murdered that night . . . by you and your boyfriend?"

Karla acknowledged she was "very excited about doing different crazy, violent things," but quickly she sidestepped King's queries and soon was talking about parole pals, those dolls she and her fellow female inmates on death row made for sale.

As the interview came to a close, King brought the conversation around to what folks could do to support Karla. "If people want to write you, they can write you, right?"

Karla said yes.

"Mountain View Unit, Texas Department of Criminal Justice, Gatesville, Texas. And can average citizens, ordinary citizens, write to the governor?"

Karla told him they could.

"I guess they can and to the parole board, right? Supporting you or not supporting you?"

"Yes," Karla said.

"It would be interesting to hear their opinion."

"Uh-huh."

So when my father asked me to write to Bush on his behalf, I did some homework: I read up on the murders and glimpsed TV footage of Karla. I got sufficiently disturbed by the heinous acts she and Danny Garrett committed in that Houston apartment and cringed at the details. My stomach soured at the mere contemplation of what Deborah Thornton must have heard as she cowered under the bed sheet. The thud of the hammer against Jerry Lynn Dean's head. The gurgling. The caving flesh and splitting bone when the pickax fell.

It seemed worse than any nightmare my subconscious could have conjured. And then there was the fear that must have shot through Deborah Thornton when the sheet came off her head and she bore witness to the visuals. And what about her two children, who were now grown adults—saddled with a lifetime of loss?

But there was no question I'd write this letter to Bush. I viewed it as a personal challenge—as though Dad were tacitly telling me, *Okay, you've been calling yourself a writer for years now, I've got an assignment for you. Let's see you write something that makes a difference.* "You put down the words," he told me, "and I'll sign my name."

At the time Dad made this request, he was seventy years old. He was on the verge of retiring from the post office after thirty-eight years of service. What none of us knew was that right now a cancer had developed in his prostate. If we had known, he could have been getting treatment to contain it. But we didn't know, so sometime soon, maybe in the next few months, the cancer spread, and by the time Dad learned he had it, it was already in his lymph nodes.

The letter would be easy to write. Though I had cast my first ever vote for Bush's father in 1988, over the last few years I had adopted a series of beliefs that caused Dad to characterize me as a liberal, which ranked even lower than *novelist* in his taxonomy. I had vague beliefs and untested ideals, which occasionally triggered enough personal outrage to spike my blood pressure before subsiding into general malaise and lingering cynicism. Among my present dubious notions was the conviction that capital punishment was wrong. I wasn't what anybody would call *political* about it—I didn't participate in marches or sit-ins or refuse to pay my taxes until the death penalty was overturned. I hadn't been mobilized, in any discernible way, to action.

If there was a single event that contributed more than anything else to my opposition to the death penalty, it was probably seeing the movie *Dead Man Walking* and reading Helen Prejean's book upon which it was based. Susan Sarandon's portrayal of Prejean so flummoxed me that I felt directly confronted by the sheer authenticity of the character's Christianity. I felt personally indicted by her brand of faith and how feeble and convenient mine felt by comparison. I suppose film critic Roger Ebert captures my response in his review: "It is so rare to find a movie character who truly does try to live according to the teachings of Jesus . . . that it's a little disorienting: [Sarandon's] character will behave according to what she thinks is right, not according to the needs of a plot, the requirements of a formula, or the pieties of those for whom religion, good grooming, polite manners and prosperity are all more or less the same thing."

But what my letter came down to, really, had little to do with politics or religious faith. Simply put, my letter would result from a desire ancient in its impulse: I wanted to make my old man proud. I wanted to show him that writing wasn't just a hobby or a pastime or diversion from the important matters at hand. My words could make a concrete, verifiable difference in the world.

During a visit to my parents' house, I sequestered myself in my old bedroom and composed the handwritten letter on a couple sheets of college-ruled notebook paper. For a feverish hour, I labored over two or three paragraphs. I told Bush I believed Karla was remorseful. Knowing that he, like my father, was an evangelical Christian, I reminded him of our moral obligation to forgive. I said I believed Karla when she claimed God had already forgiven her. By the time I finished the letter, I had convinced myself I'd made a pretty compelling argument, and felt invested in the outcome.

I carried it with pomp and circumstance into the den where Dad was watching TV. He turned down the volume and listened attentively as I read it aloud to him. As I reached the end, he fell quiet for a few moments. "That's a real nice job you did," he finally said. He nodded appreciatively. Then, "Add one more thing. Write 'P.S. Jesus loves Karla Faye Tucker.'" When I put this final addendum at the bottom of the page, I handed my letter over. Dad scrawled Governor Bush's address on an envelope and tucked the papers inside. He fastened a stamp. He said he would carry it with him to work at the post office tomorrow morning, and say a prayer over it when he dropped it in the bucket of outgoing mail.

Chapter 12

THE BALLAD OF KARLA FAYE TUCKER

It was in Europe, during the 1500s, a century before the first newspapers appeared, that broadsides became the means of disseminating news, entertaining the public, and frequently fusing the two in ways we're still trying to untangle. Print was revolutionizing Western culture, and broadsides—those large, one-sided sheets that could slide through the press in one pass—became its vehicle. A letter of indulgence printed by Gutenberg in 1454, before he printed his Bible, apparently serves as the earliest dated example. Stephen Daye's "The Oath of the Free-Man"—printed in Cambridge, Massachusetts, in 1639—is generally considered the first American broadside, though no known copy still exists.

In terms of content, broadsides were a hodgepodge of what scholars today call "ephemera": current events, government affairs, announcements of public meets and performances, promotions of political and social causes, advertisements of commercial products and services. Street hawkers and peddlers sold them for a nominal cost, a penny or a halfpenny, or sometimes even distributed them free of charge in the town squares, taverns, or churches, where they were posted for public viewing. Even by comparison with today's media, they were disposable and more akin to the tabloid press than reputable newspapers. As such, they were crudely produced and often appealed to the public's basest instincts. And relevant to what

I want to say about Karla Faye Tucker, they also featured speeches or songs that could be read or sung aloud.

According to music critic Peter Gammond, these broadside ballads often were "written by journalistic hacks of the day to cover such news as a robbery or a hanging, to moralize, or simply to offer entertainment.... The use of crude verse or doggerel was common, as this was thought to heighten the dramatic impact." Frequently they were illustrated with engravings, dramatizing the execution or the crime scene. Whenever there was a hanging, the hacks would appear on the scene, in advance, to make record of the goings-on and sell them as souvenirs of the event. It was in the 1730s that these broadsides gained immense popularity. A breakthrough in the genre was *The Last Speech and Dying Advice of Poor Julian* (1733). A Native American held as a servant (and likely a slave), poor Julian briefly escaped bondage before getting recaptured. He in turn killed the bounty hunter who had returned him to captivity.

Written in the voice of the condemned, confessions like Julian's followed a stock formula: the condemned acknowledged his crime ("I . . . confess especially my drunkenness and Sabbath-breaking," says poor Julian), expressed contrition ("I have abused God's Patience and Goodness to me"), accepted his punishment ("for my Sins I am now to die"), and sought redemption ("I am a dying Man, just going to leave this World, and the Thoughts of it terrify me, knowing how unfit I am to appear before my Judge"). Typically, he also implored others to avoid taking the same path to ruin ("I call to you now as one come from the Dead, to turn from your evil Ways while you have Time"). Was Julian's confession really "written with his own Hand," as it declared? Or was it composed entirely by one of the opportunistic scribblers on a deadline? Nobody can be certain. Probably, nobody cared.

The popularity of broadsides and broadside ballads led eventually to the sensationalized (and typically fictionalized) crime lit of the nineteenth century. Among the most well-known of these is *Life and Confession of Ann Walters, the Female Murderess!!* (1850). (I love the double exclamations!!) It begins in rather sensational manner:

It has probably never fallen to the lot of man to record a list of more cruel, heart-rending, atrocious, cold-blooded and horrible crimes and murders, than have been perpetrated by the subject of this narrative, and that too in the midst of a highly civilized and Christian community; and deeds, too, which for the depravity of every human feeling seems scarcely to have found a parallel in the annals of crime.

And it seems doubly shocking and atrocious, when we find them committed by one of the Female sex, which sex have always been esteemed as having a higher regard for virtue and a far greater aversion to acts of barbarity, even in the most abandoned of their sex, than is generally found in men of the same class, and we may truly say that we have never seen recorded a greater instance of moral depravity . . . as the one it becomes our painful lot to lay before our readers, in the account of ANN WALTERS, the subject of this thrilling and interesting narrative.

For my money, the implied relationship here between author and audience is worth the price of admission. "We" don't want to tell you this heinous story, and you don't want to read it. But members of a community have a mutual responsibility to one another, so all interested parties will inhale our breath and set aside our more virtuous selves so that we can survey this prurient material together. It is, after all, our civic duty.

The anonymous authors of *Life and Confession of Ann Walters* are confident that readers will appreciate the veracity of the narrative. "As regards the truth or authenticity of the facts contained in the foregoing pages," they write, "we presume it will not be doubted by any." Bad presumption, as it turns out. Or maybe it's just a request of readers to willingly suspend their disbelief as they would any piece of fiction. In any case, contemporary scholars regard *Ann Walters* as entirely contrived, or at best a greatest hits assortment of murders from the time. But the greater point is why the narrative exists in the first place: "It is hoped that in sending this narrative abroad, that it may be the instrument of some misguided youth from similar offences." Through this, again our civic duty, we're doing no less than conserving virtue and preserving civilization for posterity.

From the likes of Poor Julian and murderess Ann Walters, we in turn get murder ballads—the story of such confessions set to song. They came primarily from the British Isles to America via Anglo settlers in Appalachia and have become a lasting expression of American folklore. As the name implies, these songs focus exclusively on homicide. Typically, they relay the tale of a man killing somebody; often, their victim is a woman; frequently, she is of lower socioeconomic status than her killer, and pregnant, her unborn child an inconvenience that must be disposed of in timely fashion. As such, murder ballads typically are both violent and misogynistic—yet the listener is encouraged to sympathize with the killer, not the victim. With lyrics resonant of Deborah Thornton's fate, "Pretty Polly" is just one example: "He opened up her bosom / As white as any snow / He stabbed her through the heart / And the blood did overflow." Another is "Tom Dooley," a North Carolina folk song about the 1866 murder of a woman named Laura Foster. The Kingston Trio's 1958 version popularized murder ballads for a modern and mass audience. "I met her on the mountain," the singers harmonize, "There I took her life / Met her on the mountain / Stabbed her with my knife." Still another is "Pearl Bryan," about a pregnant Kentucky woman who was decapitated in 1896, which directly addresses "young girls, if you'll listen," and serves as a cautionary tale for those who should reform their wayward behavior while there's still time.

A scant few murder ballads are from the perspective of a woman who was killed. Even so, their male murderer is usually portrayed with a bizarre sort of sympathy, as though he too is at the mercy of fate and shares victimhood with the woman. Scholars contend that this sympathy is a response to growing fears of how the sexual freedom of Appalachian women was viewed as a symptom of the sweeping industrial change that threatened the cultural traditions of the past. As such, as Christina Ruth Hastie asserts, the murders of females in these songs "speak to a cultural idiom interested in limiting women's freedoms." In Doc Watson's version of "Omie Wise," about the 1808 murder of Naomi Wise, the victim pleads, "Have mercy on my baby and spare me my life / I'll go home as a beggar and never be your wife." Likewise, in "Pearl Bryan," before she loses her head, literally, the female victim asks her lover, "What have I done, Scott Jackson, that you should take my life? / I've always loved you dearly. I would have been your wife."

But almost none of the traditional murder ballads come from the point of view of a woman who did the killing. One notable exception was Patsy Montana, who in 1949 gave us "I Didn't Know the Gun Was Loaded." The lyrics tell the story of a woman who apparently fends off an attempted date rapist by shooting him in the knee. "I didn't know the gun was loaded," she sings. "And I'm so sorry, my friend / I didn't know the gun was loaded / And I'll never, never do it again." And in 1966, Wanda Jackson gave us "The Box It Came In," in which the narrator laments the fact her husband has run off with another woman and taken "everything with him that wasn't nailed down," including the box containing her wedding dress. In response, she makes a chilling vow: "He's got a new sweetheart to fill my wedding gown / But somewhere I'll find him / Then I'll have peace of mind / And the box he comes home in / Will be all satin lined."

But seemingly nowhere in the murder-ballad tradition do we get a tale that attempts to elicit sympathy for a woman who commits a completely unjustified and indefensible crime—a murder akin to the ones committed by the men in so many murder ballads.

That's what makes Karla Faye Tucker's letter to George W. Bush so remarkable. Composed two weeks before her scheduled execution and dated January 18, 1998, Karla's epistle to the governor stands as her confession, her plea for mercy, and—in a tradition dating back to Poor Julian and running through the murder ballads of Appalachia—a willingness to accept the fate her actions have wrought. It runs for eleven pages. Excerpts were made public, and all the ingredients of the broadside confession are there.

The crime: "I am in no way attempting to minimize the brutality of my crime. It obviously was very, very horrible and I do take full responsibility for what happened. I also know that justice and law demand my life for the two innocent lives I brutally murdered that night."

The acceptance of punishment: "If my execution is the only thing, the final act that can fulfill the demand for restitution and justice, then I accept that. I will pay the price for what I did in any way our law demands it."

The contrition: "It was in October, three months after I had been locked up, when a ministry came to the jail and I went to the services, that night accepting Jesus into my heart. When I did this, the full and overwhelming weight and reality of what I had done hit me. I began crying that night for the first time in many years, and to this day, tears are a part of my life."

The desire for redemption: "I am seeking you to commute my sentence and allow me to pay society back by helping others. I can't bring back the lives I took. But I can, if I am allowed, help save lives. That is the only real restitution I can give."

And if you were to set her letter to verse, you'd have the broadside ballad that led eventually to the murder ballads of Appalachia. This time, though, you'd also have something new and quite radical: a song of confession that puts a woman in a role previously occupied only by men. Karla has no defense. The best she can hope for is mercy on a woman.

Chapter 13

THE REAL DEBBIE THORNTON

As Karla's case attracted national attention, she gained public support from unlikely sources, including, of all people, Deborah Thornton's brother. Ronald Carlson described the evolution of his views this way: "When I found out who killed my sister I wanted to kill her. I wanted blood-lust and vengeance. I wanted to take that pick ax and ax her to death and leave it in her heart like she left it in my sister's heart." But Ronald Carlson claimed Jesus had taken it upon himself to touch him in the very same way he had touched Karla. "And what I see in Ms. Tucker today is Jesus. . . . I want Karla Tucker to have a chance to continue to serve the Lord as she is doing."

Likewise, even one of Governor Bush's twin daughters pleaded with him to spare Karla's life. In his 1999 autobiography *A Charge to Keep*, Bush tells the story of how, two days before the scheduled execution, Jenna "looked up at the dinner table and told me she had decided she opposes capital punishment." He describes how he gave ear to her grievances, told her how much he respected her opinions, and, in his words, "welcomed the moment."

But as sympathy for Karla began to gain traction through these unlikely sources, Deborah Thornton's husband Richard Thornton dug in his heels. "February 3 will be a date that will be the beginning of the rest of my life," Richard Thornton said. He found it offensive that people were portraying Karla as "Rebecca of Sunnybrook Farm. She is and always will be the antithesis of that description." He said the "only reason this is even an issue is that Texas is known for protecting mom and apple pie, and here comes Karla Faye Tucker, who's pleasant to look at, who can fit the mold of the pure Texas gal. Well, let's not forget that this same Miss Prim and Proper was swinging a pick ax 14 years ago."

The last time he saw his wife of two and a half years alive, Richard Thornton had engaged in an apparently serious verbal altercation with her. He'll of course never know precisely what happened after he saw her last, but it's reasonable to assume his wife had too much to drink at an apartment pool party and went home with a stranger to have sex. Thornton was unconvinced of this assumption, at least publicly. "If that happened, then that happened," he said. "I don't think it happened, but I'm enough of an adult to understand that things like that happen." His summation of the event? "Debbie was in the wrong place at the wrong time."

Whatever her reasons for going to Jerry Lynn Dean's apartment, Richard Thornton saw his wife as an innocent. "She did nothing," he said. "These people had no reason to harm her. She could have been told to get out. They chose to kill her and they took away a mother, a wife, a lover, a friend—somebody I didn't want to be without. I want them to know that she begged to die. She pleaded for the mercy of death. And these monsters kept on hitting her with a pick ax."

By the time Karla's execution approached, Richard Thornton had remarried, but he nevertheless chose not to break ties to that time in his life. He kept souvenirs, including newspaper clippings of her death and a matchbook cover from a swanky restaurant where they had dined together. But the most gut-wrenching memento was a letter dated June 11, 1983—a couple of days before she died. It's in Deborah's handwriting. She promises to love him forever. His daughter tried to give it to him the night before his wife was killed. "I guess she gave it to my daughter that night to give me," he said. "I guess next time I see her I'll ask her."

But that night, when his daughter had tried to give him the letter, a peace offering to end the spat with his wife, he had responded, simply, "No."

"It was the stupidest [word] I ever said in my life," he told Kathy Walt of the *Houston Chronicle* in an interview. "It has taken me 14 years to be able to tell myself I might not be responsible."

It would seem easy to perform some amateur psychology here. We could theorize that one of the reasons Richard Thornton could find no forgiveness in his heart for Karla Faye Tucker was that he could find none for himself. In any case, he was clearly a man haunted by the sequence of events that led to her death. And now, with Karla's execution pending, he felt like the very people with whom he should share solidarity had abandoned him. Jerry Lynn Dean's sister, Peggy Kurtz, joined Ronald Carlson, Deborah Thornton's brother, among the ranks of those claiming they had forgiven Karla. Which allowed Richard Thornton to do some easy math. "I am the only voice that Deborah Ruth Davis Thornton has left," he said. So while people rallied behind Karla's efforts to convince the Texas Board of Pardons and Paroles and Bush to reduce her sentence to life imprisonment, he took to the media to speak out against it. He felt some people were overlooking some very salient facts.

"People need to understand that Karla Faye Tucker murdered two people in cold blood," he said. "She is and was a horrible person. If she has found religion, then God bless her, because maybe the Lord will be more lenient with her than he would have otherwise. Maybe the last 14 years that she has been given to bring her affairs in order, to make the peace with the Lord—maybe they were necessary for someone who is that cold to find whatever peace she can. And I hope she has, I hope she's found peace." He left no doubt, though, about what he wished to see happen. "She was found guilty, she was sentenced to death, she needs to die."

Thornton was particularly passionate about protecting his daughter and stepson from the controversy in the lead-up to Karla's scheduled execution. They were fourteen and twelve when the murders took place. "Their suffering is the greatest suffering in this whole affair," he said. Neither child finished high school. And even now when they'd gotten older, they had become very guarded when

Karla's case was making the news. "Every single time something comes up, [they] relive it all over again," he said. "It's as if each time we hear her name, someone is killing my wife all over again."

The last time Karla had been up for execution, Richard Thornton asked his children to write letters to the Pardons and Parole Board. He wanted them to tell the board about the impact of their mother's death on their lives. His stepson, however, could not summon the strength to write the letter. "My son . . . lost his mother in a way no child should ever have to comprehend," Thornton said. "It was the most horrific thing imaginable. . . . I cannot imagine being 12 years old and hearing on the television that my mother was hacked to death with a pick ax and the pick ax was still embedded in her chest when they found her. Now, that 12 year old boy heard that, and as I tell it to you and you hear about it, we're adults. It is a heinous crime. It is terrible. But I'm not 12 years old, and it's not my mother."

His daughter did in fact write a letter. But when the courts postponed Karla's execution, it was never sent. During the run-up to Karla's new execution date, he still had his daughter's letter.

To Richard Thornton, of all the injustices associated with his wife's death, one that ranks near the top is the fact that, while Karla and Danny Garrett were convicted of murdering Dean, neither was ever officially convicted for the slaying of his wife. He feared that this injustice would trigger another: he wouldn't be able to witness Karla's execution. He wanted to be there. "I can't say I hate Karla Faye Tucker," he said. "What she did was the wrongest thing that can be done. [But] when she leaves this Earth, I hope the next person she sees is my wife." Which seems like a curious thing to say. Did he presume that Karla and Deborah Thornton would come face-to-face in heaven? That is, was Richard Thornton saying that he believed the woman who killed his wife would spend eternity in Beulah Land? "If the Lord as I know him is there, yes. I would hope that he would forgive everyone all of their sins. I don't know that . . . I would like to think God is merciful enough in his own right to do something for her.

"But my beliefs have always told me she would go to hell."

On January 5, 1998, Richard Thornton set up a website in remembrance of his wife. It was at once a tribute to Deborah Thornton and a determined attempt to suppress the rising tide of public support for Karla. It featured a picture of Deborah: a candid shot, unrehearsed, as though she's paused for a brief moment to stare at the photographer (presumably Richard?) and consent to a snapshot. She's wearing a white shirt and what appears to be bib overalls. Not the kind you wear when you're slopping pigs or shucking corn. The New West kind, the *Urban Cowboy* kind, with fresh blue denim and a tapered cut. She has dirty blond hair, parted in the middle, a style straight out of *Charlie's Angels*. Sunglasses, brown lenses, propped on top of her head. A broad smile lights up her face. She looks irrepressibly happy. Behind her, there's what appears to be a line of telephone wires strung like guitar strings across the horizon.

Under the photograph is a caption: "This is the real Debbie Thornton. This is the woman who was my wife. This picture virtually captures her in all that she was and is to me."

Then a reminder that what you're glimpsing is a confidential memento that belongs exclusively to Richard Thornton, something he's sharing with you only with the clear understanding that you're being invited to witness a private grief that you can only imagine because this kind of horror has not come your way: "Photograph is not to be copied, published or saved without the express written permission of Richard Thornton."

Then the page contains a summary of how he learned the news of his wife's death. In relaying the narrative, he makes the curious choice to render the telling in second person, as though he wants you to inhabit his mindset as he learns the devastating news. "It is a sound that you will always remember," he begins. "You may not remember exactly what the words were, but you will always remember where you were when the policeman told you that your wife was dead." He goes on to describe his initial denial, his inability to process the information, his refusal to believe what he was hearing. Then he brings his daughter into the story. She is "quietly crying in the other room," he writes. "She knows." Knows . . . how? Because she overheard the policeman's explanation? Because she has the intuitive knowledge that only a child can possess when she feels her mother leave her mortal body?

"Then you hear it for the first time," Richard Thornton continues. "It is on the evening news." He describes the visuals—the bodies covered with sheets as they're carried from the apartment and the mention of the murder weapon, a pickax. Still, there's denial—"This must be some kind of science fiction show, it isn't really the news"—until out of the corner of his eye he glimpses something blue. An old pickup truck. Nothing out of the ordinary until he sees the license plates: "Oh my god, those are her plates, that is her truck, oh no, oh my God no. It is here that you think your life has ended. It is now that you know what a broken heart is." The question then becomes who did this, and why? He describes a phantasmagoric dreamscape in which people rush toward him, some in a posture of consolation with open arms and others with guns drawn as though vowing revenge.

It's here that his story takes on a decidedly polemical tone, as he laments the government's unwillingness to protect the innocent. Listen to him:

> The dreams I had as a youth of the government wrapping me in a warm blanket of help when a disaster such as this came along were just that; dreams. I was unable to find out anything. I was not made to feel like I was part of anything that was going on. When Karla Faye Tucker and Daniel Garrett were finally arrested and charged with the murder of Jerry L. Dean and my wife, Deborah Ruth Davis Thornton, I was made to feel like an outsider, someone who had absolutely no bearing on the incident. I could not believe it. I could not get anyone to even tell me when the trial was. Everything that I learned about the case I learned through the media. There was no one who was advising me as to what was going on, or what would happen next. I felt like I was farther down on the list than the criminals themselves.

In closing, he makes an appeal for the rights of victims' families, celebrates the support of a group called JFA, Justice for All, and signs off as Richard Thornton, husband to Deborah Davis Thornton, murdered by Karla Faye Tucker on June 13, 1983. Below his valediction is an airbrushed photo of a young woman in a dancer's pose, with a poem titled "Dancing in the Moon Light." There's a link to a guest book. A small collection of people signed it, most of them apparently strangers to Richard, all of them telling him what a moving memorial he'd assembled for his wife on this webpage. People offer their blessings and wish Richard peace and happiness. They assure him they'll be praying for him. One, signed "A Caring Canadian," takes the Indigo Girls to task for writing a song called "Faye Tucker" that, in the writer's opinion, makes a hero of a murderer: "I am appalled at the amount of coverage in the media and on the internet devoted to Faye Tucker and the scarcity of attention devoted to your wife." Another must have initially come as a shock to Richard: it's signed *Deborah Thornton*. "Entered my name in google search," it says, "and read your story. I was saddened to read of the loss of your loved one in such cruel and shocking way my thoughts go with you."

In 2006, the guest book abruptly stopped accepting visitors. There was a final note from a woman called Betty, wishing him well, that God will be with him and his family, then this from Richard himself: "Due to spammers who have viciously overloaded this guestbook with their self-serving JUNK, this guestbook has been closed."

In 2020, the website was taken down altogether.

In mid-January, two weeks before Karla's execution, a group of Houston ministers and other death penalty opponents held a press conference to plead for Karla's life. David Atwood, the panel's moderator and member of the Texas Coalition to Abolish the Death Penalty, said the world was watching. "The international attention is growing significantly," Atwood said. "I seriously think George W. Bush should think about this if he has aspirations of becoming president."

While Karla's lawyers continued petitioning the court system, George Bush gave no sign that he would treat her case any differently than the others that had ended in execution. "I feel my job is to uphold the laws of the state of Texas," Bush said. "We should treat this case like any other case: Was the law broken? And was this person afforded all the resources of the courts of law?" In particular, he seemed to be serving notice that Karla's gender would not play a factor in his decision-making. "Gender does not matter to me," he said. "What matters to me is life in general. The business of the death penalty is emotional for a lot of people, and I can understand why people are all very emotional about this, particularly given the amount of publicity in this case. But my job in the state of Texas is to administer the law fairly and justly, and this case, in my judgment, should be treated as any other case." Indeed, Bush was doing everything possible to project objectivity and to remind everyone of his limited jurisdiction, to distance himself from the legal and moral responsibilities of Karla's case. He was persistent in reminding his constituency that Texas statutes restricted his authority to granting one thirty-day reprieve, unless the Board of Pardons and Paroles recommended broader clemency.

But the fact of the matter was that Bush possessed great power here. Almost all board members were appointed by none other than Bush himself, and the full board never met as a group to consider death sentences. It was suggested that a few spoke to one another on the phone, occasionally, but no one knows for sure if clemency appeals were even read by all members. Bush had full authority to intervene and suggest a course of action before the board made its recommendation. But as February 3 drew closer, Bush was making no such effort to influence their decision.

Two blocks away from the governor's mansion, on the steps of the Capitol, over two hundred people gathered to rally support for Karla's cause. Among those in attendance was Gloria Steele, whose son, Michael Moore, was on death row. She and her husband had mixed emotions about their participation. "As a woman I'm for her," Steele said, "as a Christian I'm for her, as an abolitionist I'm for her.

But why so much for her, but not my Christian son that's down the road? He's not going to get this kind of support.... There's a lot of men on death row just as Christian as her, but they're not going to get this kind of support."

Chapter 14

SOUTHERN GOTHIC

On New Year's Day 1998, the state of California banned smoking in all bars and restaurants. Three days later, El Nino triggered a massive winter storm that swept through New England and Canada, downing power lines, destroying forests, plunging people into darkness for sometimes weeks, and killing countless livestock animals and thirty-five people. On January 14, researchers in Dallas presented findings about an enzyme that could slow aging and cell death and potentially prolong life. On January 17, Paula Jones, a former Arkansas state employee, sued President Bill Clinton for sexual harassment, precipitating impeachment proceedings in the House of Representatives. On January 25, the Denver Broncos became the first AFC team in fourteen years to win the Super Bowl, beating the Green Bay Packers 31–24.

And on January 26, a week before Karla's scheduled execution, President Clinton addressed the American people in a nationally televised address. "I did not have sexual relations with that woman," he told viewers. That woman was of course Monica Lewinsky, and the Lewinsky scandal took over the national conversation and nudged Karla's appeals to the back burner. The next day, the 27th, Hillary Clinton appeared on the *Today Show* and told interviewer Matt Lauer that her husband was a victim of a "vast right-wing conspiracy." Pat Robertson, for his part, accused Clinton of turning the Oval Office into a "playpen for the sexual freedom of the poster child of the 1960s." Then, in a sudden fit of alliteration, Robertson called Clinton a "debauched, debased, and defamed" leader of the nation. Jerry Falwell would be more succinct in his critique of the president: "There's no question that Bill Clinton has lowered the moral bar for political officeholders in America."

Clinton of course was an Arkansan, so we southerners paid special notice to his unfolding drama. But down here, another story arrested our attention and distracted us from both Clinton and Karla. On January 29, Eric Robert Rudolph set off a bomb disguised as a flower pot in the yard of a Birmingham abortion clinic, spraying nails as shrapnel and instantly killing Robert Sanderson, a security guard, and severely injuring a nurse, Emily Lyons. Nobody yet knew that this was Rudolph's third bombing since the one that began his reign of terror at the '96 Olympics in Atlanta, when he had planted an explosive inside a backpack in Centennial Olympic Park and proceeded to call 911, inform them of the bomb, and warn that it would detonate in thirty minutes. The next day, as the games continued, news organizations started receiving anonymous letters crediting the bombing to an extremist religious group called Army of God.

A southerner, an Army vet, and a professed Christian, Rudolph later would declare that the purpose of the Olympic games attack was "to confound, anger and embarrass the Washington government in the eyes of the world for its abominable sanctioning of abortion on demand. The plan was to force the cancellation of the games, or at least create a state of insecurity to empty the streets around the venues and thereby eat into the vast amounts of money invested." While law enforcement bumbled through their attempts to identify a suspect in the wake of two deaths and 111 injuries—they initially targeted Richard Jewell, a security guard—Rudolph became emboldened. In January of '97, he struck a second time, planting an explosive at a suburban Atlanta abortion clinic that injured four people. Then in February, he set off a bomb that injured five at a lesbian nightclub in Atlanta.

About a week before Karla Faye Tucker was scheduled to be executed, a bystander saw a truck with North Carolina plates departing the scene, and scribbled down the tag number. Apparently unaware that he'd been identified, Rudolph rented a video called *Kull the*

Conqueror and ate at a Burger King near his home in Murphy, North Carolina. But by the time FBI showed up at his trailer, they found only the door swinging open and the lights on. That Rudolph boy was gone.

He fled to the Nantahala wilderness of the state, where the thicket grows so dense that the forest even at midday exists in perpetual shade. He knew intimately the labyrinthine maze of caves and abandoned mines, and spent the next five winters living on the lam and eluding law enforcement, likely via the aid of his Appalachian brethren. The FBI set up its headquarters in the local armory and helicopters patrolled the sky. They brought out bloodhounds and motion sensors. They put him on the Most Wanted List and a million-dollar reward on his head, leading a posse of bounty hunters to show up looking to cash in. Maybe it was a forest-for-the-trees kind of incompetence on the part of the FBI—but then again, with a military background and survivalist expertise, maybe Eric Rudolph was just really good at hide-and-go-seek. Reports of Rudolph sightings became the stuff of an expanding Bigfoot-like legend. He briefly surfaced at a health food store in Andrews, where he stole seventy-five pounds of food and a pickup truck and left behind $500 for the trouble he'd caused. The truck was later found abandoned near a trailhead with a note requesting return to its rightful owner. Occasionally a cabin owner would report a break-in, claiming socks, underwear, or toiletries had been stolen, but no property was ever destroyed. Hiding out amongst the laurel and rhododendron, Rudolph otherwise subsisted on acorns, stolen vegetables, wild turkey, venison, salamanders that he'd swallow whole, and the occasional can of tuna left behind by a sympathizer. Meanwhile, something called the internet became a breeding ground for chatter praising Rudolph as a hero and calling for similar acts of violence inspired by his.

The nurse at the Birmingham clinic, Emily Lyons—she was blinded in her left eye; her right eye was so damaged that she lost sight for five weeks; her hair was burned to a crisp; a hole the size of a fist split her abdomen, necessitating the removal of ten inches of intestines; her hand was mangled and her leg shattered; so much of her flesh was burned that skin grafts covered much of her lower body. Even today, her body contains so much shrapnel that a magnet will stick to her skin. In the aftermath of the bombing, Lyons received hundreds of letters, the vast majority of them offering kindness but a few condemning her. One, in particular, told her that if she didn't repent for her participation in abortions and change her ways, she'd burn in a "lake of fire," which is a predicament far more dire than losing an eye.

By 2000, the manhunt for Rudolph would be scaled back considerably, and by 2002 only a dozen agents were still active on the case. Many figured Rudolph had died out there somewhere in that rugged terrain. But on May 31, 2003, a rookie cop in Murphy was doing routine patrol at 4:00 a.m. when he spotted a man in a camouflage jacket and new sneakers dumpster diving behind a Save-a-Lot store. The officer, Jeffrey Postell, initially thought the suspect was carrying out a burglary. The man tried to flee, taking off running and hiding behind a stack of milk crates, but soon enough he complied and gave himself up. Deputy Sean Mathews assisted Postell with the arrest. "I thought he had an uncanny resemblance to Eric Robert Rudolph," Mathews said. "I just had a hunch when I seen his eyes." He was thirty or forty pounds lighter than when he disappeared into the woods five years ago, but his fingernails were clean, his hair cropped short and his mustache trimmed. He hardly looked like the wild Bigfoot-type creature many expected to see.

A statement from US Attorney General John Ashcroft was quickly forthcoming. "American law enforcement's unyielding efforts to capture Eric Robert Rudolph have been rewarded," he announced. "Working with law enforcement nationwide, the FBI always gets their man."

In addition to the Birmingham bombing, Rudolph eventually pled guilty to the Centennial Olympic Park bombing, as well as the blasts at the abortion clinic in the Atlanta suburbs and the lesbian bar in the city. He expressed no remorse; he was proud to characterize his actions as a just response against the legalization and practice of baby killing.

Perhaps the most bizarre moment in the whole story came when Eric Rudolph's brother took to protest in the most personal of ways. To protest what exactly? Something so undefinable and ineffable that to express it, no picket sign or mere letter to Congress would do. All I can say, really, is this: if you're ever fuzzy on the definition of Southern Gothic, fix on Daniel Rudolph. While his brother was out there somewhere in those woods, Daniel decided the right and proper thing to do was to go into his garage. There, alone, replete in a white shirt and tie—good God, he was wearing a *tie*—he rigged up a camcorder on a tripod. Made certain he had just the right angle. Then he started videoing himself. "This is for the FBI and the media," he said, and then, turning toward a radial-arm saw—what you might call a circular saw—he proceeded to do what you feared all this was leading up to, the very thing he couldn't possibly go through with: he lopped off his entire left hand. And then he did the only thing remaining to do after you've amputated yourself. He applied a tourniquet, then drove himself to the emergency room.

Somebody from the hospital came back to the garage to fetch Daniel's hand. They reattached it surgically. It's unclear whether Daniel wanted its return. How did he respond when they showed up with his hand?

The FBI apparently didn't get what he was saying about his bloodline. "Daniel Rudolph's decision to maim himself is regrettable and unexpected," they said in a formal response. They didn't get the irony of how severing a limb from his body could express his inseverable familial bonds. All that red on the video said plenty about a bloodline that ran deeper than their understanding.

I'm thinking again of Julius Mount Bleyer and his obsession with finding what he believed would be the most humane way of putting someone to death. "A man may lose a finger or a hand," Bleyer wrote, "by the action of a rapidly revolving circular saw, *and feel no pain at the instant.*"

While Eric Rudolph awaited trial, Emily Lyons was dividing her life into two parts, BB and AB—"Before the bomb and after the bomb," she called it. "If he's executed, I'd love to be in the front row." But a plea bargain guaranteed Rudolph would spend the rest of his life behind bars, exempt from the death penalty. He identified the location of 250 pounds of dynamite he'd stockpiled in the forest and saved his life with the revelation.

Though Rudolph agreed to a plea bargain, he did not do so willingly, and he still maintained his commitment to what he believed was a righteous cause. "The fact that I have entered into an agreement with the government," he stated, "is purely a tactical choice on my part and in no way legitimates the moral authority of the government to judge this matter or impute my guilt." He persisted in his claim that the bombs were a just response to abortion and gay sex. Regarding the latter, he possessed, well, different views on the subject than Tammy Bakker had; he made this assertion:

> Homosexuality is an aberrant sexual behavior, and as such I have complete sympathy and understanding for those who are suffering from this condition. Practiced by consenting adults within the confines of their own private lives, homosexuality is not a threat to society. Those consenting adults practicing this behavior in privacy should not be hassled by a society which respects the sanctity of private sexual life. But when the attempt is made to drag this practice out of the closet and into the public square in an "in your face" attempt to force society to accept and recognize this behavior as being just as legitimate and normal as the natural man/woman relationship, every effort should be made, including force if necessary, to halt this effort.

Whatever its consequences, in the end Rudolph's plea bargain allowed him to claim for himself a kind of immortality. "I have deprived the government of its goal of sentencing me to death," he said.

On February 2, four days after Rudolph bombed the Birmingham clinic, the Texas Board of Pardons and Paroles rejected Karla's appeal. Sixteen of the eighteen board members voted to deny clemency. Two abstained. Bush acknowledged his power to intervene. "I guess I could have tried to tell the board how to vote," he admitted. "The members were, after all, mostly my appointees. But that isn't how I operate. . . . I select people who are qualified, who share my conservative philosophy and approach to government, and then I expect them to make the calls as they see them."

That afternoon, the Supreme Court reinforced the board's decision by declining to act as well.

If it was true the last woman executed by the state of Texas, Chipita Rodriguez, readied for a haunt whenever a woman was scheduled to die, then somewhere in the bottomlands she was set to roam. Her noose circling her neck, her hand squeezing the other end of the rope, she was about to loose her chilling moan. Maybe she'd be able to stop it again.

Otherwise, with Karla's death scheduled in a mere twenty-four hours, only one hope remained.

Though Bush had never commuted any death-row inmate's sentence, Karla believed larger forces were at work here. When Larry King had asked why she remained optimistic about her fate, she answered, "Because my hope is in the Lord. He can change hearts. If he could change my heart and how I was fourteen and a half years ago, he can change anybody's heart . . . and what I firmly believe is, if God is going to allow this to happen, he has a purpose for it. If he has a purpose for my life to continue on, he'll change the hearts of the governor and the parole board. He will help them to see what can be done through a commutation."

Chapter 15

THIS MESS THAT SOME PEOPLE CALL LIFE

In 1968, a man named Arthur Blessitt opened what he called a "Jesus coffee shop" next door to a topless go-go bar on Sunset Boulevard in Los Angeles. His Place, as Blessitt called it, was "halfway between a church and a nightclub." He had come to Hollywood from Greenville, Mississippi, wearing a flattop haircut and nursing a burning desire to proselytize. Soon enough he took on the standard accoutrements of California counterculture, growing sideburns and moppy hair, but his mission to spread the gospel remained the same. He orchestrated a ritual he called "toilet baptism" in which hippies flushed their pot and LSD down the john and announced they were "high on the Lord."

Blessitt says he felt like the Lord wanted him to put a cross on the wall of his business—he needed one big and strong enough to hold a man like Jesus, so he settled on four-by-four California redwood, twelve feet tall with a crossbeam six feet wide. In keeping with his growing reputation as the "minister of Sunset Strip," Blessitt occasionally took his cross off the wall and began carrying it down the boulevard, sharing his message among Hells Angels and Black Panthers, flower children and protestors, and giving out food and the plan for salvation to anybody who didn't run from the weird guy dragging his cross. He soon realized the wood at the end of the cross would wear away at a rate of an inch a day, so he attached a tricycle wheel to the base.

Again called by God, he set out on Christmas Day in 1969 on a journey by foot, aiming to shoulder his cross from one side of America to the other, from LA to DC—and throughout the world. Over the next fifty years, Arthur Blessitt would make it to 315 nations, over all kinds of terrain, in all types of weather, with his cross in tow. He tightroped felled trees over deep ravines, and navigated dense jungles, blistering deserts, insurmountable mountains, and snow-laden tundra. Eventually Guinness would officially credit Blessitt with the longest walk in human history. His cross was a conversation starter in every country from Abkhazia to Zimbabwe, with stops in Eritrea, Kiribati, Svalbard, Tajikistan, Vanuatu, and Zanzibar along the way. He let Indian beggars take turns shouldering his cross. He perched small Somalian children in the intersection of the boards and pulled them through the village. He led pep rally-style chants of "J-E-S-U-S" in the remotest of locations. In Antarctica he told penguins that Jesus loved them. He taught Honduran children to sing "Jesus Loves Me." He led elderly Cubans through the Sinner's Prayer in Spanish. He crossed the Iron Curtain. He's got video footage from CNN of Yasser Arafat kissing him on each cheek in welcome to west Beirut and praying for peace in his land and a picture of the two of them sitting side-by-side at a table—Arafat is holding up a cross pendant with a broad smile. In foreign lands, Blessitt would meet utter strangers who were from *other* countries and tell them he had visited their homeland because he had visited *every nation in the world*. Along the way, he traversed fifty-two war zones, was heckled mercilessly, arrested twenty-four times, even taken before a firing squad to be shot. It's estimated that he circled the equivalent of one and a half times around the earth at the equator, covering over thirty-eight thousand miles, taking seventy-six million steps, and toting sixteen billion pounds of cross. "And Jesus was with me every step," he claimed.

He fed food to people unable to raise their heads, clipped their fingernails, trimmed their beards. And when they were able to listen, he told them what he had carried his cross all this distance to say.

Blessitt sums up his message this way:

So many people feel like the cross is against them. They look at the cross and they think, "Oh, the cross is against my sexual orientation. Or I've had an abortion. Or I drank beer. Or I smoked cigarettes. And so, God hates me." The cross is the sign, absolutely, clearly, indelibly imprinted, that "I love you." That's what the cross says. "I care. I came down and I got involved in this mess that some people call life and became flesh." [Jesus] sacrificed himself with his hands nailed to that cross, with his feet nailed, with his side pierced, saying "I'm with you, I love you, I care." I learned many, many years ago that the way to change the world is letting Jesus come and change us from the inside out. We don't need a hand slap, we don't need a pointed finger of condemnation. People know they got problems, they know they're not perfect. But they're looking for a way out. That is what real conversion is all about. If any person be in Christ, they are a new creation, a new existence. Christ, who died and rose again, now lives in them and they're changed.

It's a message tailor-made for a woman on death row. A woman who's come into an apartment in the middle night and taken up a pickax and killed two people. It's also a message that, in 1984, a man in Midland, Texas, apparently needed to hear. He heard it, in fact, and believed it. He'd been drinking heavily, having trouble with his wife—he was in danger of losing his family. And his business interests were tanking too. This was a man in need of grace, a man who desperately wanted redemption.

The man's name was George Walker Bush.

Indeed, in his journeys Arthur Blessitt made a pass through Midland, an oil town of around eighty thousand residents on the southern plains of western Texas that earned its name in 1881 as the midpoint between Fort Worth and El Paso on the Texas and Pacific railway. He was leading a revival called "Decision '84."

It was a six-day run in early April. He spent his days carrying his cross through the streets and speaking around the city. Thousands turned out for the meeting each night, plus thousands more on a local radio broadcast. Bush was one of the listeners. Blessitt's voice no doubt translated well to radio—he speaks in story, his voice often filled with pathos, and he cries easily and freely. Apparently Bush was moved by what he heard, because he asked one of his well-connected friends to arrange a meeting with Blessitt to talk religion. The friend, oil man Jim Sale, told Blessitt that Bush didn't feel comfortable attending a revival at the Chaparral Center, but he had been listening on the radio.

According to Blessitt, their meeting began with cordial exchanges, but it took no time for Bush to get to the issue at hand. Bush shook his hand, fixed him in his gaze, and "with a calm, steady look," he said, "'Arthur, I did not feel comfortable attending the meeting, but I want to talk to you about how to know Jesus Christ and how to follow Him.'"

Blessitt says he whispered a silent prayer: "Oh, Jesus, put your words in my mouth and lead him to understand and be saved."

Blessitt asked Bush what was his relationship to Jesus.

Bush said he wasn't sure.

Blessitt asked if Bush were to die this moment, did he have assurance he would go to heaven?

Bush said no.

"Then let me explain to you how you can have that assurance and know for sure that you are saved."

"I'd like that," Bush said.

Maybe Bush was seeking redemption for more than his recent troubles. You've probably heard the stories of his wayward youth and fratboy antics—the urinating on cars, the hollering obscenities at police officers, the trashing a rental home and refusing to pay damages, the drinking Wild Turkey instead of Chivas Regal in order to prove his Texas bona fides. Those days, oil prices were dropping, unemployment lines were long, the First National Bank of Midland collapsed. The whole region was in need of some divine intervention.

And so Blessitt led Bush through the traditional Sinner's Prayer, telling him all had sinned and fallen short of the glory of God. He told that both of them, Arthur and George, were sinners, and that the wages of sin is death, but the gift of God is eternal life through Jesus Christ our Lord. Bush could receive that gift if he understood that Jesus paid the price for our sins by dying on the cross for our sins, and if he would vow to take up his own cross and follow Christ.

"Would you rather live with Jesus in your life or live without Him?" Blessitt asked.

"With him," Bush replied.

"Had you rather spend eternity with Jesus or without Him?"

"With Jesus."

"Jesus changes us from the inside out," Blessitt told Bush. "The world tries to change us from the outside in. Jesus is not condemning you. He wants to save you and cleanse your heart and change your desires. He wants to write your name in the Book of Life and welcome you into His family, now and forever."

Blessitt led Bush through the prayer line for line, and Bush repeated each and every word.

When they were done, Blessitt declared George W. Bush a new creature. "There is rejoicing in Heaven now!" Blessitt declared. "You are saved!"

Then the man who had toted his cross around the world recited Luke 15:7 to the new convert: "There is more joy in heaven over one sinner who repents than over ninety-nine just persons who need no repentance."

Moving forward, George W. Bush would have plenty of opportunity to think about the nature and value of repentance. In early '98, he would have more.

Bush's testimony of his conversion from borderline alcoholic to born-again believer was well documented, but Blessitt's version of the story was not the one Bush chose to share publically. Instead, Bush went with a more conventional and perhaps safer version of events, likely because he sensed that for all its inherent spectacle, it might not play well for a candidate with serious aspirations of one day becoming president. After all, Blessitt was offbeat, maybe a little kooky. His seventies-style psychedelic Jesus Movement shtick in which he encouraged folks to get "naturally stoned on Jesus!" seemed a little, well, far out there. The better alternative was to tell the world about how mainstream evangelist Billy Graham—the same one who had served as spiritual advisor for every president since Truman—had planted what Bush called a "mustard seed" in his heart in 1985, a year after Bush was led to the Lord by Blessitt.

It was at a Bush family reunion where Graham, who'd been invited as a special guest, joined the family for a few days of golf, tennis, and swimming at Kennebunkport, Maine. One afternoon, George W. and Graham took a stroll along the beach and soon wandered into the waters of the Atlantic. There, with the waves rolling over their feet, it wasn't quite a baptism that occurred, but Graham would later call it "our beginning." Bush told Graham that he suspected reading the Bible might make him a better person. In exchange, Bush said Graham "told me about one of the Bible's most fundamental lessons: one should strive to be better, but we're all sinners who earn God's love not through good deeds, but through his grace." Later during his stay, Graham asked Bush if he could send him a Bible. Bush would say of his time with Graham, "There was no lecture, no grabbing of the shoulders.... It was the beginning of me reading the Bible. A religious walk began, and still goes on today."

For his part, Graham didn't remember it exactly the same way. Though he had called his visit to Maine their "beginning," things did not go much farther. "I've heard others say that [I led Bush to Christ], and people have written it, but I cannot say that," Graham said. "I was with him and I used to teach the Bible at Kennebunkport to the Bush family when he was a younger man, but I never feel that I in any way turned his life around." Maybe Graham was practicing humility. But he knew when he'd won a convert, and the fact that he doesn't claim Bush as one seems noteworthy here.

Whether Blessitt or Graham had the bigger impact, Bush's life did in fact undergo significant changes. He quit drinking, joined a Bible study group, recommitted himself to his family and saved his marriage. Onlookers said even his physical stride evinced a new confidence and self-assurance. Jim Wallis, editor-in-chief of *Sojourners* magazine, says when he met Bush, "I felt that he was sort of a self-help Methodist—meaning, someone whose faith had made a difference in his personal life. Solved some drinking issues and some family issues, and changed him. Gave him purpose. That's part of Methodism. Always has been. Kind of a 12-step God." Throughout his political career, Bush received strong political backing from Christians; a significant portion of his base identified as evangelical and no doubt supported him in large part because he professed religious values resembling theirs.

But now he was faced with a decision that promised to please some of his fellow Christians—and make the rest question the state of his very soul.

Chapter 16

I WILL WAIT FOR YOU

On the courthouse square in Huntsville, between Rogers Shoe Store and Ernst Jewelers, the Texas Prison Museum maintained a display case full of contraband weapons. There was a knife concealed in a shower sandal; memorabilia from John Wesley Hardin and Bonnie and Clyde; and a replica execution chamber featuring Old Sparky, the electric chair in whose lap 361 prisoners died between 1924 and 1964. This macabre tourism industry is what you get when your town contains the state's death house. The economy depends on the prison system, which employs over seven thousand people. "If Texas felons suddenly reformed or went elsewhere to rob banks or shoot their wives," claims Virginia Stem Owens, "the Wal-Mart superstore out by the Interstate would have to shut its automatic doors."

According to Owens, a writer with *Christianity Today* who hails from Huntsville, the town had been anticipating Karla Faye Tucker's execution with an excitement bordering on delirium. "A week before her sentence was scheduled to be carried out," Owens wrote, "camera crews, international news teams, Amnesty International representatives, and victims'-rights advocates crowded our town to chronicle the event. Every motel room was booked, the town's restaurants packed, the Enterprise car rental office overwhelmed. Even the stylist who did Bianca Jagger's hair for the occasion got interviewed by the press."

Despite the circus atmosphere, however, there was concern among the townsfolk over how Huntsville would be portrayed nationwide. Owens continued, "Everyone knew that rowdy fraternity boys, drinking beer and waving Rebel flags, would treat the execution like a human fox hunt. Yet even diehard death-penalty advocates shuddered at the bad impression of our town these unseemly shenanigans would make. We expected that the world's media, camped on our small doorstep, would portray Huntsvillians as uniformly sanctioning and collectively responsible for killing this repentant woman."

On Monday, February 2, Karla was flown from her prison in Gatesville to Huntsville, eighty miles north of Houston, where state executions are conducted. That night, her final one before her scheduled execution, she got little sleep. She thought much, no doubt, about her savior's final hours. She had told Larry King, "When I think about what Jesus asked, before he went to the cross, he asked God for the cup to be removed, and if he can ask it, I don't have to feel ashamed to ask that either. I would love to be able to live on."

> [32] And they came to a place which was named Gethsemane: and he saith to his disciples, Sit ye here, while I shall pray. [33] And he taketh with him Peter and James and John, and began to be sore amazed, and to be very heavy; [34] And saith unto them, My soul is exceeding sorrowful unto death: tarry ye here, and watch. [35] And he went forward a little, and fell on the ground, and prayed that, if it were possible, the hour might pass from him. [36] And he said, Abba, Father, all things are possible unto thee; take away this cup from me: nevertheless not what I will, but what thou wilt.

The next morning, February 3, three thousand calls reached the governor's office, eighty percent of which asked Bush to commute the sentence. The last of 2,369 total letters—most of them from out of state, one of them mine—poured in. Over two thousand of them pled for clemency. Pat Robertson called. Pope John Paul II sent a note.

Even Karla's ex-husband, Stephen Griffith, spoke publicly about their marriage in hopes of saving her life. He praised her willingness to clean the house, cook his meals, get him to work on time. "I hate to see [her execution] happen," he said. "We spent quite a bit of our lives together. I loved her dearly." He wanted to see her live, but if things turned out otherwise, well, he would still go to work tomorrow. "I have carpentry work to do. I just can't sit and watch. In all due honesty, it would break my heart."

Karla woke at dawn and was able to stomach only a few crackers and a soft drink. Throughout the day, she met with family members and friends—a screen separating her from those who'd come to say farewell. She cried after saying a prayer with her husband of two and a half years, Dana Brown. She was not permitted a kiss goodbye.

A couple of hours before guards would escort her into the death chamber, Karla handed the chairman of the Texas Board of Criminal Justice three pieces of paper. If her letter to Bush two weeks ago had been an earnest plea for mercy, these pages served as her evaluation of the prison system she had lived within these last fourteen years. On them she had handwritten what she titled "A Rehabilitation Plan for Inmates." Her most distinct proposal was that prisoners should be paid for their work with money that they would in turn give back to the state in exchange for their food, clothing, housing, and medical care. "When a person enters," Karla wrote in the letter she handed to Allan Polunsky, who typically met with condemned inmates prior to their executions, "they are fed three square meals a day, have a roof over their head, are given clothes to wear, schooling, medical and many other things FREE. . . . Having everything given to us free and told how to do everything has a big tendency to condition a person to be irresponsible [sic] and become very dependant [sic] upon the people in care of them." Apparently she anticipated pushback, because she added, "I believe Texas needs to pay the inmates a wage for working. But wait! Every bit of money you pay us will go right back into your system or to actions for restitution. Basically you won't be paying us at all. It would be sort of a self-sufficient, full-circle thing."

She was worried about the high rate of recidivism throughout the prison system. "Show them that one must work to eat in here just like one must work to eat out in the normal world," she wrote. Then she recommended an appropriate punishment: a food loaf. A food loaf is a meal generally served to prisoners in solitary confinement. It consists of whatever items are on a given day's menu, which are mixed together and served as a kind of meatloaf that inmates find, for all intents and purposes, inedible. "If an inmate refuses to work," she wrote, "I say put them in segregation and put them immediately on a food loaf! No TV, no recreation, just a food loaf and showers."

The time drew closer and people began congregating outside—approximately twelve hundred people and two hundred reporters from around the world. People held signs stating AXE AND YOU SHALL RECEIVE Texas 2:3 and FORGET INJECTION USE A PICK AX and YOU PICKED YOUR DEATH and DIE LIKE A MAN. Others held a sign reading, JESUS WAS A VICTIM OF THE DEATH PENALTY. A group chanted "She sliced, she diced, and now she's got to pay the price!" while another sang "Amazing Grace." A man dressed as the Grim Reaper circulated through the crowd, accompanied by a woman in witch attire. A pizza delivery man navigated his way among the glut of bodies. A giant TV screen showcased video footage of Karla dancing and using sign language to communicate the lyrics of a gospel song proclaiming, "When the time comes I want to be ready, I want to be ready when Jesus comes to take me away, when my precious Savior comes to take me away." A music store in downtown Huntsville featured an ad that read, KARLA FAYE TUCKER SALE—KILLER PRICES—DEALS TO DIE FOR! Deborah Thornton's husband, Richard Thornton, reveled in the sensation that vengeance was nigh. "Make no mistake," he said. "This is *not* Karla Faye Tucker's day. This is Deborah Ruth Davis Thornton's day."

Every major news source in the US was covering the event live. Hovering helicopters showed overhead views of police corralling crowds behind yellow tape lines. Commentators debated back and forth about the significance of Karla's gender and her white skin, her "petite, photogenic, rosy-lipped" appearance and her "flowing brown curls." CNN legal analyst Greta Van Susteren shared her reaction to a prior execution she had attended. Fox News anchor Jon Scott cautioned viewers that the network was about to display "extremely graphic" pictures and that parents might want to escort children away from the television. They then aired several photos from the crime scene, including one showing the pickax lodged in Deborah Thornton's chest.

Meanwhile, Karla remained upbeat. "She prayed and said she was right with the Lord," said Texas Department of Criminal Justice spokesman Glen Castlebury. "She was calm and composed."

The US Supreme Court rejected two eleventh-hour appeals to halt the execution. The Court offered no comment.

In 1931, George Orwell wrote a short essay called "A Hanging," about his experience watching an Indian man die in Burma when he had served with the British Imperial Police. As they walk toward the gallows, the prisoner, flanked on either side by two guards, sidesteps a puddle of rain water in his path. However slight, the gesture triggers in Orwell a moment of philosophical insight. "When I saw the prisoner step aside to avoid the puddle," he writes, "I saw the mystery.... This man was not dying, he was alive just as we were alive. All the organs of his body were working—bowels digesting food, skin renewing itself, nails growing, tissues forming—all toiling away in solemn foolery. His nails would still be growing when he stood on the drop, when he was falling through the air with a tenth of a second to live. His eyes saw the yellow gravel and the grey walls, and his brain still remembered, foresaw, reasoned—reasoned even about puddles. He and we were a party of men walking together, seeing, hearing, feeling, understanding the same world; and in two minutes, with a sudden snap, one of us would be gone—one mind less, one world less."

At 4:00 p.m., prison guards served Karla her final meal. She had been given the privilege of ordering anything she wanted from the food available in the prison pantry, but she barely touched the peaches, a banana, or tossed salad with ranch dressing she'd requested. She also was offered a sedative but declined.

At 5:30, members of nearby Saint Stephen's parish met at the church to pray—not in demonstration for or against capital punishment, but for everyone who had played a role in bringing about this whole scene: the attorneys, the judges, the jury, the Board of Pardons and Paroles, the governor, the executioner, and yes, this woman who was about to die.

And then the news came minutes before her scheduled execution, at about 6:20, that Governor Bush was making an announcement.

In the video footage, he trudges wearily into the room where the press is gathered to hear his decision. As everyone is seated and the space grows quiet, he expels a long, pent-up sigh. "When I was sworn in as the governor of Texas," his statement begins, "I took an oath of office to uphold the laws of our state, including the death penalty. My responsibility is to ensure our laws are enforced fairly and evenly without preference or special treatment."

Bush stands at the podium looking a little frumpy, his face gaunt and hair unkempt, his eyes maybe a bit swollen from sleeplessness or tears, as though this arduous decision has taxed him both physically and spiritually. His whole demeanor suggests he has made this momentous decision in the past five minutes, and with his mind now made up, he has come straight to us without delay to deliver his position. Cameramen jockey for elbow room; bulbs flash across the room like heat lightning. "Many people have contacted my office about this execution," he says. "I respect the strong convictions which have prompted some to call for mercy and others to emphasize accountability and consequences.

"Like many touched by this case, I have sought guidance through prayer. I have concluded judgment about the heart and soul of an individual on death row are best left to a higher authority."

He reminds us that Karla knows she is guilty. He reminds us that everything about this case has proceeded according to the rule of law. "The courts," he says, "including the United States Supreme Court, have reviewed the legal issues in this case, and therefore I will not grant a 30-day stay."

He refuses to answer any questions from the press.

His final words: "May God bless Karla Faye Tucker and may God bless her victims and their families."

Just before 6:00 p.m., she showered and changed into a fresh white prison uniform with white shoes—practically the only attire she'd worn for the past fourteen years. Her hair still damp, she was escorted from her holding cell behind the execution chamber and led twenty feet to the place they called the death house. Karla had seen its door but never the other side, until this moment. The space was Spartan, about the size of a hospital room, with blue-green cinder-block walls. In the middle was a slim gurney with a pillow, stark white sheets, five leather straps, and arms containing one strap each. A microphone extended from the ceiling toward the gurney. It was separated from an observation area by large, clear windows.

According to Fred Allen, captain of the death house team, Karla expressed gratitude for his kindness. "Thank you, Captain Allen, for everything you've done," she told him.

"You're welcome," he said. ("You know, that's all I *could* say," he later reported. "What else I'm gonna say?")

The warden took off his glasses, signaling for the process to begin. Those assigned such duties strapped her to the gurney, restraining her at the feet, legs, waist, chest, and arms. She lay face-up, her arms spread wide—and I guess it must be said—as though for a crucifixion.

They swabbed her arms with alcohol. Karla reportedly worried over whether they would be able to find a vein in which to insert the IV drips, one in each arm. And with good reason—all those years of heroin needles had compromised her veins such that it was quite possible they would have trouble finding ones that would not collapse. But the prison employees found suitable veins and hooked up the IVs—one to administer the drugs, the other to serve as a backup in case the first failed. The IV line ran from the gurney to a room next door, separated from Karla by a curtain.

Once she was on the gurney with the IVs ready, the witnesses were escorted into the observation area. Karla had selected five people to bear witness, the maximum allowed. Her ex-husband, Stephen Griffith, did not attend, but her current one, Dana Brown, was present. So was her sister, Kari Weeks; her friend Jackie Oncken; her lead attorney George "Mac" Secrest; and Deborah Thornton's brother, Ronald Carlson, who had spoken out against Karla's execution due to her religious conversion.

Also in attendance, on the other side of a dividing wall, was Deborah Thornton's husband, Richard Thornton. When he took his seat, he availed himself of the opportunity to ridicule Karla's husband for what he perceived as his ulterior motives. "So now Dana Brown gets to write his book," he said. His daughter, Katheryn Thornton, and Deborah Thornton's son from a previous marriage, William "Bucky" Davis, joined him in the witness room to the execution chamber. No witnesses representing Jerry Lynn Dean were present; no relatives had contacted state prison officials requesting admittance.

Four members of the media were allowed to observe.

Moments before the procedure began, the warden asked if Karla had a final statement. Still strapped to the gurney with the IVs hooked up, she spoke into the microphone in that drawl that had recently become familiar to so many Americans. "I would like to say to all of you—the Thornton family and Jerry Dean's family—that I am so sorry. I hope God will give you peace with this." Then she addressed the side of the witness room where her witnesses sat watching. To her husband: "Baby, I love you." To Deborah Thornton's brother, who had offered forgiveness: "Ron, give [Dean's sister] Peggy a hug for me." To all gathered: "Everybody has been so good to me. I love all of you very much."

Then, these last words: "I am going to be face to face with Jesus now . . . I love all of you very much. I will see you all when you get there. I will wait for you."

As Karla lay on the gurney, Richard Thornton, who was disabled with diabetes and confined to a wheelchair, was at eye level with her. Thornton uttered words to his dead wife. "Here she comes, baby doll," he said. "She's all yours. The world's a better place."

From behind a plate glass window, the executioner pushed a button. Saline flushed through her veins.

"I love you, Karla," her sister, Kari Tucker Weeks, called out.

Karla mouthed a silent prayer as the three-drug cocktail began. She gasped. She coughed twice.

First came the sodium thiopental, a powerful anesthetic that rendered her unconscious in less than a minute and paralyzed her lungs; then came pancuronium bromide, a muscle relaxant that triggered complete paralysis of all muscles, including the diaphragm, and prevented breathing; then the final drug, potassium chloride, stopped Karla's heart.

There is always the fear that something will go wrong with the anesthesiology. The person will be conscious, to whatever degree, of her inability to breathe but unable even to blink an eyelid, essentially screaming on the inside but apparently tranquil on the outside. Or the person will be aware of her skin burning as the potassium chloride takes effect. But the monitor alerted the attending physician, Daryl Wells, that this time the procedure seemed to unfold as planned and now was complete.

If Jesus spoke Karla's name, nobody heard his voice. If heaven opened and spilled light onto Karla's face, none of the mortals gathered in the room saw its glow. If ministering angels bundled Karla to their breasts and escorted her to the place where God awaited his child, no one testified of their arrival. But then again, maybe all these things happened. That's the thing about the death penalty. You have to be the one lying on that gurney to know precisely what happens in that moment when you pass from life to death.

Through the steel door, the doctor entered the chamber. He shone a light into Karla's eyes. He checked for a pulse with his fingers. Using his stethoscope, he listened for a heartbeat. He searched for any sign that this woman who claimed she had eternal life was still alive.

Eight minutes after it began, at 6:45 p.m., Dr. Wells pronounced Karla Faye Tucker dead. The warden repeated the time. The curtain was pulled over the observation window, separating the onlookers from their view of the gurney.

The door opened. A guard gestured toward it. "Family members first," he said.

Chapter 17

THE STATE OF TEXAS, OFFICE OF THE GOVERNOR, AUSTIN

When the news spilled outside the prison walls, death penalty advocates cheered. Some threw their arms over each other's shoulders and broke into chorus. "Na na . . . na na na na . . . hey, Hey, HEY, GOODBYE!" they sang, over and over, till their voices grew hoarse, their throats dry as flint. A handful of local college kids held signs reading *Hello Mom* and *Send Money* and searched frantically for the television cameras.

Forty-five minutes after her execution, Richard Thornton met with reporters outside. "Justice for Deborah Thornton is complete," he told them. "I want to say to every victim in the world, demand this. *Demand* this. This is your right."

Later, he would take to the media to air his lingering resentment toward Karla. He remained convinced she had lied about her salvation, and had pretended her way through years of prison ministry. "I don't believe her Christianity," he claimed, "I don't believe her conversion. I never did; I never will." He maintained that anti-capital punishment advocates had manipulated his wife's brother, Ron Carlson, and persuaded him to commit a kind of treason. Though now remarried, he relished Deborah Thornton's opportunity to settle the score in the afterlife. He posited the hereafter as a setting where souls resolve their lingering earthly disputes in a kind of spiritual warfare and balance the scales of justice once and for all. Karla had been "sent to the place that we're all going to go sometime, someplace my wife already is. She will deal with Karla Faye Tucker. I promise you, it won't be pretty." And the whole ordeal had made him recognize the futility of attempting to reconcile his anger with his faith. "My religion says to forgive, turn the other cheek," he said. "I'm not a perfect man. I've tried very hard. I still cannot do it."

Six weeks after Karla's execution, a group of death penalty opponents issued two stamps memorializing her. Both featured her face, smiling. In one she appears before a prison gurney resembling the one on which she was executed. The other shows her opposite an American flag with an oil rig. Though the stamps could not be used to mail letters or packages and were more akin to Easter Seals for envelopes, Richard Thornton resented the very idea that anyone would want to commemorate a murderer. "It is most unfortunate," he said, "that the artists who were motivated to produce this work were so horribly misinformed as to the true character of the person portrayed by them. The work would have been closer to the truth if it had included a pickax and a great deal of blood."

Deborah Thornton's brother, Ron Carlson, had become the first known member of a victim's family to witness an execution on behalf of the condemned. Many wondered how he managed it, emotionally. "I drew strength from the Lord," he explained, "and I knew he was here. God reached out of heaven to hold us in his hands and cradle us with his love and compassion. Karla died with a smile on her face. They took her body, but they didn't kill her spirit." He seized the moment to tell the world this event also had brought about personal transformation for him, adding,

> The world is not a better place because the State of Texas executed Karla Faye Tucker. Even though Karla murdered my only sibling—my sister, Deborah, who had raised me after our mother died—I stood with her as one of her witnesses when she was executed. I was there to stand up for the Lord, for the strength of his love. Karla and I had both done a lot of wrong in our lives. We

had both turned to drugs to heal our pain; we had both hurt a lot of people. But the love of Jesus Christ transformed us. We were able to forgive ourselves and each other. "I love you, Ronnie," was one of the last things Karla said. I still carry that love with me.

Two days after Karla's execution, a man named Fred Allen had a nervous breakdown. Allen was captain of the death house and a member of the "tie-down team." There were five of them altogether, members of the team, and each one was assigned to strap a different part of the condemned inmate's body to the gurney. Two for the legs, two for the arms, and one charged with making sure the inmate stayed down if she tried to get up. ("Once you're up there, you're up there," Allen said.) Allen always took care of the left leg. They were trained to do it cleanly and efficiently. It took about fifteen seconds to get the prisoner completely strapped down. They waited until the execution was complete, then they removed the straps again. Allen was not new to this. He had participated in 130 executions. He'd been promoted to captain in 1990 and often did two executions per week. He usually spent the entire day, eight to ten hours, with the inmate in the lead-up to the execution.

Allen's breakdown was unexpected and came on without any apparent indication that his routine role in Karla's death would affect him any differently than the others had. "I was just working in the shop [at his home]," he said, "and all of a sudden something just triggered in me, and I started shaking. And then I walked back into the house and my wife asked, 'What's the matter?' And I said, 'I don't feel good.' And tears, uncontrollable tears, was coming out of my eyes and she says, 'What's the matter?' And I told her. I said, 'I just thought about that execution that I did two days ago, and everybody else's that I was involved in.' And what it was, something triggered within, and it just, everybody—all of these executions all sprung forward."

Allen described his breakdown as a "shake. Like, I couldn't . . . why am I shaking?" He had a hard time finding words to describe the experience, anything beyond the physical pain it triggered. "All of a sudden I just . . . this is *hurtin*. I remembered her, and this was two days afterwards. I remembered her execution . . . hers was no different than anybody else but it was *hers*."

He called a chaplain, who came over and sat with him in a swing outside his home. For a time, they just sat together silently, listening to the roosters and the doves. "I can't do it no more," Allen finally told the chaplain. "That's it. I'm done. I can't . . . I can't go back there anymore." He couldn't understand why this was happening to him— why this time was any different from all those past executions. It just didn't make any logical sense.

He said the chaplain started talking to him about vases. "Every time you put a drop of water in, it fills up," the chaplain explained. "One last drop of water, it overflows . . . That's how you might want to look at the way you did the executions. You did so much, your vase is full now and you're done. You're spilling over."

George W. Bush had called the window of time between when he left his press conference and Karla was pronounced dead "the longest twenty minutes of my tenure as governor." He had returned to his office, where a staff member told him it was a good thing that he was affected so emotionally by his decision, that he was hurt by its weight. If it wasn't a hard thing to do, the staff member had told him, now *that* would have been cause for concern. Bush's deputy counsel, Donna Davidson, established communication with the death chamber and relayed the play-by-play from Karla being led from her cell; to the gurney; to the insertion of the needle; to the administration of the lethal dose. "I felt like a huge piece of concrete was crushing me as we waited," Bush said. Finally came the news of Karla's death. Bush's next act was to call his wife Laura. He told her he was on his way home but, really, "I wanted to hear her voice," Bush said. By his account, everything about this decision whether to intervene in Karla's case had exhausted him physically and emotionally.

But less than five months later, Bush chose to grant clemency to a man he described as "contemptible, a one-eyed drifter, a proven liar, and a killer who wore a surly scowl and at one time confessed to police that he had committed more than six hundred murders." In actuality, investigators into Henry Lee Lucas's confessions suspected he had committed only a handful of murders. The rest, they decided, had resulted from law enforcement urging him to confess, because they were so anxious to solve unsolved crimes. In particular, they believed he had not murdered an unidentified woman known only as Orange Socks. The woman had been strangled, her body thrown over a guardrail off Interstate 35 north of Austin and dumped in a culvert. She was naked but for two orange socks. Lucas claimed he had killed her and raped her corpse. He later recanted his confession.

It was later confirmed that Lucas wasn't in the state of Texas when the murder of Orange Socks was committed. That, and the fact that he was already serving six life sentences for other murders, convinced Bush to act. Before the Board of Pardons and Paroles made a recommendation, he intervened, which in turn resulted in a 17–1 vote to commute Henry Lee Lucas's sentence to life imprisonment. Bush could accept their recommendation or decline it and allow the execution to proceed.

He accepted.

Lucas died of heart failure in 2001, in prison.

In *Talk* magazine in 1999, conservative journalist Tucker Carlson recounted an interview he conducted with Bush about Karla's execution. Bush was recalling Bianca Jagger and a number of high-profile protestors coming to Austin to demand clemency for Karla.

"Did you meet with any of them?" Carlson asked Bush.

According to Carlson, Bush was angered by his question. "No, I didn't meet with any of them," he snapped. "I didn't meet with Larry King either when he came down for it. I watched his interview with her, though. He asked her real difficult questions, though, like 'What would you say to Governor Bush?'"

Carlson asked how Karla responded.

According to Carlson, Bush began whining in mock desperation. "Please," he whimpered through pursed lips, "Please don't kill me."

Bush of course denied this exchange occurred. "Mr. Carlson misread, mischaracterized me," he said. "He's a good reporter, he just misunderstood about how serious that was. I take the death penalty very seriously. I take each case seriously. I just felt he misjudged me. I think he misinterpreted my feelings. I know he did."

Point of fact: nowhere in the transcript of Karla's appearance on Larry King's show does she appeal to Bush for clemency.

Europe's Renaissance, of course, gave us all those renderings of Christ's crucifixion, but American art has offered little commentary on the death penalty. Perhaps Andy Warhol's silkscreen-printed canvas *Electric Chair* stands as the most recognized piece. It's part of his *Death and Disaster* series that he began in 1962, which also depicted newspaper images of car and plane crashes and suicides and celebrities like Marilyn Monroe and Jacqueline Kennedy in the throes of tragedy. The chair in Warhol's piece employs a 1953 press photo from the death chamber at New York's Sing Sing Prison, where the Rosenburgs were executed for passing information about the atomic bomb to Russia during World War II. It's an empty chair in an otherwise empty execution chamber. Buckles and straps dangle from the arms and cling serpentine-like to the legs of the high-back chair. A cable runs from under the seat and curls in front of it. There's a table against the back wall and a sign that reads "SILENCE" on the margins of the image. It's unclear whether we're gazing on the chair hours before the next victim takes his seat, or hours after the last one occupied the space. In any case, it's as still and quiet as death itself. It reminds me of those first few seconds in silent movies from the turn of the century as the film rattles through the projector. It's got that grainy, unfocused texture. The image is repeated once on ten separate sheets. The successive sheets feature the chair in different, often garish colors—yellow, pink, orange, and red among them. The final one is perhaps the most arresting. It appears as though the room has been struck by lightning, or maybe a stray surge of electricity has left us with an aftershock.

Warhol's fascination with these images seemed related to our ever-increasing desensitization toward violence. "When you see a gruesome picture over and over again," he said, "it doesn't really have any effect." The media gratuitously repeats these images without creating intimacy between us and the victim. We philosophize death, but we don't internalize it in any emotional way.

Despite the attention Karla's case brought to the debate over the death penalty, Warhol's canvas seems an appropriate signifier. During his tenure as governor, Bush would ultimately preside over 154 executions—a number eclipsing that of any other governor in any state in modern history. (His successor, Rick Perry, would far surpass Bush's record, executing 234 people.) Just six days after Karla died, on February 9, a man named Steven Renfro was executed in Huntsville. He'd been on death row only 263 days. The circus frenzy that had surrounded Karla's death was entirely absent for this white man who had shot three people, including his common-law-wife. Renfro's final words: "I would like to tell the victims' families that I'm sorry, very sorry. I am so sorry. Forgive me if you can. I know it's impossible, but try. Take my hand, Lord Jesus. I'm coming home."

It would be less than two months before Florida electrocuted Judy Buenoano, the state's first woman to die since 1848 when a slave woman named Celia was hanged in Jacksonville for murdering the man who owned her. Buenoano too had converted to Christianity and lived an exemplary life on death row, and it was easy to draw parallels between her case and Karla's. But she did not engender the same intensity of debate. "Judy may not have been as photogenic, as young or as pretty as Karla," claimed a relative, "but she was just as good a Christian."

And it would be a little over two years before one of Karla's companions on death row, Betty Lou Beets, became the next Texas woman put to death.

In 1984, the year Karla and Danny Garrett murdered Jerry Lynn Dean and Deborah Thornton, three men were executed in the state of Texas. During the nineties, the number of executions began to increase dramatically—seventeen in '93, fourteen in '94, nineteen in '95. After the number again fell to three in '96, it leaped to thirty-seven in '97. Karla was the first of twenty Texans to die in '98. Over the next few years, the number of executions in the state vacillated, ranging from forty in 2000 to ten in 2014, but the practice continued steadily, and support among Texans remained high. Elsewhere in the US, support languished and implementation of the death penalty became increasingly rare. But Texas dug in. John B. Holmes Jr. was district attorney in Harris County for twenty-one years and presided when Karla died. As sympathy for her was building, he had been prepared, if necessary, to go public with those brutal images of the crime scene. "Texans have a right to say what their rules are," he declared. "Tell the people of Vermont that if they don't like Texas' death penalty rules, they ought to commit their murders in Vermont."

At a program on clemency in February 1999, a year after Karla's execution, televangelist Pat Robertson continued to support the death penalty for what he called "vicious killers," but also spoke out forcefully against capital punishment for offenders who had a "genuine change of heart." He opposed the existing "culture of death," saying, "We need to be pro-life across the board." About Karla Faye Tucker, he doubled down on his longstanding support, saying, "The woman who had been convicted wasn't there any longer. This was a different person. To execute her was an act of barbarity that was totally unnecessary." He lamented the "unseemly air of vengeance" outside the prison, and asked, "What kind of animal vengeance is it in a society where people take such delight in this?"

And though abolitionists applauded Robertson for drawing attention to the issue, many felt he did not go far enough. "With a few exceptions he has ignored the other 3,300 people on death row," said Kurt Rosenburg, who founded the Friends Committee to Abolish the Death Penalty. "I don't want to minimize his turnaround on this issue. He needs to continue to process it and ultimately come out against the death penalty in every instance."

Indeed, Robertson drew his line in the sand against those like Rosenburg. A spokesman at Robertson's Christian Broadcasting Network made clear that Karla represented an exception to his general take on the subject. "Mr. Robertson's views of the death penalty have not changed, despite what participants gleaned from his [recent] remarks."

Sister Helen Prejean, author of *Dead Man Walking* and inspiration for the movie, suspected more was going on inside Robertson than he was willing to publicly declare. "Is there a possibility that perhaps every human being is more than the worst act of their lives, and that they can be open to redemption?" she asked. "Perhaps this has been part of the fermentation in his soul and in his conscience and in his faith that is moving the Pat Robertsons of the world more in the direction of compassion and mercy. Perhaps it can move him eventually to a principled position—not just make an exception on the Karla Faye Tuckers, but in fact no human being should be subjected to that torture."

Whatever inner conflict Robertson was experiencing, a notable shift was occurring within the evangelical world as a collective body. Two months after Karla's death, *Christianity Today* published what proved to be a groundbreaking editorial about the death penalty. Citing its unfair and discriminatory application and its failure to deter future crimes or console society, the editorial exposes injustices of the practice. True to the evangelical worldview, though, these theories are subject to what the Bible expresses about the issue. "The law of Moses put the brakes on vengeance, but the other stream of biblical thought calls for its end," the editorial argues. "God's first, and perhaps most characteristic, response to murder was not law but grace: he placed a protective mark on Cain, protecting him from those who would avenge Abel's blood, and warning others of a dangerous man." The editorial asserts the death penalty has "outlived its usefulness," and has failed to make the US a safer or more equitable country. "The potential of life imprisonment without parole and other protective measures, however, offer better options for the state, which must continue to deal with 20,000 murders each year."

Since then, Christians have remained divided on the issue. In 2015, the National Association of Evangelicals updated their official position. Now, as a collective body, they were climbing on the proverbial fence. The same group who in 1973 argued that "if no crime is considered serious enough to warrant the death penalty, then the gravity of the most atrocious crime is diminished accordingly," now adopted a new resolution: "Evangelical Christians differ in their beliefs about capital punishment, often citing strong biblical and theological reasons either for the just character of the death penalty in extreme cases or for the sacredness of all life, including the lives of those who perpetrate serious crimes and yet have the potential for repentance and reformation. We affirm the conscientious commitment of both streams of Christian ethical thought."

In the two decades since Karla's death, support for the death penalty has steadily declined nationwide, dropping from almost 80 percent in 1998 to 56 percent today. And among evangelicals, the number has dropped to 59 percent. Many attribute this shift to the growing number of minorities in evangelical churches—especially Latinos—who recognize racial bias in application of the death penalty. But even white evangelicals seem to be growing disillusioned with the practice.

In the nineties, Karla's support from evangelicals was indeed unexpected. But she objected to accusations she had solicited their assistance and described their allegiance this way: "I didn't get them for me. God did. . . . what they're really speaking out for is for the cause of Christ. I believe that they see what Jesus Christ has done in a life, the way he has transformed a life. And what they're speaking out for is saying, he's real." She claimed if Jesus could transform a life like hers, he could transform anybody's. "And he can take a person that is out there doing something horrible," she continued, "and he can stop them from doing that, and . . . Jesus can turn them around and use that as a witness and a testimony to stop others from doing it. I can witness to people who have been on drugs or into prostitution or into all of that, and they'll listen to me because they know I understand and can relate to them. And I can keep them from going down that road, because I can let them know. I changed. You can too. So that's what they're speaking up for."

In our loyalty to and practice of the death penalty, the South outpaces the rest of America by a considerable margin. In fact, it's fair to say capital punishment is a southern thing. And by South, I mean the thirteen states that made up the original Confederacy. To date, no former Confederate state is among the twenty-nine that have either abolished the death penalty or conducted fewer than three executions since capital punishment was reinstated in 1976 (Kentucky has executed exactly three). Overall, of the 1,531 executions that have occurred in the US between 1976 and 2019—seventeen of whom were women—over 81 percent happened in the South.

Like most southern things, these facts and figures have much to do with race. We of course could talk about the people put to death, how Black inmates themselves have been executed at percentages entirely disproportionate to their representation in the American demography. But another way of looking at it is to consider the way race and capital punishment have intersected historically in the South and how the legacy of that intersection has led to the execution of people of *all* races at a ratio far exceeding that of elsewhere.

Our habit of putting people to death at a disproportionate rate started in the 1700s. The spike in executions corresponded directly to the influx of African slaves to the region. Slave owners began demanding state assistance in disciplining the ever-growing population of enslaved people, promoting productivity, and protecting themselves against the kind of violence or revolt that sheer numbers made seem alarmingly possible. Incarceration did not serve as a deterrent to slaves, so the state often resorted to more extreme measures to maintain order. As punishment for uprisings and insurrections, slaves were often burned at the stake or their bodies were displayed for public viewing—all dire warnings of the consequences of rebellion. Slave owners were even compensated by the state when their property was executed.

While Michigan, Rhode Island, and Wisconsin became the first three states to outlaw capital punishment between 1846 and 1853, the antebellum South saw no states follow suit. In fact, abolition of both the death penalty and slavery overlapped in many northern and midwestern states, but the link between the two led both to fail mutually in the South. Over time, the same swath of Bible Belt states that made up the Confederacy also became known as the *Death Belt*.

Even after the Civil War, when slavery was abolished, the same desire to "restrain a primitive, animalistic black population" fueled the preservation of the death penalty in the former Confederacy. A particular fear was the sexual aggression posed by recently freed Black men. Hence, the charges of "outrage" accusing Black perpetrators of assaulting white women and the resulting spike in lynchings between 1880 and 1930, when more than three thousand blacks became victims of extrajudicial mob activity in southern states. The practice was so prevalent that, in 1907, one defense attorney insisted his Black client was innocent of all charges of rape precisely because otherwise he surely would have been lynched by now.

It's this relationship between race and death that explains why the South would continue to outpace other regions in capital cases through the Jim Crow era and beyond. By the time of the civil rights movement, this kind of legacy meant our relationship to the death penalty was deeply ingrained in our culture, often resulting in arbitrary administrations of it. In fact, it was the South's distinctive practice of the death penalty that eventually led the Supreme Court to declare it unconstitutional in 1972. When Justice Potter Stewart condemned the capriciousness of the death penalty, saying, "These death sentences are cruel and unusual in the same way that being struck by lightning is cruel and usual," he was talking primarily about the South.

The South's commitment to executions has a dramatic ripple effect on the United States' impact on capital punishment rates worldwide. The US stands apart from virtually all Western countries in its commitment to executions, which annually puts us among China, North Korea, Vietnam, Syria, Iran, Saudi Arabia, Iraq, Egypt, Pakistan, and Somalia for leading the world in capital punishment.

A state's number of documented lynchings historically and its number of executions today is one of the more compelling correlations to observe. It's reasonable to predict that the changing demographic in the South eventually will lead to shifts in how the region views the death penalty and applies it. As the percentage of white southerners decreases, the ratio of capital punishment supporters will likely mirror this decline.

But what do we do with a woman like Lisa Montgomery?

There would be others—there always would be others—but as I was writing this, Lisa Montgomery became the latest woman to summon our attention. She was scheduled for a January 2021 execution, in the waning days of Trump America. If she were put to death, she would be the first American woman to meet that end since Kelly Gissendaner in 2015. She was a federal death-row inmate; the United States government had not executed a female prisoner since 1953, when two women died, the murderous Bonnie Brown Heady in the gas chamber and the treasonous Ethel Rosenberg in the electric chair.

In 2004, Lisa Montgomery drove 175 miles from her home in Melvern, Kansas, to Skidmore, Missouri, where she ostensibly planned to adopt a rat terrier puppy from a pregnant twenty-three-year-old dog breeder named Bobbie Jo Stinnett. Instead, she strangled Stinnett with a rope and proceeded to conduct a crude C-section, cutting the fetus from Stinnett's womb and leaving her to bleed to death. Montgomery fled with the baby, which had been eight months in utero, with plans to raise it as her own. The child, a girl, survived.

If left to stand alone, that narrative prompts very little sympathy for Lisa Montgomery. To anyone with even a remote respect for the death penalty, her January 12, 2021, execution date seemed appropriate and justified. But when we consider mitigating circumstances—the kind of life history and mental health testimony that typically is considered during the punishment phase of a capital trial but was decidedly neglected by Montgomery's own lawyers in her case—a very different picture emerges. If we see little humanity in Lisa Montgomery, maybe there are reasons. Maybe very little of her treatment by others fell within any category we could call humane.

She was diagnosed with a catalog of disorders—bipolar, PTSD, dissociative—as well as psychosis and temporal-lobe epilepsy. But it seems they resulted not from an unfortunate imbalance of chemicals allotted her by fate, but from a level of abuse and violence few of us can even imagine. Lisa Montgomery's life story began as a series of unpleasant but not entirely atypical misfortunes—her mother drank heavily during her pregnancy with Lisa; her father left when she was a baby; and her extended family was riddled with mental illnesses ranging from depression to schizophrenia. But even her toddler years suggested her life was quickly becoming a nightmare of a different, unspeakable type. For example, to keep her silent, her mother sealed her mouth with duct tape so regularly that Lisa learned not to cry. Her first words were "Don't spank me. It hurts."

And then came adolescence, when her stepfather commenced sexually assaulting her at age thirteen. On the side of the family's trailer, he built a shed with its own entrance and invited friends to rape Lisa, often three at a time, for hours. Her mother was no ally; she would make her other children go outside while Lisa was being abused, and often prostituted her to pay repairman who did work on their house. At age eighteen, Lisa married her twenty-five-year-old stepbrother (the son of her mother's fourth husband), who proceeded to sexually assault her with bottles and hold knives to her throat. By age twenty-three, when she was sterilized, she had four children; she was not a good mother, frequently failing to feed or bathe them, or herself (she had lice for five years without noticing it). In the thirty-six years before she went to prison, she lived at sixty-one different addresses.

MRI scans of Lisa Montgomery's brain indicated severe brain damage. PET scans showed brain dysfunction. It's believed these injuries were as much the result of psychological trauma as physical abuse. The jury in her trial never saw any of these scans before they sentenced her to death.

Maybe her half sister, Diane Mattingly, had a point when she said we should not count Lisa Montgomery among "the worst of the worst" for whom the death penalty is intended. Instead, "she is the most broken of the broken." But it is such brokenness that might cause us to view death, even via lethal injection, as relief. More than sorrow for her, maybe Lisa Montgomery's brokenness is the kind that makes us feel sorry for *us*.

In the last months of his presidency, Donald Trump revived the federal death penalty after a seventeen-year hiatus. In six months' time, the US government completed thirteen executions, triple the number it had conducted in the previous six decades. One person put to death was Lisa Montgomery, just a week before Trump left office.

Typically inmates are permitted a spiritual advisor in the room during an execution. Lisa, however, was not extended this mercy. Her lawyer, Kelley Henry, said this decision was one of the biggest disappointments of her story. There had been a specific plan in place for the spiritual advisor. He had a role to fill. "He was going to sing her 'Jesus Loves Me' while the chemicals flowed," she said.

The website for Forest Lawndale cemetery, which occupies three hundred acres on the banks of Brays Bayou in Houston's East End, says this: "Over the years, [the cemetery] has become the final resting place for hundreds of local dignitaries and notable people. This includes our founder, J. D. Eubanks; J. Robert Neal, founder of Maxwell House coffee; Walter Fondren, founder of Humble Oil Company, now Exxon Oil Company; Senator Lloyd Bentsen; Robert E. "Bob" Onstead, founder of Randall's Food Markets; and others." These "others," these "notable people," include Karla Faye Tucker. Her burial spot is marked by a flat slab, with her name, dates of birth and death, and a cross and flowers carved in the granite.

Indeed, Karla is in the grave now, and so is my father, and, as I write this, it was a month ago that my mother joined them both. After Mom's funeral, I sorted through some of my parents' belongings in their brick ranch in suburban Atlanta. In one of the bedrooms I came across a drawer full of Dad's stuff—items I hadn't seen in years or, in some cases, ever. There was a copy of his birth certificate and his military discharge papers. The bill of sale for five acres he bought in the North Georgia mountains. A pocketknife and a milestone pin he received from the post office for accruing sick leave. And Mom's handwritten record charting his physical decline after his cancer diagnosis. Important things he and my mother kept out of necessity, nostalgia, or both.

Buried near the bottom of the drawer, I found an envelope from the State of Texas, Office of the Governor, Austin. It was stamped March 12, 1998—a little over a month after Karla Faye Tucker was executed. When I glimpsed the envelope, my pulse quickened, because I never knew Dad received any official response to the letter I had written on his behalf. I hadn't asked about it, and he didn't say anything more about it either. Once we heard the outcome, we simply dropped the conversation, our shared disappointment too much to dredge up.

But when I took the envelope in hand and slid my finger inside where it had been knifed opened twenty years ago, I found, curiously, nothing. It was empty.

I rummaged through every item in that drawer, thumbing through all manner of paperwork—Dad's Baptist deacon ordination, his retirement compensation, and a dozen copies of a poem a friend had written to memorialize him at his funeral.

The correspondence had been a form letter, no doubt, a single sheet of office stationery offering thanks to my father for expressing his views, explaining how it was a difficult decision indeed, but informing him that Karla Faye Tucker had received due process and the courts had spoken. It had probably noted God's ultimate jurisdiction in matters of this kind. Surely it had merely repeated what Bush stated when he told the world he would not be commuting her sentence.

But I'll have to settle for conjecture. Whatever that envelope once held now was gone.

Chapter 18

THE SON'S EXECUTION DATE

I suppose it was during those few weeks leading up to Karla Faye Tucker's execution that I broke ties once and for all with the faith of my youth. I was still calling myself a Christian, but I had a hard time reconciling how easily my Bible Belt brethren navigated their own belief system, picking and choosing according to what seemed like convenience, making an exception when they came upon a killer in whom they unexpectedly saw themselves. When I watched interviews with Karla, I indeed saw a changed woman, perhaps even—as Falwell called her—a woman of God, but for me this change confirmed more about the vagaries of the death penalty than it did the redemptive power of Jesus. And when the state of Texas finally put the needle in her vein, I grew ever more frustrated with the Pat Robertsons, George Bushes, and all their ilk who spoke constantly of compassion but typically acted with an utter absence of it. I felt a bone-deep embarrassment that I'd ever gotten caught up in their agenda in the first place. I felt foolish that I had written a letter. Had I really believed it could make a difference? I remembered the words of Pat Robertson three weeks before Karla was executed, when he appeared on *Larry King Live*, trying to drum up support for her. King asked Robertson if it would help for people to write the governor. "Well, it never hurts to write," Robertson answered. "But I think the parole board is going to make up its own mind.... It's going to take a miracle to get this sentence commuted and I don't think it's going to be done by writing letters." Did I need Robertson to tell me that? Hadn't I known what the outcome would be before I ever composed a word? At the time, it seemed as though I had never written anything.

Which turned out to be as appropriate a segue to the next stage of my writing life as any I could have received. That experience of saying something, only to hear in response the echo of your own voice—well, I was learning that every writer has to get used to that.

That August, six months after the execution, I crammed all my earthly belongings into my car and drove six hours from Atlanta to the piedmont of North Carolina, where I started grad school in hopes of writing another novel. There, I began believing I'd found a new transparency to lay over the story of my life—who I was Before and After announcing to the world, and to myself, I was a writer. I hadn't been able to save Karla's life with my words. Maybe I could save my own.

But even now, as I look back at that time from a distance of two decades, I keep coming back to moments that transpired during that window of time when Karla was heading to the death chamber and I was figuring out if I still belonged among the Born Againers. In those days, my father and I didn't know that a cancer was growing inside him, that it had begun in his prostate but by this time was spreading to other parts of his body. We didn't know that this woman the newspapers were calling the Pickax Murderess would turn out to be one last cause we could unite behind. I certainly didn't know that she would snag in my consciousness precisely because she seemed to embody questions I would spend the rest of my life trying to find satisfactory answers to. What is the nature of forgiveness? When have we atoned for our sins? Who can be redeemed? How far can God's love reach? Even now, one moment in particular still haunts me. Maybe because it answers some of the questions. Or maybe because it only deepens the mystery.

January 1998: it was mere days before Karla's execution. Pat Robertson's *The 700 Club* sent a correspondent named Terry Meeuwsen to Gatesville, Texas, to interview Karla. They conducted the whole of their conversation through a glass partition, but when you watch the video, there's an unmistakable intimacy between these two women that no wall can separate. They lean toward each other, make deep eye contact. As though communicating via telepathy, they finish each other's sentences—versed in the same evangelical rhetoric, they speak a common language. When Karla claims that if she has to go on February 3, Jesus is going to come and "escort" her to heaven, Meeuwsen smiles and nods her head and tilts her chin as though she understands precisely what Karla is talking about. Meeuwsen admits we don't know what God's plan is in all this, but—and here her voice drops to a hoarse whisper filled with compassion—"Well, there's just a lot of us praying for you." The camera zooms in on Meeuwsen and you can see how glassy her eyes have gotten and how her lower lip is trembling when she fixes Karla in her gaze and says, "In truth, it's not even about you—it's all about *Him*."

They're still holding out hope, all right, but they seem resigned to Karla's fate. Much of their talk is about how thankful they are to have experienced this ordeal together, and how much they look forward to becoming reunited in heaven. They seem to be seizing this opportunity to celebrate the significance of Karla's life because they know that, yes, she is going to be executed. Meeuwsen even goes as far—and I have to say, this comes across as rather curious—to draw comparisons between Karla's impending death and Jesus's crucifixion. Jesus, too, did not want to die, but he knew it was going to happen. "I think of how God the father knew the son's execution date," Meeuwsen says, "and how perfect that son of God was . . . I know I wouldn't be thinking that way if I wasn't here with you today, so I thank you for the honor of walking with you." The two women close with a prayer, Meeuwsen on one side of the glass, Karla on the other.

Then comes the moment I can't shake.

When the prayer concludes, Karla lifts her head, breaks into a buoyant smile, and stares toward the camera—toward you and me. "I love you guys—bye!" she says. "We'll see you when you get there!"

ACKNOWLEDGMENTS

Many scholars of history and religion have devoted their lives to studying evangelicals, the South, and the death penalty, and perhaps have forgotten more about these subjects than I will ever learn. If at times in these pages I come across as an amateur, thrilled at discovering information that, in professional circles, is common knowledge, it's because I am. I hope the historical and cultural context I offer reads as an earnest attempt to ascertain where Karla Faye Tucker's story fits into the larger story of American culture circa the eighties and nineties. I am especially indebted to Frances Fitzgerald and her excellent survey *The Evangelicals*; Steven P. Miller's analysis of late-twentieth-century religion and politics in *The Age of Evangelicalism*; and Stuart Banner's overview of capital punishment in *The Death Penalty*. Also, the archives of the *Houston Chronicle* allowed me to investigate the crime and trial of Karla Faye Tucker in what felt like real time. Thanks, too, to Robyn Martin, librarian extraordinaire at the Lovett School, for her aid in trekking down information. And I'd be remiss if I failed to note that I am not the first writer to attempt to merge memoir with Tucker's story: Beverly Lowry's excellent 1992 book *Crossed Over* served as a source of both information and inspiration.

Thanks to my students, colleagues, and friends at the Lovett School.

Thanks to Julia Franks and Jonathan Newman, good writers and good pals, who read significant portions of the manuscript and offered their always insightful feedback.

Thanks to Lisa McMurtray and all the fine people at the University Press of Mississippi who gave this book a home and believed in it.

Thanks to my big brother, David, and my oldest friend, Biss.

Thanks to my mother, who passed during the writing of this book, and to whom it is dedicated.

And to Bernadette, Chloe, and Leila: thank you will never be enough. My greatest pleasure is living out the story of our lives, together.

NOTES

PROLOGUE: ALL FIVE

5 "I should have pushed her": Lindsey Bever. "Georgia's Only Woman on Death Row Set to Die for Husband's Murder Despite Religious Conversion," *Washington Post*, March 2, 2015.

6 "She's all that we have left": "A Message from the Children of Kelly and Doug Gissendaner," Youtube, Posted September 20, 2015, https://www.youtube.com/watch?v=M8pgceAhqJo.

6 "cloudy": Alan Blinder. "Georgia Executes Woman on Death Row Despite Clemency Bid and Pope's Plea," *New York Times*, September 29, 2015.

7 "Bless y'all": Dan Shepherd, Tracy Connor, and Gabe Gutierrez. "Georgia Woman Kelly Gissendaner Sings 'Amazing Grace' During Execution," NBC News, September 30, 2015. https://www.nbcnews.com/storyline/lethal-injection/pope-urges-halt-execution-georgia-woman-kelly-gissendaner-n435566.

8 "I have never attended": Rhonda Cook. "As the State of Georgia Executes Its First Woman in 70 Years, A Chilling Dispatch From Inside the Chamber," *UK Daily Mail*, September 30, 2015. https://www.dailymail.co.uk/news/article-3255523/She-sang-Amazing-Grace-drugs-took-hold-stuttered-silence-state-Georgia-executes-woman-70-years-chilling-dispatch-inside-chamber.html.

8 "a virtual guest": Sam Howe Verhovek. "Karla Tucker Is Now Gone, But Several Debates Linger," *New York Times*, February 5, 1998.

8 "The real question": Ibid.

9 "She was a woman": Ibid.

10 A 2016 Pew Research Survey: Keri Blakinger. "Death Penalty Nearing Historic Lows in Texas and Nationwide," *Houston Chronicle*, July 3, 2017.

10 After a peak of forty executions: "Executions by State and Year." deathpenaltyinfo.org.

CHAPTER 1: SWEET WOMAN OF GOD

13   "I didn't know what I was reading": Larry King. *Larry King Live* (Television Broadcast). New York: Cable News Network, January 14, 1998.

13   "Whoso sheddeth man's blood": Genesis 9:6, King James Translation.

13   "a really huggy, touchy-feely person": Sam Howe Verhovek. "As Woman's Execution Nears, Texas Squirms," *New York Times*, January 1, 1998.

13   "If no crime": "Capital Punishment 1972." National Association of Evangelicals, 1972. https://www.nae.net/capital-punishment-1972.

14   "I'd prefer to be shot": "Gary Mark Gilmore." http://www.clarkprosecutor.org/html/death/US/gilmore001.htm.

14   "I just knew instantly": "Man, Woman, Death and God," *Economist*, February 5, 1998. Economist.com.

14   "lets this sweet woman of God die": "Governor Faces Death Row Dilemma," BBC, January 30, 1998. News.bbc.co.uk.

14   Texas executed thirty-seven people that year: Execution Database. Death Penalty Information Center. Deathpenaltyinfo.org.

15   "[I]t's the difference": George W. Bush, *A Charge to Keep* (New York: Perennial Press 1999), 147.

15   "I'm not afraid of dying": Mike Trickey. "No Reprieve for Tucker: Texas Woman Executed after Failed Supreme Court Appeal," *Ottawa Citizen*, February 4, 1998.

17   "concerns the sexual predilections": 'Soap' or No 'Soap.'" *New York Times*, September 4, 1977.

CHAPTER 2: YOUR VERY OWN GETHSEMANE

19   My God, my God: Mark 15:34, King James Translation.

20   But if ye do not forgive: Mark 11:26, King James Translation.

CHAPTER 3: LOOKING FOR SOMETHING TO DO

29   "It was all a bunch": "The Significance? In Texas Capital Punishment Is Only to be Applied in Cases of Clear Premeditation!" LifeWay Church, Tep.online.info.

30   "I'd been married to a biker": Ibid.

30   "We were very wired": Beverly Lowry, *Crossed Over* (New York: Vintage Books 1992), 42.

30   "the temp was in the low seventies, but the humidity exceeded ninety percent": "Houston, TX Weather," Wunderground.com.

31   "We never went anywhere": "The Significance? In Texas Capital Punishment Is Only to be Applied in Cases of Clear Premeditation!" LifeWay Church. Tep.online.info.

32 "What's going on?": Lowry, 52.
32 five-seven and 142 pounds: Ibid., 54.
32 "Don't move, motherfucker": Ibid., 55.
32 "My idea of getting even": "The Significance? In Texas Capital Punishment Is Only to be Applied in Cases of Clear Premeditation!" LifeWay Church. Tep.online.info.
33 "That sound": Lowry, 168.
34 "I reached over and grabbed it": Ibid., 58.
34 "like an aquarium pump": Ibid., 170.
34 "She finally got the ax out": Ibid., 170.
35 "tucked tail and ran": Ibid., 58.
36 "Oh God, it hurts": Ibid., 62.
37 "Maybe Lynyrd Skynyrd": Mike Ward. "Witness to Butchery Has Little Sympathy for Tucker," *Austin American Statesman*, January 24, 1998.
37 Or maybe something like Loverboy's: "U.S. Top 40 Singles for the Week Ending June 18, 1983," Top40weekly.com.
37 "I seen the girl": Lowry, 163.
37 "I tried to run back": Ward. "Witness to Butchery . . ."

CHAPTER 4: EVANGEL

39 "Twenty-two million dollars": William Stracener. "Falwell Dives Down Water Slide to Fulfill Fund-Raising Promise," Associated Press, September 10, 1987.
39 "summer of survival campaign": Ibid.
40 "I may break my fool neck": Ibid
41 "God that holds you": Jonathan Edwards, "Sinners in the Hands of an Angry God," 1741.
42 "for the purpose of carrying": "Constitution of Southern Baptist Convention," May 8, 1845, Sbc.net.
43 "October 6. I rose at 6 o'clock": William Byrd, *The Secret Diary of William Byrd, October 1709*.
43 "considering numbers, nature, and natural means only": Thomas Jefferson, *Notes on the State of Virginia*, 1785.
44 "Our relationship to African-Americans": Southern Baptist Convention. "Resolution on Racial Reconciliation on the 150th Anniversary of the SBC, June 1, 1995," https://web.archive.org/web/20140408064550/http://www.sbc.net/resolutions/899.
44 "We lament and repudiate": Ibid.
45 "America's present need": William Harding. "Readjustment," Speech delivered June 29, 1920, https://www.loc.gov/item/2016655168.
45 "I believe in part of evolution": Edward Larson, *Summer for the Gods: The Scopes Trial and America's Continuing Debate over Science and Religion*, (New York: Basic Books 2006).

46	"You insult every man": Jeffrey Moran, *The Scopes Trial: A Brief History with Documents* (New York: Bedford Press 2002).
46	"tin pot pope": H. L. Mencken, *H. L. Mencken on Religion*. Ed. by S. T. Joshi, (Amherst, New York: Prometheus Books 2010).
47	"I repudiate him entirely": Alan Wolfe. "Among the Non-Believers," *New Republic*, April 12, 2004.
47	"I sat there staring": Randall Balmer. "The Real Origins of the Religious Right," *Politico*, May 27, 2014.
48	"Gallup estimated": "Poll Finds 34% Share 'Born Again' Feeling," *New York Times*, September 26, 1976.
48	"God Almighty does not hear": Frances Fitzgerald, *The Evangelicals*, (New York: Simon and Schuster 2018), 314.
48	"I looked at Mr. Reagan": Daniel Hummel. "Revivalist Nationalism since World War II: From 'Wake up, America!' to 'Make America Great Again,'" *Religions* 7(11), 2016.
49	"the most famous lines": Steven P. Miller, *The Age of Evangelicalism*, (Oxford UP 2016), 62.
49	"I know you can't endorse me": Ronald Reagan. "National Affairs Campaign Address on Religious Liberty." Americanrhetoric.com.
49	"a perpetual ward": Ibid.
49	"Under the pretense": Ibid.
50	"We gave him": W. Scott Lamb. "35th Anniversary of Reagan's 'I Know You Can't Endorse Me, But I Endorse You' to Evangelicals," *Washington Times*, August 21, 2015.
51	"the feminists' anti-God": Concerned Women for America, https://concernedwomen.org/about/our-history.
51	"purchased $10 million in radio commercials": Jimmy Carter, *White House Diary*, (New York: Farrar, Straus, and Giroux 2010), 469.
51	"the greatest thing that has happened": Miller, 66.
51	"probably the most evangelical president": Miller, 67.

CHAPTER 5: FISH AND KETCHUP

53	"We had killings like that": T. J. Milling. "Karla Faye's Last Chance," *Houston Chronicle*, February 1, 1998.
53	"all-time high of 701 homicides": Jennifer Leahy. "Houston Homicide Rate May be Worst in a Decade," *Houston Chronicle*, October 21, 2006.
54	"As far as the actual crime scene": T. J. Milling. "Karla Faye's Last Chance," *Houston Chronicle*, February 1, 1998.
55	"I was so spaced out on drugs": Larry King. *Larry King Live* (Television Broadcast). New York: Cable News Network, January 14, 1998.
55	"She always said": Allan Turner. "Ex-Husband Loved Her Despite 'Wild Streak,'" *Houston Chronicle*, February 3, 1998.

- 56 "Got a nut": Beverly Lowry, *Crossed Over* (New York: Vintage Books 1992), 65.
- 56 "freaked", "it was there", "Well, hell yes": Ibid., 91, 91, 174.
- 57 "[Danny's] brother came in": Larry King. *Larry King Live* (Television Broadcast). New York: Cable News Network, January 14, 1998.

CHAPTER 6: PUPPET SHOW

- 62 "I had a Harley Davidson": "Karla Faye Tucker's Story," Discipleship Unlimited, April 24, 2010. Discipleshipunlimited.org.
- 62 "We got along fairly well": Ibid.
- 63 "idolized": Beverly Lowry, *Crossed Over* (New York: Vintage Books 1992), 100.
- 63 "I don't think any of this": Ibid., 99.
- 64 "Siamese twins": "Texas v. Karla Faye Tucker," http://nobillsman.tripod.com/karlawrit3.html.
- 65 "pill doctor": "The Significance? In Texas Capital Punishment Is Only to be Applied in Cases of Clear Premeditation!" LifeWay Church, Tep.online.info.
- 65 "He'd once been": Ibid.
- 66 "The other Karla": Richard Cohen. "Spare Karla Faye Tucker," *Washington Post*, January 6, 1998.
- 66 "A ministry came": Larry King. *Larry King Live* (Television Broadcast). New York: Cable News Network, January 14, 1998.
- 66 "I didn't want to stay alone": Ibid.
- 66 "I stole this Bible": Ibid.
- 67 "At the time": Jesse Katz. "Should Karla Faye Tucker be Executed," *Los Angeles Times*, January 9, 1998.
- 67 "I probably brought more people to the Lord": Kathy Walt. "Execution May Haunt Texas," *Houston Chronicle*, December 14, 1997.
- 67 "I don't try and convince people": Larry King. *Larry King Live* (Television Broadcast). New York: Cable News Network, January 14, 1998.
- 67 "personification of evil": Anna Quindlen. "Public and Private; A Murder, A Mother, A Mystery," *New York Times*, September 20, 1992.
- 68 "[T]he things that were in me": Kathleen O'Shea "Killing the Killers: Women on Death Row in the United States," *Killing Women: The Visual Culture of Gender and Violence*, Annette Burfoot and Susan Lord, editors, Wilfrid Laurier Press, 2006, 80.
- 68 "It's called the joy of the Lord": Larry King. *Larry King Live* (Television Broadcast). New York: Cable News Network, January 14, 1998.

CHAPTER 7: AND THAT'S THE WAY WITH JESUS

- 72 "Listen, people": John Wigger, *PTL*, (Oxford UP 2017), 28.
- 73 "move of the spirit": Fitzgerald, 372.

73	"It's not listed in the Bible": Miller, 81.
74	"Give, and it shall be given unto you": Wigger 140.
74	"If you don't give": *20/20*, "Unfaithfully Yours," Season 41, Episode 20, January 18, 2019.
75	"If you pray for a camper": Ibid.
75	"It's kind of a hobby": *Nightline*, Interview with Ted Koppel, May 27, 1987.
75	"From this moment on": *20/20*, "Unfaithfully Yours," Season 41, Episode 20, January 18, 2019.
75	"God loves you": Wigger, 56.
76	"The Bible says we're fishers of men": William Schmidt. "TV Minister Calls His Resort 'Bait' for Christianity," *New York Times*, December 24, 1985.
77	"At what time in your life": *Tammy's House Party*, November 1985, https://www.youtube.com/watch?v=GjXXdQ6VceQ.
78	"Thank God for a mom": Ibid.
78	"And that's the way with Jesus": Ibid.
78	"Steve, have you ever had": Ibid.
79	"How sad that we as Christians": Ibid.
79	"We had to face some . . . realities": *Nightline*, Interview with Ted Koppel, May 27, 1987.
80	"I went with the intention": *20/20*, "Unfaithfully Yours," Season 41, Episode 20, January 18, 2019.
80	"It just happened": Wigger, 124.
81	"I thought this was going": *20/20*, "Unfaithfully Yours," Season 41, Episode 20, January 18, 2019.
81	"pro-life, pro-traditional family": Peter Applebome. "Jerry Falwell, Leading U.S. Religious Conservative, Dies," *New York Times*, May 15, 2007.
82	"an evangelical who is mad": Wigger, 276.
82	"You're the only preacher I trust": "Nothing Sacred in Holy War," *Orlando Sentinel*, May 28, 1987.
83	"I don't see any repentance there": Wigger, 291.
83	"Jim, since that time": *Nightline*, Interview with Ted Koppel, May 27, 1987.
84	"Jim, I must tell you": Ibid.
84	"wreck": Ibid.
85	"probably the greatest scab": Miller, 83.
86	cinnamon rolls: Wigger, 316.
86	"sympathy stunt": Art Harris. "Bakker Mental Tests Ordered," *Washington Post*, September 1, 1989.
86	"manhandled, strip searched": *20/20*, "Unfaithfully Yours," Season 41, Episode 20, January 18, 2019.
86	"those of us who do have a religion": June Preston. "Tammy Faye Describes Plight of Her Caged Husband," UPI, September 6, 1989.
87	"I have a song for ya!": *20/20*, "Unfaithfully Yours," Season 41, Episode 20, January 18, 2019.

87	"It's not over": Ibid.
88	"I wish people could look": Martha Sherrill. "Tammy Faye, Unblinking," *Washington Post*, November 3, 1996.
88	"Oh, I don't care": Ibid.
88	"Well, about a quarter": Larry King. *Larry King Live* (Television Broadcast). New York: Cable News Network, August 7, 2007.
89	"It showed me what kind of girl she was": Sherrill. "Tammy Faye, Unblinking."
91	"go ye therefore": Matthew 28:19, King James Translation.
91	"I had everything you could ask for": Fitzgerald, 380.
91	"call him home": Keith Schneider. "Oral Roberts, Fiery Preacher, Dies at 91," *New York Times*, December 15, 2009.

CHAPTER 8: WELL, HELL YES

94	"The day I was appointed": Jesse Katz. "Should Karla Faye Tucker be Executed?" *Los Angeles Times*, January 9, 1998.
94	"I just remember": Beverly Lowry, *Crossed Over* (New York: Vintage Books 1992), 13.
94	"I was advised by my attorneys": "Excerpts from Karla Faye Tucker Letter to Governor Bush," January 20, 1998, http://www.tep-online.info/laku/usa/dp/tucker437.htm.
95	"hacked to death": Lowry, 163.
96	"the girl was a tough motherfucker": Ibid. 61.
96	"I picked him": Ibid. 65.
96	"The murder occurred in 1983": Florence King. "The Misanthrope's Corner," *National Review*, Volume 50, Issue 4, March 9, 1998.
97	"The evidence is overwhelming": Lowry, 176.
97	"Intentionally cause the death": Lowry, 161.
98	"strange fire": Leviticus 10:1, King James Translation.
98	"Go, and sin no more": John 8:11, King James Translation
99	"death is different": Nina Totenberg and Domenico Montanaro. "Supreme Court Closely Divides on 'Cruel and Unusual' Death Penalty Case," NPR. April 1, 2019.
99	"I wanted to tell the truth": Lowry, 141.
99	"used to share drugs like lipstick": Lowry, 129.
100	"I've hurt a lot of people": "Texas v. Karla Faye Tucker," http://nobillsman.tripod.com/karlawrit3.html.
100	"I have not heard one cuss word": Ibid.
100	"playing church": Ibid.
100	"Mrs. Griffith": Mary Welek Atwell, *Wretched Sisters: Examining Gender and Capital Punishment*, (New York: Peter Lang Inc. 2014), 68.
101	"If she had known": Atwell, 74.
101	"Should Karla Faye Tucker be Executed": Lowry, 180.

CHAPTER 9: THE THING IS QUICKLY ENOUGH DONE

103 "spectacle for warning": Stuart Banner, *The Death Penalty: An American History*, (Cambridge, MA: Harvard UP 2009), 73.

103 "After I had passed": "Letter from Paul Revere to Jeremy Belknap, circa 1798," Massachusetts Historical Society, http://www.masshist.org/database/viewer.php?item_id=99&img_step=1&mode=transcript#page1.

104 "bungling and barbarous": Julius Mount Bleyer. "Best Method of Executing Criminals," *Medico-Legal Journal*, February 1888, 426, https://archive.org/stream/medicolegaljourn05medi#page/424/mode/2up.

104 "sometimes sudden, painless": Ibid. 428.

104 "dangling between heaven and earth": Banner, 2.

104 dance of death: Gilbert King, *The Execution of Willie Francis*, (New York: Perseus Books, 2008), 216.

104 "and we have the bloodiness": Bleyer, "Best Method . . ." 428.

105 "on account of the fact": Julius Mount Bleyer. "Instant Death by Decapitation an Impossibility According to Biological Analysis," *Medico-Legal Journal*, 1898, 515–16, https://archive.org/stream/medicolegaljourn16medi#page/515/mode/2up.

105 "I concede that consciousness": Ibid. 530.

105 "After all, there must remain": Ibid. 531.

105 "to receive impressions still": Ibid. 532.

105 "I was not, then, dealing": Nancy McKeon. "After the Fall . . . Last Thoughts on the Guillotined King," *Washington Post*, July 14, 1989.

106 "decorous, involving no brutal or barbarous": Bleyer. "Best Method . . ." 429.

106 "Life is undoubtedly extinct": Ibid. 429.

106 "before bystanders": Ibid. 432.

106 "incidental advantage": Ibid. 432.

106 "equally painless . . . eminently suitable": Ibid. 432.

107 "administers six grains": Ibid. 434.

107 "The thing is quickly enough done": Ibid. 437.

107 "the man simply goes to sleep": Ibid. 436.

107 "dying game": Ibid. 436.

107 "brutal mirth": Michael Madow. "Forbidden Spectacle: Executions, the Public and the Press in Nineteenth Century New York," *Buffalo Law Review*, vol. 43, Number 2, Oct. 1, 1995, 464.

107 "What a group": Ibid. 503.

107 "The place and occasion": Banner, 182.

107 "made strenuous efforts": Madow, 516.

108 "she importuned the Sheriff": Ibid. 516.

108 "a high wooden fence": Ibid. 517.

108 "I think that for capital punishment": Larry King. *Larry King Live* (Television Broadcast). New York: Cable News Network, January 14, 1998.

109	"The velocity of the electric current": Banner, 180.
109	"Gentlemen, I wish you all good luck": "Far Worse Than Hanging," *New York Times*, August 7, 1890.
109	"twisted into a ghastly grin": Ibid.
110	"purplish foam": Ibid.
110	"quick, no delay": Ibid.
110	"An awful odor": Ibid.
110	"It had nauseated": Ibid.
110	"They would have done better": King, 219.
110	"There is the culmination": "The Electric Chair," Cayuga Museum of History and Art. http://cayugamuseum.org/the-electric-chair.
110	"The first experiment": King, 185.
111	"regular, methodical, and dignified": Banner, 188.
111	"fry . . . sit in the hot seat": King, 220.
111	published the pic on the cover: *New York Daily News*, January 13, 1928.
112	"nothing but a mass": Deanna Pan and Jennifer Berry Hawes, "An Undying Mystery," *The Post and Courier*, March 25, 2018.
112	"I have just talked": Ibid.
113	"a round instrument": Ibid.
114	"wisps of smoke": Ibid.
114	"Take it off!": King, 25.
115	"It seemed like they were in an awful hurry": Ibid. 26.
115	"a mouth full of cold peanut butter": Ibid. 31.
115	"I'm right interested": Ibid. 222–23.
115	"my Sunday pants": Ibid. 269.
116	"I, at this very moment": "Death Row Information," Texas Department of Criminal Justice, Charlie, Brooks, Jr., https://www.tdcj.texas.gov/death_row/dr_info/brookscharlielast.html.

CHAPTER 10. HERE AND HAPPY

119	"so I could take these two hands": "Supporters Try to Prevent Woman's Execution," *Austin American Statesman*, June 15, 1992.
119	"I lay in my bed": Christy Drennan. "On Death Row, Pickax Murderer Finds a 'New Life,'" *Houston Chronicle*, March 28, 1986.
119	"God helps me": Ibid.
120	"When you're drug-free": Ibid.
121	"I'm not going to say": Ibid.
121	"caring person. That's hard for people": Rachel King, *Don't Kill in Our Names: Families of Murder Victims Speak Out Against the Death Penalty*, (New Jersey: Rutgers UP, 2003), 67.
121	"I'm not saying that at the time": "Inmate 777." *60 Minutes*, CBS, 1997.

121	"The other Karla": Richard Cohen. "Spare Karla Faye Tucker," *Washington Post*, January 6, 1998.
121	"I think she is different now": Christy Drennan. "The Embodiment of Evil? Opinions Have Changed Over Pickax Murderer Karla Faye Tucker," *Houston Chronicle*, March 28, 1986.
121	"If she is executed": Ibid.
122	"When we sent a reporter": Pat Robertson. "Transcript of Speech on Religion's Role in the Administration of the Death Penalty," *William and Mary Bill of Rights Journal*, Volume 9, Issue 1, December 2000.
122	"beautiful picture": Earl Marks. "No Sympathy for This Born Again Murderess," June 23, 1992.
123	"From what I know of Karla": Kathy Fair and Carol Rust. "Death Row Inmate Dies of Natural Causes: 10 Years After Conviction in Pickax Murders, Prisoner Was to Receive New Trial," *Houston Chronicle*, June 16, 1993.
124	"It sounds silly": Carol Rust. "'Gender Shouldn't be an Issue': Death Row Inmate Claims Responsibility for Crimes," *Houston Chronicle*, December 14, 1997.
124	"I was drawn to the spirit inside of her": Ibid.
124	"We let everyone know": Ibid.

CHAPTER 11: UNTIL SHE BE DEAD

126	"There is something inside of us": Larry King. *Larry King Live* (Television Broadcast). New York: Cable News Network, January 14, 1998.
126	"For years, women's groups have been screaming equal rights": Rebecca Leung. "Texas Executes Tucker," ABC News, February 3, 1998.
126	"Women have been placed on pedestals": Charlotte Sutton. "Death Row Is Path Few Women Tread," *Tampa Bay Times*, October 17, 2005.
127	"You must consider": Rev. Henry Channing, *God Admonishing His People of Their Duty*, New London, CT, 1786.
127	"thanked the Sheriff for his kindness": Julie Stagis. "A Girl, 12, Is Hanged in Connecticut for Murder in 1786," *Hartford Courant*, April 1, 2014.
127	only one (.002 percent) of the 432 executions had been female: Sam Howe Verhovek. "As Woman's Execution Nears, Texas Squirms," *New York Times*, January 1, 1998.
127	women committed one in eight murders: Ibid.
127	"When it comes to the death penalty": Ted Gregory. "Execution of Women Still Rare Nationwide," *Chicago Tribune*, January 16, 1996.
128	"If it was Karl Tucker": Jesse Katz. "Should Karla Faye Tucker be Executed?" *Los Angeles Times*, January 9, 1998.
128	"are going to be totally horrified and unnerved": Kathy Walt. "Path Clear for Woman's Execution: Karla Faye Tucker Loses Court Appeal," *Houston Chronicle*, December 9, 1997.

129 "*no soy culpable*": Steve Ray. "Chipita's Execution Haunts Local Memory," *Corpus Christi Caller Times*, February 2, 1998.
129 "She will be taken to the place of execution": Wallace L. McKeehan. "The Hanging of Chipita Rodriguez," *Sons of Dewitt Colony Texas*, Sonsofdewitt colony.org.
130 "She didn't have a decent dress": Ray "Chipita's Execution Haunts..."
131 "well developed and well nourished colored man": "Emma Oliver v. State," *Court of Criminal Appeals of Texas*, December 13, 1950.
131 "I didn't mean to kill him": Jerry Bledsoe, *Death Sentence: The True Story of Velma Barfield's Life, Crimes, and Execution*, (New York: Diversion Books, 1998), 7–8.
132 "had a shy smile": Mara Bovsun. "Death Row Granny," *New York Daily News*, May 2, 2009.
132 "my gateway to heaven": William Schmidt. "First Woman Is Executed in U.S. Since 1962," *New York Times*, November 3, 1984.
133 "I didn't notice": Ibid.
133 "a little tired sometimes": Larry King. *Larry King Live* (Television Broadcast). New York: Cable News Network, January 14, 1998.
133 "It gets a little more exciting": Ibid.
136 "It is so rare to find a movie character"· Roger Ebert. "*Dead Man Walking* Review," January 12, 1996, RogerEbert.com.

CHAPTER 12: THE BALLAD OF KARLA FAYE TUCKER

138 "written by journalistic hacks": Peter Gammond, "Broadside Ballads," *The Oxford Companion to Popular Music* (Oxford: Oxford UP, 1991), 82, https://archive.org/details/oxfordcompaniontoogamm/page/81/mode/2up.
138 "I ... confess especially my drunkenness": "The Last Speech and Dying Advice of Poor Julian, Who Was Executed the 22d of March, 1733. For the Murder of Mr. John Rogers of Pembroke." https://americanantiquarian.org/earlyamericannewsmedia/files/original/3c655b20846e6b5bc78985762ae24f3e.jpg.
139 "It has probably never fallen": *Life and Confession of Ann Walters, The Female Murderess!!*, 1850, 3, http://reader.library.cornell.edu/docviewer/digital?id=sat:2609#page/2/mode/1up.
139 "As regards the truth or authenticity": Ibid. 22.
139 "[I]t is hoped that sending this narrative abroad": Ibid. 22.
140 "He opened up her bosom": Paul Slade. "Timber Wolf: Pretty Polly," http://www.planetslade.com/pretty-polly.html.
140 "I met her on the mountain": Paul Slade. "Infectious: Tom Dooley," http://www.planetslade.com/pearl-bryan-04-06.html.
140 "young girls, if you'll listen": Paul Slade. "Pearl Bryan: Chapter Four Continued," http://www.planetslade.com/pearl-bryan-04-06.html.

140   "speak to a cultural idiom": Christina Ruth Hastie, *"This Murder Done": Misogyny, Femicide, and Modernity in 19th-Century Appalachian Murder Ballads* (Knoxville: University of Tennessee, 2011), 117, https://trace.tennessee.edu/cgi/viewcontent.cgi?article=2127&=&context=utk_gradthes&=&sei.

141   "Have mercy on my baby": Karen Hogg. "The History of Murder Ballads and the Women Who Flipped the Script," March 17, 2020, https://sheshreds.com/the-history-of-murder-ballads.

141   "What have I done, Scott Jackson": Ibid.

141   "I didn't know the gun was loaded": Ibid.

141   "everything with him that wasn't nailed down": Ibid.

141   "I am in no way": "Excerpts from Karla Faye Tucker's Letter," *Houston Chronicle*, January 21, 1998.

CHAPTER 13: THE REAL DEBBIE THORNTON

143   "When I found out": Kathy Walt and T. J. Milling. "Karla Faye's Last Chance: Words on Life or Death," *Houston Chronicle*, February 1, 1998.

143   "And what I see in Ms. Tucker": Ibid.

143   "welcomed the moment": George W. Bush, *A Charge to Keep*, (New York: Perennial, 1999), 147.

143   "February 3 will be a date": Stefanie Asin and Kathy Walt. "Execution of Tucker Scheduled for Feb. 3," *Houston Chronicle*, December 19, 1997.

143   "Rebecca of Sunnybrook Farm": Ibid.

143   "only reason this is even an issue": Jesse Katz. "Should Karla Faye Tucker Be Executed?" *Los Angeles Times*, January 9, 1998.

144   "If that happened, then that happened": Kathy Walt. "She Was Sentenced to Death; She Needs to Die," *Houston Chronicle*, December 13, 1997.

144   "She did nothing": Ibid.

144   "I guess she gave it to my daughter": Ibid.

145   "I am the only voice": Ibid.

145   "People need to understand": Ibid.

145   "Their suffering is the greatest suffering": Ibid.

146   "My son . . . lost his mother": Ibid.

146   "I can't say I hate Karla Faye Tucker": Ibid.

147   "This is the real Debbie Thornton": Richard Thornton. Personal Website.

147   "Photograph is not to be copied": Ibid.

147   "It is a sound that you will always remember": Ibid.

147   "quietly crying in the other room": Ibid.

148   "Then you hear it": Ibid.

148   "This must be some kind": Ibid.

148   "Oh my god": Ibid.

148   "The dreams I had as a youth": Ibid.

149   "I am appalled": Ibid.

NOTES

149 "Entered my name": Ibid.
149 "Due to spammers": Ibid.
149 "The international attention": Eric Berger. "A Date with the Executioner: Ministers, Groups Plead for Tucker's Life," *Houston Chronicle*, January 15, 1998.
150 "I feel my job": Matt Schwartz and Clay Robison. "Tucker's Lawyers Plan to File Clemency Petition Next Week," *Houston Chronicle*, January 16, 1998.
150 "As a woman I'm for her": Kathy Walt. "'Moment of Truth': Death Penalty Opponents Rally at State Capitol," *Houston Chronicle*, January 18, 1998.

CHAPTER 14: SOUTHERN GOTHIC

152 "I did not have sexual relations": "President Clinton Denies Sexual Relations with Monica Lewinsky," January 26, 1998, Abcnews.go.com.
152 "a vast right-wing conspiracy": David Maraniss. "First Lady Launches Counterattack," *Washington Post*, January 26, 1998.
152 "playpen for the sexual freedom": Thomas Edsall. "Resignation 'Too Easy,' Robertson Tells Christian Coalition," *Washington Post*, Sept. 19, 1998.
153 "There's no question": Joe Scarborough. "Trump Has Made Courage Scarce. But There Are Still Brave Leaders Out There," *Washington Post*, December 23, 2019.
153 "to confound, anger, and embarrass": Eric Rudolph. "Full Text of Eric Rudolph's Written Statement," April 13, 2005. http://www.armyofgod.com/EricRudolphStatement.html.
155 "lake of fire": Ed Pilkington. "Right to Choose? British Director Tackles the Debate that Divides U.S.," *The Guardian*, October 23, 2007, https://www.theguardian.com/world/2007/oct/23/usa.film.
155 "I thought he had an uncanny": "FBI Holds Press Conference on Rudolph's Capture," CNN, May 31, 2003, http://transcripts.cnn.com/TRANSCRIPTS/0305/31/se.01.html.
155 "American law enforcement's unyielding efforts": Associated Press. "Attorney General John Ashcroft Confirms Capture of Rudolph," *New York Times*, May 31, 2003.
156 "This is for the FBI": Allan Gurganus. "Why We Fed the Bomber," *New York Times*, June 8, 2003.
156 "Daniel Rudolph's decision": Ibid.
156 "A man may lose a finger": Julius Mount Bleyer. "Best Method of Executing Criminals," *Medico-Legal Journal*, February 1888, 429, https://archive.org/stream/medicolegaljourn05medi#page/424/mode/2up.
157 "Before the bomb and after the bomb": Patricia Guthrie. "Clinic Bombing Survivor Emily Lyons: 'I Live in Pain Every Day,'" *Atlanta Journal-Constitution*, January 26, 2003.
157 "The fact that I have entered": Eric Rudolph. "Full Text of . . ."

157	"Homosexuality is an aberrant": Ibid.
157	"I have deprived the government": Ibid.
158	"I guess I could have tried": George W. Bush, *A Charge to Keep* (New York: Perennial Press 1999), 151.
158	"Because my hope is in the Lord": Larry King. *Larry King Live* (Television Broadcast). New York: Cable News Network, January 14, 1998.

CHAPTER 15: THIS MESS THAT SOME PEOPLE CALL LIFE

159	"Jesus coffee shop": Arthur Blessitt. "Praying with George W. Bush," blessitt.com
159	"halfway between a church": Ronald Enroth, Edward Erickson, and C. Breckenridge Peters, *The Jesus People: Old-Time Religion in the Age of Aquarius* (Grand Rapids, MI: Eerdmans, 1972), 69.
159	"toilet baptism": Craig Unger. "How George Bush Really Found Jesus," *Salon*, November 8, 2007.
159	"high on the Lord": Ibid.
160	"And Jesus was with me": Arthur Blessitt. *The Cross: The Arthur Blessitt Story* (Movie), Youtube, https://www.youtube.com/watch?v=anIOob6TIkQ.
161	"So many people feel": Ibid.
162	"with a calm, steady look": Tim Dickinson. "A Prayer for W," *Mother Jones*, December 2005.
162	"Oh, Jesus, put your words": Blessitt. "Praying with George W. Bush," blessitt.com
164	"naturally stoned on Jesus": Arthur Blessitt, *Life's Greatest Trip*, World Books, 1971.
164	"a mustard seed": Bush, 136.
164	"our beginning": Mark Updegrove. "How Billy Graham and George W. Bush Connected on Faith," *Parade*, November 14, 2017.
164	"told me about one": George W. Bush. "How Billy Graham Changed My Life," *Wall Street Journal*, February 23, 2018.
164	"There was no lecture": Ibid.
164	"I've heard others say": Craig Unger. "How George Bush Really Found Jesus," *Salon*, November 8, 2007.
165	"I felt that he was sort of": "Interview Jim Wallis." *Frontline*, November 12, 2003, https://www.pbs.org/wgbh/pages/frontline/shows/jesus/interviews/wallis.html.

CHAPTER 16: I WILL WAIT FOR YOU

166	"If Texas felons suddenly": Virginia Stem Owens. "Karla Faye Tucker's Final Stop," *Christianity Today*, July 13, 1998.

166 "A week before her sentence": Ibid.
167 "Everyone knew that rowdy fraternity boys": Ibid.
167 "When I think about what Jesus asked": Larry King. *Larry King Live* (Television Broadcast). New York: Cable News Network, January 14, 1998.
167 "And they came to a place": Mark 14:32–37, King James Translation.
167 "I hate to see": Allan Turner. "Ex-Husband Loved Her Despite 'Wild Streak,'" *Houston Chronicle*, February 3, 1998.
168 "When a person enters": Sam Howe Verhovek. "Near Death, Tucker Gave Suggestions to the Prison," *New York Times*, February 8, 1998.
169 AXE AND YOU SHALL RECEIVE: Kathleen O'Shea. "Killing the Killers: Women on Death Row in the United States," *Killing Women: The Visual Culture of Gender and Violence*, Annette Burfoot and Susan Lord, eds, (Wilfrid Laurier Press, 2006), 73.
169 "Make no mistake": Kathy Walt. "Tucker Dies After Apologizing," *Houston Chronicle*, February 3, 1998.
169 "petite, photogenic, rosy-lipped": Jesse Katz. "Should Karla Faye Tucker be Executed?" *Los Angeles Times*, January 9, 1998.
170 "She prayed and said": Corky Siemaszko. "The Day the Pickax Killer Karla Faye Tucker Was Executed in 1998," *New York Daily News*, February 3, 2016.
170 "When I saw the prisoner": George Orwell. "A Hanging," The Orwell Foundation, https://www.orwellfoundation.com/the-orwell-foundation/orwell/essays-and-other-works/a-hanging.
171 "When I was sworn in": George W. Bush, *A Charge to Keep* (New York: Perennial Press 1999), 154.
171 "Many people have contacted my office": Ibid. 154.
172 "The courts": Ibid. 154.
172 "Thank you, Captain Allen": *Into the Abyss* (Movie), Directed by Werner Herzog, IFC Films, 2011, Youtube, https://www.youtube.com/watch?v=kCmlE17iUTo.
173 "So now Dana Brown": Kathy Walt. "Tucker Dies After Apologizing," *Houston Chronicle*, February 3, 1998
173 "I would like to say to all of you": "Last Statement—Karla Faye Tucker," Texas Department of Criminal Justice, https://www.tdcj.texas.gov/death_row/dr_info/tuckerkarlalast.html.
174 "Here she comes, baby doll": Walt, "Tucker Dies After Apologizing."
174 "I love you, Karla": Ibid.

CHAPTER 17: THE STATE OF TEXAS, OFFICE OF THE GOVERNOR, AUSTIN

176 "Na na, na na na na": Sam Howe Verhovek. "Execution in Texas: The Overview," *New York Times*, February 4, 1998.
176 "Justice for Deborah Thornton": Ibid.

NOTES

176 "I don't believe her Christianity": Stephanie Salter. "A Convert to the Church of Vengeance," *SFGate*, February 15, 1998.

177 "sent to the place": Michael Graczyk. "Texas Executes Karla Faye Tucker," Associated Press, February 4, 1998.

177 "My religion says": Ibid.

177 "It is most unfortunate": Eric Berger. "Two New Stamps Memorialize Tucker," *Houston Chronicle*, March 16, 1998.

177 "I drew strength from the Lord": "Ron Carlson to Speak at 11th Annual March to Abolish the Death Penalty on October 30 at Texas Capitol," Texas Moratorium Network. September 14, 2010. http://www.texasmoratorium.org/archives/1367.

178 "Once you're up there": *Into the Abyss* (Movie), Directed by Werner Herzog, IFC Films, 2011, Youtube, https://www.youtube.com/watch?v=kCmlE17iUT0.

178 "I was just working in the shop": Ibid.

178 "shake. Like, I couldn't": Ibid.

179 "I can't do it no more": Ibid.

179 "Every time you put a drop of water": Abramson, Stacy. "Interview with a Tie-Down Officer," *Texas Observer*, December 6, 2002.

179 "the longest twenty minutes": George W. Bush, *A Charge to Keep* (New York: Perennial Press 1999), 155.

179 "I felt like a huge piece of concrete": Ibid. 155.

179 "I wanted to hear her voice": Ibid. 155.

179 "contemptible, a one-eyed drifter": Ibid. 155.

180 "Did you meet with any of them?": Timothy Noah. "Bush's Tookie," *Slate*, December 2, 2005. Slate.com.

180 "Mr. Carlson misread, mischaracterized me": Ibid.

181 "When you see a gruesome picture": Guggenheim, "Orange Disaster #5," Guggenheim.org.

182 "I would like to tell the victims' families": "Last Statement—Steven Renfro," Texas Department of Criminal Justice, https://www.tdcj.texas.gov/death_row/dr_info/renfrostevenlast.html.

182 "Judy may not have been as photogenic": Kathleen Sweeney. "No Victims' Kin to See 'Black Widow' Die," *Jacksonville Sun*, March 31, 1998.

182 During the nineties, the number of executions began to increase dramatically: Execution Database, Death Penalty Information Center, Deathpenaltyinfo.org.

182 Thirty-seven in '97: Sam Howe Verhovek. "Execution in Texas: The Overview," *New York Times*, February 14, 1998.

183 "Texans have a right": John Holmes, Jr. "Dealing Out Death," *Texas Monthly*, July 2002.

183 "vicious killers": Teresa Malcolm. "Tucker's Death Affected Robertson's Views." *National Catholic Reporter*, Volume 35, Issue 25, April 23, 1999.

183 "culture of death": Ibid.

NOTES

183 "With a few exceptions": Ibid.
183 "Mr. Robertson's views": Ibid.
184 "Is there a possibility": Ibid.
184 "The law of Moses": "The Lesson of Karla Faye Tucker," *Christianity Today*, April 6, 1998.
185 "If no crime": "Capital Punishment 1972," National Association of Evangelicals, 1972. https://www.nae.net/capital-punishment-1972.
185 "Evangelical Christians differ": "Capital Punishment 2015," National Association of Evangelicals, 2015, https://www.nae.net/capital-punishment-2.
185 dropping from almost 80 percent: Execution Database, Death Penalty Information Center, Deathpenaltyinfo.org.
185 "I didn't get them for me": Larry King. *Larry King Live* (Television Broadcast). New York: Cable News Network, January 14, 1998.
186 1,531 executions: Death Penalty Information Center, "Facts About the Death Penalty," January 17, 2021, https://documents.deathpenaltyinfo.org/pdf/FactSheet.pdf.
187 "These death sentences are cruel": Andrew Glass. "Supreme Court Strikes Down Death Penalty, June 29, 1972," *Politico*, June 29, 2017, https://www.politico.com/story/2017/06/29/supreme-court-strikes-down-death-penalty-june-29-1972-239938.
189 "Don't spank me": Rachel Louise Snyder. "Punch After Punch, Rape After Rape, a Murderer Was Made," *New York Times*, December 18, 2020.
189 "the worst of the worst": Tim Hrenchir. "Lisa Montgomery, a Woman Who Cut a Baby from Her Mother's Womb, Was Executed by the Federal Government," *Topeka Capitol-Journal*, January 13, 2021.
190 "He was going to sing": Hannah Murphy. "Lisa Montgomery Suffered Years of Abuse and Trauma. The United States Killed Her Anyway," *Rolling Stone*, January 22, 2021, https://www.rollingstone.com/culture/culture-features/lisa-montgomery-kelley-henry-death-penalty-capital-punishment-1117592.
190 "Over the years, [the cemetery] has become": Forest Park Lawndale Funeral Home, Dignitymemorial.com.

CHAPTER 18: THE SON'S EXECUTION DATE

192 "Well, it never hurts to write": Larry King. *Larry King Live* (Television Broadcast). New York: Cable News Network, January 15, 1998.
194 "escort" her to heaven: "Karla Faye Tucker: Forevermore Interview #2," Youtube, Posted May 20, 2009, https://www.youtube.com/watch?v=vdVCl9vUwIo.
194 "I think of how God the father": Ibid.

ABOUT THE AUTHOR

Mark Beaver is author of *Suburban Gospel* (Hub City, 2016), a memoir about growing up in the 1980s Bible Belt. His prose has appeared in many publications, including *North American Review*, *Crazyhorse*, *River Teeth*, *Gulf Coast*, *Ninth Letter*, and elsewhere. He is a graduate of UNC Greensboro's MFA program and lives with his wife and daughters in his native Atlanta.